Approaches to Teaching Collodi's *Pinocchio* and Its Adaptations

Approaches to Teaching
World Literature

Joseph Gibaldi, series editor

For a complete listing of titles,
see the last pages of this book.

Approaches to Teaching Collodi's *Pinocchio* and Its Adaptations

Edited by

Michael Sherberg

The Modern Language Association of America
New York   2006

©2006 by The Modern Language Association of America
Printed in the United States of America

For information about obtaining permission to reprint material from MLA book
publications, send your request by mail (see address below), e-mail
(permissions@mla.org), or fax (646-458-0030).

Library of Congress Cataloging-in-Publication Data
Teaching Collodi's Pinocchio and its adaptations / edited by Michael Sherberg.
    p.   cm. — (Approaches to teaching world literature)
Includes bibliographical references and index.
ISBN-13: 978-0-87352-595-4 (cloth : alk. paper)
ISBN-10: 0-87352-595-7
ISBN-13: 978-0-87352-596-1 (pbk. : alk. paper)
ISBN-10: 0-87352-596-5
1. Collodi, Carlo, 1826–1890. Avventure di Pinocchio. 2. Collodi, Carlo, 1826–1890—
Study and teaching. I. Sherberg, Michael. II. Series.
PQ4712.L4A7393 2007
853'.8—dc22   2006015592
ISSN 1059-1133

Illustration by Luigi Cavalieri and Maria Augusta Cavalieri for chapter 3,
Le avventure di Pinocchio, Firenze: Salani, 1924.

Published by The Modern Language Association of America
26 Broadway, New York, New York 10004-1789
www.mla.org

CONTENTS

PREFACE TO THE SERIES

In *The Art of Teaching* Gilbert Highet wrote, "Bad teaching wastes a great deal of effort, and spoils many lives which might have been full of energy and happiness." All too many teachers have failed in their work, Highet argued, simply "because they have not thought about it." We hope that the Approaches to Teaching World Literature series, sponsored by the Modern Language Association's Publications Committee, will not only improve the craft—as well as the art—of teaching but also encourage serious and continuing discussion of the aims and methods of teaching literature.

The principal objective of the series is to collect within each volume different points of view on teaching a specific literary work, a literary tradition, or a writer widely taught at the undergraduate level. The preparation of each volume begins with a wide-ranging survey of instructors, thus enabling us to include in the volume the philosophies and approaches, thoughts and methods of scores of experienced teachers. The result is a sourcebook of material, information, and ideas on teaching the subject of the volume to undergraduates.

The series is intended to serve nonspecialists as well as specialists, inexperienced as well as experienced teachers, graduate students who wish to learn effective ways of teaching as well as senior professors who wish to compare their own approaches with the approaches of colleagues in other schools. Of course, no volume in the series can ever substitute for erudition, intelligence, creativity, and sensitivity in teaching. We hope merely that each book will point readers in useful directions; at most each will offer only a first step in the long journey to successful teaching.

Joseph Gibaldi
Series Editor

PREFACE TO THE VOLUME

The essays offered in this volume testify to the remarkable power of an inexplicably animate piece of wood to endear itself to readers for well more than a hundred years. When Carlo Collodi, born Carlo Lorenzini, began to write *La storia di un burattino* ("Story of a Puppet") in 1881, primarily to earn some money, he surely had no idea of the impact his trifle would have. And while he lived long enough to see its fame accelerate as several editions were published before his death in 1890, he could not have imagined its leap across national borders and continents, spawning an industry in every extant medium, including some that had yet to be invented.

Indeed, the unpretentious *Adventures of Pinocchio* enjoys pride of place alongside other great Italian exports, though Collodi's final image of the puppet slumped on a chair appears to have been prescient. Pinocchio's iconic status has often reified him, erasing much of his complex dynamism. But the novel, and the best of its adaptations, does not lack for an artistry as engaging as the instantly charismatic Pinocchio himself. The brilliance of Collodi's achievement, both in the overarching story and in its details, belies the novel's pragmatic birth. Carlo Collodi did not aspire to write a great novel; he simply sought to pen a pleasant children's story, at his own pace and on his own terms. His was an accidental genius, producing a work that has given to world literature one of its most compelling protagonists.

The essays that follow cover three areas: the presentation of the novel in the classroom, various historical and critical contexts in which to read it, and *Pinocchio*'s legacy in various works and genres. In its own way each essay attempts to identify a key to Collodi's art, either admiring the novel itself or elucidating how the tradition it spawned has revered it. These diverse approaches and interests all emphasize a common point: the extraordinary adaptability of *Pinocchio* as a teaching tool. American students in particular will find their encounter with the puppet rewarding, inasmuch as it may evoke earlier experiences of one or another version of Collodi's story. Moreover, as college students themselves straddle childhood and adulthood, the two life stages that the novel puts in play, they can both appreciate Pinocchio's transgressive behavior as reminiscent of their own and identify with the norms to which the novel subjects its young puppet. Most significant perhaps, as several of these essays recall, is the novel's discourse on the value of education. Collodi's work reflects, albeit in a more puerile way, students' own tensions about learning, particularly the tension between their intellectual acceptance of the need to buckle down in order to achieve economic autonomy and their desire to flee to a hedonistic world where study does not matter.

By reading the novel and writing about it, students also enter the stream of criticism that has flowed almost endlessly since the late nineteenth century, gathering momentum in the most recent decades. They can learn about the extraordinary wealth of the critical tradition, discovering the vitality of a text and its avatars that challenge us in countless ways. To ask students to join this conversation is to ask them to participate in the very thing that Pinocchio sought: his humanity, which is a reflection of our own. For in what is perhaps the novel's central irony, it is the puppet's deeply affecting humanness, measured paradoxically against a desire to become biologically human, that sparks so many poignant epiphanies about ourselves.

Part One

MATERIALS

Editions and Translations

The modern critical edition of the novel is *Le avventure di Pinocchio*, edited by Ornella Castellani Pollidori and published by the Fondazione Nazionale Carlo Collodi in 1983. Castellani Pollidori's edition also forms the basis for other, more accessible imprints, most notably *Le avventure di Pinocchio / The Adventures of Pinocchio*, edited by Nicolas J. Perella for the University of California Press. Perella's volume contains both the Italian original of Collodi's novel and a facing-page English translation, as well as the original illustrations and notes. While Perella adopts Castellani Pollidori's critical text, he carefully notes some of the questions surrounding her choices. Her text appears as well in Collodi's *Opere* ("Works"), edited by Daniela Marcheschi, which also amply annotates on the novel.

Teachers of *Pinocchio* in English who do not require the Italian text may choose among several economical translations currently available. The oldest is Mary Alice Murray's translation, revised by Giovanna Tassinari and published by Penguin. The illustrations, by Charles Folkard, first appeared in a 1911 edition of Murray's translation. Oxford University Press has published Ann Lawson Lucas's translation of the novel, which, being more recent, is based on Castellani Pollidori's edition. One caveat: readers who thanks to Disney associate the name "Geppetto" with the Pinocchio story may be disconcerted at first by Lucas's translation of the name as "Old Joe." This edition also contains original illustrations. Most recently Nancy Canepa has published a translation with Steerforth Italia, containing original illustrations. Her translation is also based on Castellani Pollidori's edition.

Instructors teaching the work in Italian may want to avoid the California volume, as students will likely have trouble resisting the temptation to read the translation instead of the original. But these instructors face something of a challenge: although there are many Italian editions of *Pinocchio*, none offers the sort of straightforward linguistic glosses that are often necessary when confronting Collodi's Tuscan in the classroom. The edition published in Perugia by Edizioni Guerra contains some helpful notes but also suffers from poor proofreading. Every major Italian publisher has its edition of the novel. The Oscar Mondadori edition contains a few useful notes but none that address some of the details of Collodi's Italian. The Einaudi Tascabili edition has the advantage of containing Giovanni Jervis's excellent essay as well as one by Italo Calvino, but it is based on an earlier critical edition prepared by Amerindo Camilli and first published by Sansoni in 1946 and contains no notes. Finally, the Feltrinelli edition, prepared by Fernando Tempesti, offers a superabundance of notes that would certainly answer just about any question an undergraduate might have, linguistic and otherwise. True to his surname, Tempesti can be somewhat irksomely polemical at times, but in general he is an exceptionally well-informed commentator, and his paperback edition is far less costly than the likewise well-annotated edition prepared by Daniela Marcheschi for the Mondadori leather-bound Meridiani series. Unfortunately the Feltrinelli edition no longer includes the two famous essays by Tempesti that came in an earlier edition of the novel, "Chi era il Collodi" ("Who Was Collodi") and "Com'è fatto Pinocchio" ("How Pinocchio Is Made"), though Tempesti has integrated some of the information contained therein into his notes. It appears that he followed Camilli's text of the novel, though he does not say so explicitly.

Instructors interested in exposing students to the novel in its original context, the *Giornale per i bambini*, face some challenges. In 1990, under the aegis of the Fondazione Nazionale Carlo Collodi, there was issued a three-volume facsimile edition of the *Giornale* covering 1881 to 1883. Unfortunately the publisher, L'Acacia in L'Aquila, is no longer in business, and copies of the reprint are nearly impossible to find. More recently Pagliai Polistampa published a facsimile edition just of the novel, with original illustrations. This slender paperback volume is not expensive at all and may be a useful addition to the instructor's library. While students would not be able to get a full sense of the content of the *Giornale*, this edition does enable them to see the novel's original typographical format as well as to study the text in its serialized form, before it was revised for publication in a single volume in 1883.

Required and Recommended Reading for Undergraduates

All the English translations mentioned above contain useful introductions; Perella's is by far the longest and most thorough. Instructors who do not adopt his edition may recommend an earlier version of the essay, "An Essay on *Pinocchio*," which appeared in the journal *Italica*. The other introductions offer general biographical and historical information that will help students understand the background of the novel. Also recommended, for its focus on *Pinocchio* in America, is Richard Wunderlich and Thomas Morrissey's *Pinocchio Goes Postmodern*.

Readers of Italian will appreciate Alberto Asor Rosa's lengthy essay "*Le avventure di Pinocchio: Storia di un burattino* di Carlo Collodi," which appears in his *Genus italicum*. The two essays by Tempesti mentioned above deserve attention. Rodolfo Tommasi's *Pinocchio: Analisi di un burattino* may also prove useful.

The Instructor's Library

A vast literature on *Pinocchio* appears in both English and Italian, as well as in many other languages, and the novel is often taught in contexts other than Italian, such as courses on children's literature. For that reason at some points in what follows I separate the Italian references from the English.

For a thorough bibliography of the novel through 1980, consult Luigi Volpicelli's *Bibliografia collodiana, 1883–1980*. Renato Bertacchini offers a more analytic approach to the history of *Pinocchio* criticism in "Pinocchio tra due secoli: Breve storia della critica collodiana" and "'Pinocchio' centenario e vent'anni di critica collodiana."

For detailed biographical information about Collodi, one must refer to Italian sources. These include Bertacchini's *Il padre di Pinocchio: Vita e opere del Collodi*, Pietro Pancrazi's "Vita di Collodi," and Tempesti's "Chi era il Collodi." Daniela Marcheschi provides a thorough chronology in her Mondadori edition of Collodi's *Opere*.

Instructors wishing to familiarize themselves with the social and political history of Italy in Collodi's time may consult John A. Davis's *Italy in the Nineteenth Century, 1796–1900* and Albert Russell Ascoli and Krystyna Clara von Henneberg's *Making and Remaking Italy: The Cultivation of National Identity around the Risorgimento*. Also recommended are John Agnew's "The Myth of Backward Italy in Modern Europe" and Harry Hearder's *Italy: A Short History*.

Information about the history of European puppetry may be found in Henryk Jurkowski and Francis Penny's *A History of European Puppetry* as well as in Dora Eusebietti's *Piccola storia dei burattini e delle maschere*.

Other book-length studies of interest are Sandra Beckett's *Recycling Red Riding Hood*, Peter Coveney's *The Image of Childhood*, Willard Gaylin's *Adam and Eve and Pinocchio: On Being and Becoming Human*, Lois Kuznets's *When Toys Come Alive*, Alison Lurie's *Boys and Girls Forever: Reflections on Children's Classics*, Ganna Ottevaere–van Praag's *Le roman pour la jeunesse*, Eric S. Rabkin's *Fantastic Worlds: Myths, Tales, and Stories*, Glenn Edward Sadler's *Teaching Children's Literature: Issues, Pedagogy, Resources*, Harold B. Segel's *Pinocchio's Progeny*, and D. W. Winnicott's *Playing and Reality*.

Articles about Le avventure di Pinocchio

Among the useful articles about *Pinocchio* in English are Jean-Marie Apostolidès's "Pinocchio; or, A Masculine Upbringing," Martha Bacon's "Puppet's Progress: *Pinocchio*," Glauco Cambon's "*Pinocchio* and the Problem of Children's Literature," John Cech's "The Triumphant Transformations of *Pinocchio*," Stelio Cro's "Collodi: When Children's Literature Becomes Adult," Allan Gilbert's "The

Sea-Monster in Ariosto's *Cinque Canti* and in *Pinocchio*," James W. Heisig's "Pi-nocchio, Archetype of the Motherless Child," Ann Lawson Lucas's "Enquiring Mind, Rebellious Spirit: Alice and Pinocchio as Nonmodel Children," Patricia Merivale's "The Telling of Lies and 'The Sea of Stories,'" Perella's "An Essay on *Pinocchio*," Wunderlich and Morrissey's "Death and Rebirth in *Pinocchio*," Wunderlich's "De-radicalizing *Pinocchio*," Jack Zipes's "Toward a Theory of the Fairy-tale Film: The Case of *Pinocchio*" and "Carlo Collodi's *Pinocchio* as Tragic-Comic Fairy Tale," which appeared in his book *When Dreams Came True*.

Articles that address the problem of children's literature more generally are Leslie Fiedler's "An Eye to Innocence" and Perella's "When Children's Litera-ture Becomes Adult."

Important critical articles in Italian are Asor Rosa's "*Le avventure di Pinoc-chio*," Giorgio Bàrberi-Squarotti's "Gli schemi narrativi di Collodi," Fredi Chi-appelli's "Sullo stile del Lorenzini," Concetta D'Angeli's "L'ideologia 'moderata' di Carlo Lorenzini, detto Collodi," Rodolfo Di Biasio's "Il notturno in *Pinocchio*," Franco Ferrucci's "Il teatro dei burattini," Alberto Frattini's "Appunti sulla tec-nica del racconto e sulle strutture espressive nelle *Avventure di Pinocchio*," Jone Gaillard's "Pinocchio sovversivo," Marino Parenti's "Il papà di Pinocchio," Gianni Rodari's "Pinocchio nella letteratura per l'infanzia," Riccardo Scrivano's "Gioco del caso e fantasia nelle *Avventure di Pinocchio*," Tempesti's "Come è fatto Pi-nocchio," and Ferruccio Ulivi's "Manzoni e Collodi."

Collections of Essays

There are several collections of essays in Italian, most notably those prepared by the Fondazione Nazionale Carlo Collodi. These include *Carlo Lorenzini-Collodi nel centenario*, *C'era una volta un pezzo di legno*, *Interni e dintorni del Pinoc-chio* (Clemente and Fresta), *Omaggio a Pinocchio*, *Pinocchio fra i burattini*, *Pi-nocchio nella pubblicità*, *Pinocchio oggi*, *Pinocchio sullo schermo e sulla scena*, *Scrittura dell'uso al tempo del Collodi*, and *Studi collodiani*. The Fondazione Nazionale regularly sponsors congresses on *Pinocchio* and Collodi, so one may expect to see future essay collections as well. Another important collection, stemming from a 1991 conference about the novel held at the University of Urbino, is Le avventure di Pinocchio: *Tra un linguaggio e l'altro*, edited by Is-abella Pezzini and Paolo Fabbri.

Books about Le avventure di Pinocchio

The most important recent English-language book-length study on *Pinocchio* is Wunderlich and Morrissey's *Pinocchio Goes Postmodern*. One may also consult Nancy Sachse's *Pinocchio in USA*.

Among book-length studies of the novel in Italian are Giacomo Biffi's *Contro maestro Ciliegia*, Rossana Dedola's *Pinocchio e Collodi*, Emilio Garroni's *Pinocchio uno e bino*, and Tommasi's *Pinocchio: Analisi di un burattino*.

Two other books published in Italy may be of particular interest to instructors. The first, Carlo Martini's *Pinocchio nella letteratura per l'infanzia*, is a topically organized anthology of criticism covering a wide range of approaches. The second, *Le notti di Pinocchio: Riflessioni per giovani, provocazioni per adulti*, by Luigi Guglielmoni and Fausto Negri, is an interpretation of the novel based on its seven nights. The volume also contains numerous supplementary materials as well as suggestions for discussions aimed at both adults and children.

Audiovisual and Electronic Resources

Instructors interested in the illustration history of *Pinocchio* may consult Antonio Faeti's *Guardare le figure: Gli illustratori italiani dei libri per l'infanzia*, *L'altra metà di Pinocchio*, *L'immagine nel libro per ragazzi*, Rodolfo Biaggioni's *Pinocchio: Cent'anni di* Avventure *illustrate*, and Marta Zangheri and Roberto Maini's *Pinocchio e pinocchiate: Nelle edizioni fiorentine della Marucelliana*.

A Web search for "Pinocchio" reveals scores of sites that address the novel, the various films, or the puppet in one way or another. The most important Italian Web site is www.pinocchio.it, home page of the Fondazione Nazionale Carlo Collodi. The novel may be read in English at various sites, among them the University of Pennsylvania's Project Gutenberg: http://digital.library.upenn.edu. The first Italian edition of 1883 is available at www.crs4.it. An Italian version is also available at www.linguaggioglobale.com and at www.artemotore.com, which contains information about adaptations of the novel as well.

Many of the sites offer reviews of one or another *Pinocchio* movie or information about where to purchase them. One may also buy *Pinocchio* movie posters and toys online. Information about the Disney version of the novel may be found at www.animationhistory.com. Information about the 1996 film is available at www.movieweb.com. Readers may also want to consult www.hollywood.com. Many sites discuss the recent Roberto Benigni version.

The two most famous film versions of *Pinocchio* are the Disney version (1940) and Benigni's 2002 *Pinocchio*. To that one may add Gianluigi Toccafondo's 1999 *Pinocchio*, Steve Barron's *The Adventures of Pinocchio* (1996), Luigi Comencini's *Le avventure di Pinocchio* (1971), and the 1911 production directed by Giulio Antamoro. Pinocchio finds his way into the horror movie genre in *Pinocchio's Revenge* (1996), directed by Kevin Tenney, and into pornography in the 1971 *The Erotic Adventures of Pinocchio* (rated R or X, depending on the cut). In 1999 there appeared *The New Adventures of Pinocchio*, which quite ingeniously integrates a variety of elements from the original. It stars Martin

Landau as Geppetto and airs occasionally on cable or satellite channels. Finally, Pinocchio vaults into the future in *P3K: Pinocchio 3000*, produced by Ciné-Groupe in 2004.

Pinocchio was produced for television in 1976, directed by Ron Field and Sid Smith. Other television versions are a one-hour production in 1957 starring Mickey Rooney as Pinocchio and a ninety-minute musical from 1968 with Burl Ives as Geppetto and Peter Noone as Pinocchio. From 1984 to 1986 a *Pinocchio* television series aired, directed by Tim Reid. Fifty-two episodes of a Japanese anime version of *Pinocchio*, *Kashi no Ki Mokku*, were produced in 1972 and released in Italy as *Le nuove avventure di Pinocchio*. Another anime series, *Pinocchio Yori Piccolini no Bokken* (Eng. *The Adventures of Piccolino*, Ital. *Bambino Pinocchio*), first aired in 1976 and 1977 in fifty-two episodes. The Japanese Astroboy series derives from *Pinocchio*.

The current predominance of television and film media should not obscure *Pinocchio*'s adaptations in other media as well. In 1935 George Alfred Grant-Schaefer wrote *Adventures of Pinocchio: An Operetta in Three Acts*, which included arrangements from Italian folk melodies. Yasha Frank wrote *Pinocchio: A Musical Legend* for the Federal Theatre Project, with music by Eddison von Ottenfeld and Armando Loredo; it was published in 1939. The Italian composer Renato Bellini (1895–1957) wrote a piano piece entitled "Pinocchio." *Pinocchio* also appears in poetry, as in Charles Harper Webb's "The Temptations of Pinocchio" (in his volume *Reading the Water*), Suniti Namjoshi's "Pinocchio" (in *Quiet Fire: A Historical Anthology of Asian American Poetry, 1892–1970*); and Miriam Solan's prose poem "The Pinocchio Papers" (in her volume *A Woman Combing*). The list goes on.

NOTE

Except where stated otherwise, Italian and English quotations from *Pinocchio* are taken from Nicolas J. Perella's bilingual edition *Le avventure di Pinocchio / The Adventures of Pinocchio*.

Part Two

APPROACHES

Introduction: *Pinocchio* in the Classroom

Courses Taught

Readers familiar with the Pinocchio story will recall that the puppet has trouble getting to school, and when he finally gets there, he encounters unexpected social challenges and significant distractions. Collodi's *Pinocchio* and its adaptations have made a smoother transition to the classroom, though sometimes with similar trouble and not without adjustment pains.

Instructors adopt the Pinocchio story, in both Italian and English, predominantly in courses on Italian classics, modern Italian literature, and children's literature. David Del Principe teaches it both in a survey course of modern Italian literature and in a course on Italian literature of the nineteenth century. In the survey course, *Pinocchio* serves "as an introduction to figurative language and rhetorical devices." Del Principe continues, "Mining its multiple levels of symbolism, I demonstrate how the text's allegories reflect cultural, sociopolitical, and economic realities of Collodi's time." Like Del Principe, Manuela Marchesini teaches the book in an upper-division undergraduate course in Italian. She cites Calvino's characterization of the novel for her choice: "it provides a text space to test and apply Italian culture in its many aspects and media, of the past as well as of today." Joseph Luzzi teaches *Pinocchio* in a course on Romanticism, "in which I attempt to show the ways in which Romantic aesthetic theory and practice influenced the sources, themes, and aims of Collodi's text." Rebecca West introduces *Pinocchio* both in a survey of nineteenth-century Italian prose and in courses on Italian cinema. She lauds it as "one of the most seminal books, not only for Italian literature but also for global literary and cinematic art and popular culture." Charles Klopp has adopted the text for a course in English on Italian culture from 1800 to the present. He has also used it in a course on Italian best sellers of the nineteenth and twentieth centuries, coupling it with Edmondo De Amicis's *Cuore*. Angela Jeannet has used it in a course entitled Works from the Italian Tradition, taught in English, with *Pinocchio* leading off. Michael Sherberg teaches it in a fourth-semester Italian grammar course in which the readings all address the representation of childhood in the late nineteenth and early twentieth centuries. He juxtaposes it to some of the "Racconto mensile" stories from *Cuore*, Giovanni Verga's "Rosso Malpelo," Gabriele D'Annunzio's "La madia," and Luigi Pirandello's "La veste lunga."

Pinocchio pops up in children's literature courses taught in both English and Italian. Maria Truglio has developed a course—C'era una volta: La letteratura infantile in Italia, dal 1880 al 2001—that features *Pinocchio* as well as *Cuore*, Vamba's *Il giornalino di Gian Burrasca*, and a variety of fairy tales. Complementing these readings are others about children by Don Bosco, Maria Montessori, and Giovanni Pascoli. Truglio adopts these texts because they offer "a very effective lens through which one can discover and analyze the values, the desires, and the self-image of a culture" and how those aspects are communicated to children. Holly Blackford teaches *Pinocchio* in an upper-division English course, Literature of Childhood, along with Disney's *Pinocchio* and the ABC made-for-TV movie *Geppetto*. She judges Collodi's novel "perhaps the quintessential text in which existential dilemmas of children come to the fore," but she adds that it "troubles and makes visible the Western conventions of children's literature that my students feel to be 'natural.'" Rita Mignacca teaches the novel in translation, again in an English department course on children's literature as a literary genre. The course is required for English majors preparing to enter secondary education. She encourages students to consider the "subversive aspects" of the text: issues of parental authority and of metaphysical authority, the mythology of motherhood, the concept of father as savior and its reversal.

Finally, the endlessly kinetic Pinocchio moves in other directions as well. Massimo Riva teaches about him in his courses on the relation between literature and digital media. E. Ann Matter introduces the book into her Religion and Literature course "as one of a number of inquiries into creation stories (along with *The Golem, Frankenstein*, etc.). . . . I read *Pinocchio* as a story about how creation by humans is a flawed process that must be finished by the protagonist."

Approaches and Difficulties

Pinocchio presents few difficulties in the classroom. That the novel is not long, its structure is linear, and its chapters are mostly short makes it easy to read and to include with a number of other texts in an average semester's syllabus. Collodi's Italian, aimed at children, is syntactically straightforward, and his vocabulary, while peppered with Tuscan forms and phrases, is for the most part quite accessible, even to students whose knowledge of Italian is not particularly advanced (at Washington University students read a chapter of the original text in their first-year grammar course). Instructors whose students lack the linguistic background to read the original may adopt the simplified version of the Italian original edited by Giuseppe L. Abiuso and M. Giglio, which includes grammar and vocabulary exercises. Another possibility is Gianni Rodari and Raul Verdini's *La filastrocca di Pinocchio*, which is less linguistically challenging than the original.

Instructors do note two challenges when teaching *Pinocchio*. First, they have to introduce a certain amount of background material to enable students better to understand the novel. Luisetta Chomel's assessment is typical: "I think that the text should be placed in its historical and sociopolitical context. From the beginning, however, students should be made aware of the multiplicity of *Pinocchio's* interpretations." Holly Blackford reports that she "fluctuate[s] between offering feminist readings, Marxist readings, genre readings, children's lit readings . . . deconstructionist readings, biblical readings, historical readings, cultural studies readings . . . and psychoanalytic readings." Klopp likewise reports reading the book "mostly as a portrait of social and economic realities in late-nineteenth-century Italy," though he also approaches it "as a pure fable in the Proppian sense and with some attention to myth-criticism." Rita Mignacca cites Jack Zipes's *Fairy Tales and the Art of Subversion*, Marina Warner's *Six Myths of Our Time*, and Bruno Bettelheim's works on children's psychology, specifically *The Uses of Enchantment*, as useful secondary readings; Marchesini likewise finds Bettelheim useful.

Second, instructors often have to struggle against students' preconceptions of *Pinocchio*, thanks mostly to the Disney movie that is all too familiar to young American audiences. Angela Jeannet reports that when reading *Pinocchio* "[i]nvariably, the students were surprised, first because they associated *Pinocchio* with their childhood and could not believe we were going to take it 'seriously.' Second, because they could not recognize the Pinocchio they knew in the Italian original." Sherberg has observed a similar reaction of surprise, because the novel so contrasts with childhood memories of the film and also because it represents a society that is far less protective of children than the students' own; this theme echoes in the other readings he includes.

Survey respondents related specific challenges to understanding the text. Blackford recounts student frustration at the form of the novel:

> It provides an example of picaresque (episodic structure) rather than a linear coming-of-age story in which a boy puppet actually learns to be good. Thus while the character Pinocchio falls into the rhetoric of the "good bad boy," he also defies true moral sensibility.

She also highlights the novel's contradictions, including "confusion about what makes a 'real' person, how a person develops through experience . . . and the random, episodic nature of human development."

Finally, instructors will inevitably confront one more challenge, though by no means an infelicitous one. Like all great works of literature, Collodi's novel reinvents itself with each reading, suggesting new interpretive avenues every time. It abounds with an elusive nuance, a sort of flight from order that mimics the puppet's race toward idiosyncratic autonomy. As readers return to it, *Pinocchio* both rewards and frustrates, disclosing more of its secrets while holding tenaciously on to others. Instructors thus enjoy the pleasure of rediscovering *Pinocchio* with every reading and of sharing that joy with their students.

A Note on the Essays

The essays of this volume variously address Collodi's *Pinocchio* or its translations or adaptations into other media. They share a conviction about the utility of the Pinocchio story in the classroom. While some essays discuss pedagogical experiences directly and others propose specific plans for the use of *Pinocchio* in the classroom, all suggest approaches to the novel or its adaptations that have proved successful.

The essays are divided into three sections. The first, "*Pinocchio* and the Nineteenth Century," puts the novel in contemporary social, historical, and literary contexts. Amy Boylan shows how Collodi's text reflects the culture and politics of the Risorgimento and Unification. Del Principe and Klopp both locate *Pinocchio* in the context of nineteenth-century gothic, Del Principe looking at gothic with a wide lens, Klopp narrowing the focus to Mary Shelley's *Frankenstein*. Dennis Looney discusses the importance of Ariosto's *Orlando furioso* in the nineteenth century and how that great poem may have influenced Collodi. Sherberg examines the origins of *Pinocchio* in the children's literary culture of the time.

The second group of essays, "Modern Critical Approaches," demonstrates the adaptability of Collodi's story to a variety of twenty-first-century critical contexts. Rossana Dedola subjects the novel to a Jungian reading. The essays by Carlo Testa and by Jacqueline Gmuca and Lorinda Cohoon both compare Collodi's Pinocchio to a model of the hero; Testa looks at other literary heroes, Gmuca and Cohoon look at theoretical models. Blackford and Truglio both address the novel in the important context of children's literature, Blackford outside the Italian context, Truglio within it. Cristina Mazzoni studies the novel from a feminist perspective—difficult, given the relative paucity of female characters and the problematic status of the blue-haired Fairy. Nancy Canepa examines the talking animals in the novel and their various roles. Finally, Laura Stallings proposes an integrated approach to reading and composition that advances students' abilities to understand and write cogently about the text.

The third group of essays looks at the novel's many adaptations in a variety of media. Angela Jeannet offers a sweeping overview of the puppet's fortunes, while Sandra Beckett details its many reincarnations in children's books. Rebecca West discusses several filmic adaptations of the novel. Elena Paruolo looks at the reception of *Pinocchio* in England and what that says about British culture. Marchesini offers an example of *Pinocchio*'s penetration into Italian theatrical culture through the works of Carmelo Bene. Finally, Massimo Riva takes the novel in a postmodern direction, arguing that the puppet's technological origins have found permutations in a variety of twentieth- and twenty-first-century technologies.

While the approaches suggested here by no means exhaust the possibilities, they will provide the reader with a variety of resources, both pedagogical and bibliographical, to exploit in the classroom. For all its entertainment value, *Pinocchio* asks many serious questions and asks students to think beyond the idea of the story that they carry with them from childhood. It is perhaps in that rediscovery of *Pinocchio*, through the eyes of a young adult, that the story will offer its greatest rewards, allowing students to measure the distance from their own first encounter with the puppet while discovering a value in the story that transcends their earlier appreciation of it. Rather than struggle against students' preconceptions, instructors can integrate them into the classroom, thus ensuring that the story continues to speak intimately to its readers.

Carving a National Identity: Collodi, *Pinocchio*, and Post-Unification Italy

Amy Boylan

Carlo Collodi—one of Carlo Lorenzini's many pseudonyms—is celebrated for inventing one of the world's most famous literary characters, but the details of his unconventional life are relatively obscure. While most widely known as a writer of children's stories, in particular as the author of *Le avventure di Pinocchio* (*The Adventures of Pinocchio*), the tale of a disobedient puppet who struggles to become a good little boy, Collodi in fact wore many hats—dedicated journalist, political activist, avid gambler, freewheeling bachelor, Risorgimento soldier, eccentric artist, dabbler in the occult, and civil servant, to name just a few.

He was born in Florence, in 1826, to Angela Orzali and Domenico Lorenzini. Of extremely humble means, his parents found it difficult to provide a stable environment for Carlo and his siblings, who grew up knowing firsthand the anxieties of poverty. As the Lorenzini family's financial hardships worsened, young Carlo was sent to live with relatives in Collodi, a small Tuscan village that was the birthplace of his mother and would be the source of his best-known pseudonym.

In Collodi, Carlo proved to be, not unlike his celebrated creation Pinocchio, rebellious and unruly—traits that would carry over into his life and work as an adult. He did settle down long enough to get a solid education—part of which was completed at a seminary—and to hone his skills as a journalist, while at the same time beginning to develop and express his opinions about Italy's complex and explosive political situation.

In the 1840s and 1850s, Italy was in the throes of the Risorgimento, the tumultuous and sometimes violent process of transforming the peninsula from a group of politically and culturally disconnected territories governed by foreign rulers into a single nation. Collodi adhered passionately to the ideals of the Risorgimento hero and political thinker Giuseppe Mazzini (1805–1872), who advocated a united Italy run by popular democracy.

In 1848 Collodi volunteered for the Tuscan army and fought in the First Italian War of Independence against the Austrians. The Italian victories in battle, and the accompanying glimmer of hope for independence they inspired, were short-lived; the Austrians regained their hold on the peninsula in a matter of months and increased the severity of their rule.

After his military service, Collodi returned to Florence and founded the politically satirical newspaper *Il lampione* ("The Lantern"). But soon after it was launched, the newspaper was suppressed by the Florentine government, headed by Leopold II, the grand duke of Tuscany. Although considered a relatively reasonable authoritarian leader, Leopold was under pressure from the Austrians to stifle revolutionary sentiment in the region. Collodi quickly founded another journal, *La scaramuccia* (1850–58; "The Skirmish"), less overtly political and dedicated to theater criticism.

If discouraged and disillusioned by his experiences with *Il lampione*, Collodi never lost his patriotic idealism and support for a unified Italy. When the opportunity presented itself in 1859, he enlisted to fight in the Second War of Unification, the results of which were far better for Italian patriots, as the Austrians were soundly defeated and Tuscany and other territories were annexed to Piedmont under the rule of King Victor Emmanuel II. A monarchy was not exactly what Collodi had envisioned for the new nation, but he, like many others, provisionally accepted it as the most expedient means of unification.

Returning to Florence in 1860, Collodi accepted, rather incongruously, a government job on the Florentine commission responsible for censoring dramatic works. (This job would be the first of a long line of government posts he would keep until his retirement.) But there is anecdotal evidence that he dedicated little time to actual work, spending his hours in the office instead on his favorite activity: reading journals and plays (Bertacchini, *Collodi narratore* 13).

During both his military and civil service careers, Collodi wrote articles, essays, plays, short stories, and novels. His work as a journalist, including his trademark pieces written in a sketchlike, ironic style and describing characters and scenes from Tuscan daily life, is gathered in several volumes: *Macchiette* (1880; "Sketches"); *Occhi e nasi* (1881; "Eyes and Noses"); *Storie allegre* (1887; "Happy Stories"); and *Note allegre* ("Happy Notes") and *Divagazioni critico-umorisitiche* ("Critical-Humorous Ramblings"), both published posthumously in 1892. He also composed little-known and critically unremarkable comedies, such as *Gli amici di casa* (1856; "The Friends of the Family") and *I ragazzi grandi* (1873; "The Big Kids"). His early novels, *Un romanzo in vapore: Da Firenze a Livorno* (1856; "A Novel in Steam: From Florence to Livorno") and *I misteri di Firenze*

(1857; "The Mysteries of Florence"), have interested critics and scholars but never earned him fame outside Italy.

He found perhaps his greatest writing inspiration when he set about translating into Italian the French fairy tales of Charles Perrault. *I racconti delle fate* (1875; "Fairy Tales") included such classics as the stories of Sleeping Beauty, Little Red Riding Hood, and Cinderella. Soon after completing the translation, Collodi embarked on creating a series of pedagogical books for schoolchildren that centered on the character Giannettino, a naughty little boy with whom young students could easily identify. The series includes titles such as *Giannettino* (1877), *Minuzzolo* (1878), *Il viaggio per l'Italia di Giannettino* (1880–86; "Giannettino's Trip through Italy"), *La grammatica di Giannettino per le scuole elementari* (1883; "Giannettino's Grammar for Elementary Schools"), *La geografia di Giannettino* (1886; "Giannettino's Geography") and *Libro di lezioni per la terza classe elementare* (1889; "Lesson Book for Third Grade").

It was during the thirteen-year span in which the Giannettino series appeared that Collodi also composed his masterpiece, *The Adventures of Pinocchio*. Originally published in serial form in the *Giornale per i bambini* between 1881 and 1883 under the title *The Story of a Puppet*, it was an immediate success. When he concluded the eighth installment in October 1881 with the word *fine*, Pinocchio having been hanged by assassins, there was a massive outcry by the story's young readers. The journal's editor, Ferdinando Martini, had to reassure Pinocchio's fans that "Signor Collodi has written to me that his friend Pinocchio is still alive and that [the author] has some good stories to tell about what he's been up to" (qtd. in Bertacchini, *Collodi narratore* 357). Under pressure from his readers and the editor, Collodi resumed the story in February 1882. *The Adventures of Pinocchio* was then published in a single volume in 1883.

All of Collodi's literature for children was composed during a time when the task of creating an Italian national identity was being passionately discussed by politicians, writers, and socially engaged citizens. The country had been unified from a political standpoint, but cultural and social unification had not been achieved. This unification proved to be extremely difficult, because of the far-reaching economic, social, and cultural problems facing the new nation. An unfair system of taxation exploited the lower classes; the standard of living was poor; most of the population did not want or know how to conform to the new civic and linguistic regulations being imposed on it; and political disagreements lingered.

The government promoted education and literacy as the essential solution to poverty and the general sense of civic detachment. The Casati Law of 1859 and then the Coppino Law of 1877 resulted in obligatory primary education of at least two years for all children. While the law was often enforced unevenly, it did play a part in the large drop in illiteracy between 1861 and 1911: the number of illiterate Italians decreased from 75% to 40% during those years (although the percentages were still higher among women and in the south than among men and in the north). The growth of the reading public in turn led to an increased demand for reading materials, and the proliferation of dailies and weeklies was seen as an excellent means of creating and communicating a national sensibility.

The increase in literacy, however, gave new urgency to the long-standing language question that afflicted the country: how to make standard Italian accessible to the inhabitants of all regions. Each region had its own dialect that was often unintelligible to other Italians. With the clear, dialogue-laden prose of *Pinocchio*, Collodi managed to evade the language barrier and at the same time imbue the work with a strong linguistic flavor that he felt would familiarize non-Tuscans with Tuscany's particular dialect.

Literature's pedagogical function; its influence on the public sphere, especially on children; and its ability to transmit national values and codes of behavior were much-discussed ideas during this period. Just three years after *The Adventures of Pinocchio* appeared, Edmondo De Amicis published his classic, *Cuore* (1886), a children's book aimed at instilling a sense of civic duty and class and interregional consciousness in young readers. Both works, along with the Giannettino books, were used as school readers for decades.

Collodi's Giannettino series reflects, as one may deduce from the titles, several key concerns of the newly formed Italy—particularly about education, pedagogy, and the creation of a shared sense of national identity—through presenting the various regions of Italy to audiences unfamiliar with them. *Pinocchio*, though also concerned with issues of national identity and the success of the new Italy (it emphasizes the importance of education and promotes such values of the post-Unification government as the primacy of family and a work ethic that helps Italians achieve a middle-class mentality and standard of living), was also an outlet for Collodi's ambivalence about late-nineteenth-century Italy. While *Pinocchio* has often been heralded as a mouthpiece for post-Risorgimento values, on closer examination it conveys skepticism toward the necessary sacrifice of personal freedom for the good of society.

Disillusioned as he was with the system of government Italy adopted and the continuing political disappointments of the 1880s, Collodi felt compelled to contribute to the formation of an Italian national character. Yet he did not simplistically embrace the government's insistence on education as the savior of the nation. In *Pinocchio*, he highlights the presence of poverty, especially in the form of hunger, and how it negatively affects one's ability to get an education (Perella, "Essay" [*Adventure*] 32–33, 36). In his more overtly political writing, he even called the laws backward that required primary school for children. He agreed with Mazzini's motto, "Without national education, the nation does not morally exist" (qtd. in Bertacchini, *Collodi narratore* 213), but also saw the hypocrisy with which the plan of education was carried out:

> I know as well if not better than you do that liberty is an invaluable treasure and education is a priceless gem, but do you know . . . where these two jewels should be safeguarded? I'll tell you: [in] the nourished stomach and

a secure life . . . . Let's see if by chance the sentiment of human dignity doesn't enter the bloodstream better by way of bread than by way of obligatory schooling and books.   (215)

True to his antiestablishment tendencies, he does not show Pinocchio getting the best education from school. Rather, it is from being on the road and reading during breaks on workdays (Perella 15, 22).

Collodi breaks rank again when it comes to his treatment of the family. The family was considered the most important social unit of post-Risorgimento Italy. The mother and father each had a prescribed role: she was the moral educator of the private sphere, he the ultimate authority and the breadwinner. From this foundation, Italy would propel itself into the modern, bourgeois European world. Collodi's narration of Pinocchio's struggle to accept the responsibility and thus security of being part of a family unit does fit with the official position on the all-importance of the nuclear family, but he presents a slightly off-center image of that family. First, while there is indeed a mother figure in the story, there is no true, human mother; second, Geppetto, as the father, is hardly the embodiment of patriarchal authority. Thus, even as he writes the lines, "Because when children go from bad to good, they have the power of making things take on a bright new look inside within their families too" (461), Collodi expresses a unique perspective on one of the foundations of post-Risorgimento Italian culture.

That he himself never maintained a traditional family, neither marrying nor having children, may account for his legendary loneliness later in life. He lost his mother and, his health worsening, reportedly staved off melancholy in cafés, where he drank and smoked excessively, against medical advice (Bertacchini, *Padre* 291). He continued writing until the very end. He died of a lung aneurism in his beloved Florence on 26 October 1890, at the age of sixty-six.

NOTE

All English translations supplied in this essay are mine.

Pinocchio and the Gothic

David Del Principe

In Italian literature and culture courses, I teach works that engage allegories of the Italian Risorgimento to foster students' knowledge of a period of history that is fundamental to an understanding of the Italian nation and character. One work that I use is Carlo Collodi's *Pinocchio* (1883), because it offers compelling insight into the social, cultural, and political realities of nineteenth-century Italy and because students are intrigued by the sophistication that lurks in a tale written for children. I propose an alternative, gothic reading of *Pinocchio* that emphasizes its subversive nature and dark vision. Such a reading considers the complex struggle between good and evil underlying the puppet's pranks and the tale's didactic intent.

Pinocchio deploys themes, allegories, and a tone indicative of the gothic genre, drawing on a European as well as specifically Italian tradition of the fantastic. I argue that the work is a monster narrative in its gothic doubling, its statement of reproductive crisis, and its portrayal of sociocultural fears. It conveys the tensions in families and nations that mark such historical turning points as the Unification of Italy. As Collodi wrote his tale, radical ideas of the time crept into the puppet's formation: vitalism, the spark of life; the homunculus, a miniature adult created in an alchemist's vial; Thomas Malthus's dystopian vision of reproductive potency and population; Charles Darwin's theory of evolution by natural selection; and the countless advances of industrialization and medical science of the late nineteenth century.

In teaching *Pinocchio* I propose the tale as a site for gothic practices based on the genre's proclivity to upset conventions, provoke anxiety, and incite the fear of political and cultural instability. I see its gothic character as coexisting with various aesthetic influences, including Romantic, naturalist, and decadent. Collodi's use of the tropes of recurrence and supernatural aging, which destabilize the life spans of Pinocchio and the thousand-year-old Fairy as well as the tale's ending is a fairy tale device applied to more sordid purposes. There is a palpable sense of doom and death in *Pinocchio*, suggesting that the gothic elements and motifs are an expression of the author's political disillusionment, acerbic social satire, and black humor. Teaching *Pinocchio* as a gothic work also promotes a study of Italian narrative in a comparative context, establishing a point of contact with such nineteenth-century gothic masterpieces as Mary Shelley's *Frankenstein* (1818). *Pinocchio* has taken the provocative, life-and-death metaphors that we study— reproductive, alimentary, evolutionary—on loan from the gothic. Their topical relevance in times of cultural crisis is one reason that both the tale and the genre have enjoyed renewed critical and popular interest.[1]

The puppet's sinister side stems from a pessimism inherent in Collodi's aesthetics. Collodi believes that "man is a flawed creation" (qtd. in Desideri 249), an idea that is even more ominously reflected in his original intention for the fate of the Little Girl—as a "pale emissary to the unknown realm of the dead" (Citati 215)—and of the puppet, who is wickedly hanged and left to die on the Great Oak in chapter 15. That Collodi recommits the puppet to an equally deleterious form of malice in chapters 16–36 suggests a strengthening resolve in adhering to his original, pessimistic vision. Reading *Pinocchio* as the author's recitation of an aesthetic-moral dilemma explains several thorny interpretive issues—the puppet's irrational relapses of misbehavior, a complex allegorical structure, and the contrived nature of the plot.

The puppet's vindictive nature can be credibly ascribed to a sadistic desire to take revenge for an aberrational birth. Pinocchio is born an artificial mutant; he is wooden, with two fathers and no mother. His unprocreated nature draws on a tradition of misbegotten others, such as Shelley's Creature and the vampire, whose unhuman deformities challenge and destabilize the makeup of the family. The puppet's patrilineal descent, his murky origins, and his mutability—born/unborn, alive/dead—reinscribe the matrophobic, reproductive terms laid out by Shelley's animal-human hybrid and proposes Geppetto, carpenter, inventor, and father in one, as an Italian Victor Frankenstein. The puppet's true nature is that of an iconoclastic crossbreed, merging several traditions of artificial creation—puppets, automatons, and monster figures—into a new amalgam: a wooden, bloodless, sexless form.

The incongruencies of Pinocchio's birth confer a disturbing dimension to the tale. When the uncarved wood first turns up in Master Cherry's workshop, it is already—alarmingly—animate, possessing faculties of speech and reason acquired in a dimly lit prenarrative past. Given the revelation that Pinocchio may have come from a nonhuman family, Cherry and Geppetto commit a monstrous error by trying to father a puppet child. The result is a long struggle between the partially born arboreal and human halves of Pinocchio's doppelgänger self. Cherry's mutilating, phallic blows with a hatchet to carve a table leg of the wood, which result in the disfigurement of his face and establish the pattern of punishment and reprisal that pervades the story, suggest a brutal midwifing scripted to beget a corrupted offspring. The mangling of Pinocchio's birth initiates a continuum of gothic transference and a procreative energy that, displaced throughout the narrative, is vested with increasing sociopolitical significance.

The two related meanings of Pinocchio's name, "pine wood" and "pine nut" (the second meaning predominated in Collodi's day), suggest several connotations of arboreal heritage and earthly immortality and insinuate a pagan subtext into the tale's Christian morality. What actually emerges from the puppet carving is a mutating, intermediate being who represents a fall from grace, a contemptuous nature that is reflected in his "[s]piteful wooden eyes," "impudent nose," and mocking mouth and hands (97, 99). But it is not only an uncertain past and protean form that create suspicions about the puppet's wooden body. The hasty, perfunctory nature of Geppetto's fashioning of the puppet, especially his omission of anatomical detail, marks Pinocchio's body as a site of allegorical articulation, one mediating the kind of political satire generally found in Collodi's journalistic and critical commentary. Pinocchio's impaired body elides transgressive representations of the (political) body with an aberrational birth (Risorgimento)—a manifestation of the author's growing estrangement from the sociopolitical body and commitment to individual rights. The puppet figures as a geopolitical expression on a subnational level, mirroring Italy's emergence from tyranny as an orphan state and the problematics of its (truant) pursuit of true revolution and independence.

Central to an understanding of the geopolitical allegory, and to the development of the interpretive strands of a gothic reading—the scientific, medical, ethnographic, and evolutionary—is the persistent threat of combustion that fire poses to the puppet. *Pinocchio* forsakes a contemporary frame of cultural reference to industrialization and progress in order to elaborate a Promethean symbolism based on fire and other elemental substances—wood and trees, coal, water—that, favoring a primitive domain to the realities of nineteenth-century Italy, suggests an anxiety over the puppet-nation's survival and future. The provocative pairing of a thematics of creation and fire elucidates *Pinocchio* as an idiosyncratic treatise on reproductive anxiety with ties both to the precarious family situation of Collodi's childhood and to Mary Shelley's interpretation of the Promethean myth in *Frankenstein*. Geppetto's carving of a nonhuman lifeform in a small, dark room near a "battered table" (97) evokes the conditions and ethical dilemmas of Victor Frankenstein's "workshop of filthy creation" ([ed. Hunter] 32).[2] But in a counterpoint to Victor's generative spark, *Pinocchio* recounts the Promethean myth with a decadent twist, associating fire with the puppet's combustion and death rather than with vitalism and placing it in a mechanical context. Indeed, the artificial representation of fire as a painted fireplace and steam when Geppetto creates the puppet (ch. 3) may be construed not only as a parody of Victor's generative use of fire but also as a foreshadowing of the more serious form of punishment that will be repeatedly imposed on the puppet for his aberrational birth. The specter of industrialization is raised in *Pinocchio* by negation: coal is stressed, not fire's role in supplying engine or steam power; the narrative recurrence of this raw material, scarce in post-Unification Italy, along with the themes of illiteracy and poverty, points to the social problems that jeopardized Italy's modernization.

An interpretation of the primal threat of fire in conjunction with the tale's prevailing nutritional metaphor, the dominant impulse to consume or be consumed, is essential to an understanding of a being whose shifting existence—pine wood, pine nut, puppet, and child—has multiple alimentary connotations.[3] A close look at Pinocchio's eating habits reveals a self-imposed hunger. He has ample opportunity to eat more but does not. He is finicky about eating pear peelings (127); he fails to eat the chick (115); he eats little, unsubstantially, or things that are low on the food chain—sugar (201), candy (279), vetch (263), cauliflower

(279), straw and hay (391); or he simply refuses to eat—a walnut and bread (167). By abstaining from food, he also avoids fire, the means by which it is cooked, a defense mechanism meant to ward off the threat of combustion or consumption (being eaten). Unlike Shelley's Creature, who turns to fire to cook and eat shortly after his creation, Pinocchio, a "puppet made of very dry wood" must flee from cannibalizing fire or risk death. Two examples of this threat are when Fire-Eater orders him thrown "on the fire [to] make a beautiful blaze for the roast" (147) and when Pinocchio is forced to flee the pine tree in which he has regressively taken refuge because it has been set ablaze by the assassins (179–81).

The puppet reacts to the threat of fire-consumption by countering with two kinds of nutritional resistance. He refuses to eat in order not to be eaten, and he refuses to digest or swallow—straw and hay (ch. 33), his medicine (ch. 17)—in order not to be digested. His being swallowed but not digested by the Shark illustrates this principle. His indigestibility inside the Shark is a symbolic form of defense, that is, the projection of his own refusal to digest. The episodes marked by the conjoined threat of fire and consumption also expose the artificiality and symbolic constructedness at the core of the puppet's unanatomical carving—for example, when he is transformed into a donkey because of "jackass fever" (ch. 32) and when his donkey "bark" is eaten away by fish and his wooden body is revealed (ch. 34).

The puppet's destabilizing metamorphoses—a reminder of his botanical-biological classification, which fluctuates among wood, animal, mammal, and human—invite questions about his internal organs that invoke the puppet nation's geopolitical symbolism and a racial context. His shifting bodily parameters and absent or mutating internal organs may be considered a physiological outgrowth of attitudes about the dispossessed, sociopolitical body that lies in the author's psychobiographical formation. The emphasis on Pinocchio's disembodiment, on his external and especially internal bodily spaces, is shorthand for the peninsular disembodiment and instability caused by the Risorgimento and the geopolitical decentralization of the 1860s and 1870s, when the Italian capital was transferred from Turin to Florence, the author's birthplace, and then to Rome.

The conflicted nationalism of Collodi underlies such an allegory. He was devoutly loyal to the cause of Unification but disillusioned by Italy's 1882 alliance with its former enemy, Austria, and neighboring Piedmont's jurisdiction over the Risorgimento and advocacy of a political platform that proposed the annexation of northern and central regions of Italy, including his native Tuscany.[4] If unresolved political tensions compromise the puppet nation's quest for transformation and independence, Pinocchio's resilience (ingested but never digested by the Shark) and his escape from the invader (but only under the protection of his tyrannical father) are jeopardized by a return to the subordination, deformity, and existential transience of his former family. To obtain true independence, he must abandon his puppet self and seek more radical transformation to human form, an act that points pessimistically to mounting ideological, ethnopolitical tensions and anxiety about Italy's growing imperialist ambition in the 1880s.[5] Such a context also extends to the many menacing forces in *Pinocchio*: Fire-Eater, the assassins, the rabbit pallbearers. Their presence expresses a colonized nation's racially coded fear of the imperialist other and, correlatively, a horrid fascination for its own emerging colonialist ambition.

Reading *Pinocchio* as a deconstruction of biblical iconography allows instructors to build the polyvalent symbolism that the tale endeavors to dismantle. There are indeed many biblical parallels—for example, that between Joseph and Geppetto, whose name is a derivative of Giuseppe: both are carpenters and father figures. But the parallel takes a mocking turn: Christ's conception and birth and the holy family are desacralized when the puppet is positioned as a sort of false prophet. Both Christ and Pinocchio are conceived asexually, but while Christ is flesh and blood and born to a human mother, Pinocchio is made of wood and not exactly born. The puppet's symbolic demolition of the holy family is punished by his own family's deterioration. *Pinocchio* takes the Bible's desexed account of procreation to a sacrilegiously abridged level by eliminating the mother from the reproductive equation. In monster narratives such a collapse, based on the patrilineal erasure of the womb, signals the arrival of a body whose materialization reflects, on multiple levels, a crisis of binary classification. Human and nonhuman, it exists at the border between species.

The actions of the puppet's Fairy-mother stand in stark contrast to those of the biblical Mary. She has an undead ("I am dead, too" [183]) and unstable presence: she changes from the Little Girl to the Fairy in chapter 16, to the puppet's mother in chapter 25, and to a she-goat in chapter 36. Abandoning Pinocchio at will, she is a weak counterpart to Mary. The Fairy's mysterious mobility mocks biblical virtuousness. Her irreverent rescue of the hanged puppet from his cross, the Great Oak, subverts Mary's acceptance of Christ's agony.

The most compelling example of Collodi's dark vision, persistent after his original intention to kill off the puppet, and of the deconstruction of Christian symbolism is the arboreal iconography that links the puppet's hanging to Christ's crucifixion. Whereas Christ sacrifices himself on the "tree of life" to forgive human sin and ascend to celestial immortality, Pinocchio resists suffering and death. His protracted, unborn condition suggests an earthly—indeed, vampiric—immortality; his arboreal heritage and consequent fear of fire invoke a primitive pagan domain rather than a Christian one. In chapter 17, after his hanging and resurrection, he is ready not for the reform that he claims so desperately to desire but for more mischief, malice, and lies. It is here that his nose grows so long that he cannot exit the room. Its resistance to medical treatment is only one indication of the puppet's growing invincibility on earth. In sharp contrast to Christ's mortality, Pinocchio's invulnerability is predicated on an absence of flesh and blood.

His final act evokes the transubstantiation of the Last Supper, a further sub-version of Christian symbolism. Like the disciples, who partake of bread and wine, the eucharistic symbols of Christ's body and blood and eternal life, Pinoc-chio partakes of flesh and blood in his transformation to child. But for the pup-pet such an acquisition denotes either humanness and mortality (the traditional reading) or (in the alternative reading I suggest) regenerative immortality. In ei-ther case, Christian eternity is sacrilegiously reduced to an earthly domain.

In the final scene, tensions remain unresolved. Although the child abandons his combustible half, he still does not eat—a nod to the author's belief in the in-solubility of the social issue of hunger. The puppet's final transformation to child is problematic in two ways, indicative of both gothic contrivance and the genre's tendency to impersonate a restoration of order. The nullifying deus ex machina of a dream is introduced, and Pinocchio gazes in the mirror at his human double "with a festive air about him that made him seem as happy as a holiday," then re-gards his lifeless puppet exterior, "its arms dangling, and its legs crossed and folded in the middle so that it was a wonder that it stood up at all" (459, 461). The transmission of his monstrously immortal, arboreal half to the child and the suggestion of an alarming cyclicality indicate a gothic transference more akin to the fate of the vampire than to Christ's redemption. In this way the procre-ative energy embedded in the tale is frustrated, and the ending overtly insti-gates a Jekyll-and-Hyde split. The puppet's terrestrial immortality, the trade-mark of miscreants such as the vampire, brings Pinocchio's fate to a European, gothic sphere of influence where one surmises demonic transference, such as that from Dracula to the offspring of his minion Mina Harker.

Strongly reinforcing the notion of transference in the final scene is the restora-tion of Geppetto to his carpenter-creator-positivist self. Geppetto's reversion to carving, which he acknowledges is, suspiciously, "all [of Pinocchio's] doing," en-sures the reinscription of the cycle of an artificial, wooden family (461). With only one unrepentant father (Cherry disappears in chapter 2); a moribund, phantas-mal Fairy-mother; and a son whose resurrection implies the extinction rather than salvation of a people, Pinocchio's family is as deformed as it was before. Col-lodi's ending, conferring on the puppet nation a spurious transformation result-ing from unresolved, procreative tensions, again offers the family as a crucial point of articulation for his psychopolitical and ideological conflictedness. Advo-cating unity and nationhood, he fears political paralysis and incomplete auton-omy. The hanged puppet nation's cries for rescue, emanating from a bloodless, wooden body, reverberate with the denial of a masochistic wish for submission to foreign powers, with the horror of instability. The wish is suicidal: the puppet nation would liberate itself by capitulating to the greatest threat.

The stirrings of gothic transference in *Pinocchio* are reflected in Collodi's in-vestigation of a human-evil correlative in "Pipì o lo scimiottino color di rosa" ("Pipì; or, The Little Pink-Colored Monkey"), a story about the escapades of a pink monkey published about the same time as *Pinocchio*, pointing to the development of monstrosity and a coherent motive behind his characters' actions. In "Pipì," the monkey's fear that being human means being a "frightful monster" (*Opere* 565) expresses a concept of evil that takes on greater complexity in *Pinocchio*. The innate fear of the human that Pipì confesses but the puppet suppresses explains the novel's narrative-long deferral of moral reform and conversion, proposing *Pinocchio* as Collodi's most complex exploration of the monstrous human cause of evil.

NOTES

[1] Instructors may be interested in examining the tradition of animated creation from E. T. A. Hoffmann's early nineteenth-century automatons to their reincarnation, in popular horror movies, as homicidal dummies, dolls, and toys. The tradition underlines universal themes, such as the fear of possession by nonhuman beings or the creator as a god.

[2] For a surgical-political allegory by Collodi that lends credence to my reading of Geppetto, see his "La Cometa e il Padre Antonelli" (*Opere* 759).

[3] Genot states that an outline of the entire tale could be drawn "based on food, bringing the euphoria and dysphoria into relation based on the opposition between 'to eat / to be eaten'" (307). Similarly, D'Angeli categorizes this food-based tension in *Pinocchio* as "Eat–Don't Eat–Be Eaten" (162).

[4] Collodi states in *Divagazioni critico-umoristiche*, "The complainers are not wrong when they say that Tuscany will pay a high price for annexation to Piedmont" (252; in "Il suffragio universale").

[5] Volpicelli emphasizes the nationalistic, expansionist spirit prevailing in Italy at the time of *Pinocchio*'s publication. The Triple Alliance (Austria, Italy, Germany) and the proclamation of Italy's African rights led to its expansion to Africa (Del Beccaro 193).

"Frankenstein" and Pinocchio, Nineteenth-Century Humanoids

Charles Klopp

It was the century of industrialization, of the emergence of the industrial worker and of mass society, of the machine and the valorization of science as never before. For this reason, it is scarcely surprising that the nineteenth century was fascinated by entities made by human beings that were humanlike yet not quite human. The most famous of these nineteenth-century humanoids were the nameless creature created by Doctor Frankenstein and commonly (though erroneously) referred to as "Frankenstein" and the puppet Pinocchio.

The English writer Mary Wollstonecraft Shelley first published *Frankenstein; or, The Modern Prometheus* in 1818. Collodi's novel first appeared as a book in 1883. *Frankenstein* was written by an English intellectual from a family of freethinkers. When her novel was published, she was three times a mother. *Pinocchio* was written by a journalist and confirmed bachelor from rural Tuscany who lived in Florence. Both works are birth stories that begin with the painful coming to life of a creature that has a father but no mother.

Shelley's and Collodi's creations are famous throughout the world today, thanks in part to their initial appearance during a period of intense interest in the similarities between humans and the complex tools and machines they were inventing. Hollywood too has promoted their fame, through Disney's *Pinocchio* and the classic 1931 treatment of *Frankenstein* with Boris Karloff as the Creature. (For a list of some of the more important films made on the theme, see Tropp 169–74; see also the essays collected in Levine and Knoepflmacher.) Clearly, there is something about the idea of these particular two humanoids that has earned them a permanent place in the modern and postmodern imagination.

To begin to understand this fascination, it is essential to know that *Frankenstein* and *Pinocchio* are both about transgression. The testing if not the breaking of norms is at the center of interest, though in Collodi's tale it is the social norms that are being tested, in *Frankenstein* the limits of nature itself. Although both works condemn the transgressions they describe, readers tend to sympathize more with the two transgressors than with the rules that are broken. The appalling tragedies in *Frankenstein*, many think, are not so much the fault of the pathetic Creature as they are of the overly insouciant, perhaps even criminally negligent Victor Frankenstein (e.g., see Tropp 63–65). Readers of *Pinocchio*, too, cannot help but root for the mischievous puppet.

It may be because *Frankenstein* and *Pinocchio* belong, respectively, to the literary subgenres of the ghost story and the children's fable—types of expression less valorized in both their days than were serious essays, poetry, and novels—that their creators felt entitled to introduce subversive themes into their tales. It may even be that the remarkable success of the two novels is due not so much to the wisdom of their ostensible messages as to readers' responses to the seditious notions that lay beneath the texts' respectable surface. In *Frankenstein*, there is a distinct appeal for sympathy for all outsiders and unconventional opinions, no matter how monstrous those individuals or ideas may appear. In *Pinocchio*, the glories of rebellion are contrasted with the tedium of conformity.

In both works these messages are directed at a collective rather than monadic readership. Shelley's novel was originally issued in three volumes so that several people—perhaps in the same family or circle of friends—could read and discuss it at the same time. Collodi's tale, first issued in installments in the *Giornale per i bambini*, was read simultaneously by numerous readers, who were free to discuss the progress of the story with others and to wonder what would happen next. The audiences for the two books, however, were very different. *Frankenstein* was made for consumption by adults, the mostly female, middle-class readers of the post-Napoleonic age in Europe; in terms of income and education, these readers did not differ dramatically from the characters who appear in the work. This audience delighted in gothic horror stories but was also concerned about advances in science and in the changing roles of women. *Pinocchio* was aimed not at the illiterate peasants of rural Tuscany featured in the book but at middle-class children whose parents could afford to buy the *Giornale per i bambini* and were eager to instill in their children the values that the cautionary tale appeared to advocate. That Collodi's story, which is set entirely in rural Tuscany, was published in a Roman periodical suggests that its prime audience were the offspring of the new class of government functionaries in the new (since 1871) capital of the new country of Italy. Many of these functionaries were uneasy about their recently attained positions and receptive to a story that addressed issues of obedience, honesty, discipline, and work.

When it first appeared in the *Giornale per i bambini*, Collodi's tale was titled *Storia di un burattino* ("Story of a Puppet"). As the title indicates, it is the *burattino* or puppet whose adventures are of primary importance in the book, with Geppetto playing a secondary role. *Frankenstein*, by contrast, is just as much the story of Victor Frankenstein as it is that of his Creature. The skilled student of physical science and his tormented vicissitudes receive more space in the book than does the being he created. Frankenstein and the Creature, indeed, have such a symbiotic relationship that many readers have concluded that Frankenstein's offspring is his rejected other half, a portion of his being that he does not dare acknowledge but that is nonetheless an intrinsic part of his being. Though Frankenstein and the Creature hunt each other more obsessively in the course of Shelley's book than Pinocchio and Geppetto ever do in Collodi's, the episodes that conclude both *Frankenstein* and *Pinocchio* consist of reunions after protracted pursuits. A dramatic confrontation on the ice floe ends Victor's vengeful hunt for the Creature who killed his bride. *Pinocchio* ends when the puppet finds Geppetto and obtains his forgiveness for his many transgressions. These reunions also mark the end of the humanoids as well as of their quest. With Frankenstein now dead, the Creature exits the scene predicting that he will expire "triumphantly" on a funeral pyre and then "sleep in peace" ([ed. Wolfson] 186). Pinocchio is similarly immolated by his transformation into the adventureless "ragazzino perbene" (460; "proper boy" [461]).

Though it began as a parlor game by a group of professional writers who whiled away a long evening trying to outdo one another in composing ghost stories, Shelley's novel is not without literary pretensions. Her characters have much more psychological depth than those in *Pinocchio*. Collodi's puppet rarely agonizes. The characters in *Frankenstein*, by contrast, worry about what is happening to them and frequently burst into tears and deliver long and impassioned speeches about their plight. If Pinocchio has the redeeming quality of a good heart and sometimes sheds a tear or two, expressions of sentiment in his story are undercut by heavy doses of irony that temper both the puppet's emotional outbursts and the speechifying of other characters.

These differences can be understood in part by considering the different periods in which the two books appeared. Shelley's work is a product of the Romantic period, its initial publication coinciding with the early idylls and patriotic poems of Giacomo Leopardi (1798–1837), Italy's greatest Romantic poet. In fact, many of the Creature's laments about his immense loneliness in a cold and indifferent world recall Leopardi's complaints about his abandonment in an unresponsive and empty, though beautiful, universe. *Pinocchio* expresses not the passionate idealism of a Leopardi but the anti-Romanticism and disillusionment of Italian culture during the years following the Unification. Collodi's novel shares a sense of pessimism and disappointment that can be found in contemporaries such as Giovanni Verga or Giosuè Carducci.

Economic history provides additional explanation for the differences between the two works. *Frankenstein*, though published earlier, is clearly the product of a more industrially advanced society. Mary Shelley wrote at a time when science and manufacturing were more fully developed in England than they were sixty-five years later in Italy. The Italian economy depicted in *Pinocchio* was still largely that of agricultural workers and small-scale artisans, without any hint of the "dark Satanic mills" that William Blake memorably described in a poem published the same year as Shelley's novel. Thus, Frankenstein is a scientist who in his "workshop of filthy creation" ([ed. Wolfson] 38) makes use of the latest in scientific and technological advances, while Geppetto is a country artisan.

The two humanoids belong to two different affective worlds as well. Unlike Pinocchio, who is neither handsome nor plain but simply ordinary, the Creature is spectacularly ugly. Even more important, Frankenstein's monster is a mature sexual being, while Geppetto's creation is a little boy. While the Creature wants a mate, Pinocchio desires a family—though the one he gets in the end is an oddly all-male one consisting of just the puppet and Geppetto. In this sense, the tales of both Pinocchio and the Creature could be said to end in sterility and frustration. The Creature (at least until Hollywood stepped in with *The Bride of Frankenstein* of 1935) never attains the mate he pines for. Pinocchio, once he has given up his freedom to become part of the family he now heads, loses his essential identity.

Still other differences mark the two works. Unlike the merry Pinocchio, the Creature is "a depraved wretch, whose delight was in carnage and misery," and one of his first acts is to murder Victor Frankenstein's little brother. In his own words, he is "wretched, helpless, and alone" (58, 104).[1] Pinocchio, by contrast, is not wretched; he is far from helpless (many come to his aid when he is not able to help himself) and rarely alone. Although a creature whose state of being, Alberto Asor Rosa has noted, "is a *natural* inferior condition that in fact predisposes him to temptation and guilt" (599), Pinocchio is ultimately susceptible to social redemption. The Creature, on the other hand, quickly places himself beyond the pale of civilized behavior by giving in to his violent temper, with tragic results.

Social relations in both books are frequently characterized by violence. But in *Frankenstein* almost all the violence is meted out by the Creature on innocent victims; in *Pinocchio* the puppet is himself the object of violence—or of near violence, since he usually escapes in the nick of time from whatever threatens him. *Frankenstein*'s violence is meant to produce a frisson of horror and indignation in its readers. In *Pinocchio*, especially after Pinocchio's hanging in chapter 15 proves not to be lethal, it becomes clear that the puppet will wriggle away from all the violent situations he encounters—including, repeatedly, the prospect of being eaten alive.

Both creatures are constantly on the move, in flight from their enemies or other pursuers at what is always a terrific speed (Gasparini 148–53). His ugliness, the stain of his forbidden creation on his physical countenance, inspires hatred of the Creature in everyone he meets. Pinocchio, however, from the very first episode at the puppet show, is never viewed as threatening. While always quick to sprint away from his enemies, he has little interest in fleeing from society and cannot imagine living without other people. Collodi's tale never suggests that one can live alone—out in the wilderness of Brazil, for example, where the monster longs to settle and perhaps procreate, or on the ice floe where his story comes to an end.

If less social than Pinocchio, the Creature is far more intellectual. Whereas Pinocchio knows how to talk even before being carved into a puppet—still no more than a "vocina" (82; "little voice" [83]), he begins his existence by roundly insulting first Master Cherry and then Geppetto—the Creature comes into existence aphasic and must struggle mightily to learn to use language. Unlike Pinocchio, he is not content with just learning to speak but teaches himself to read as well. He devours the books that come into his hands with an "ecstasy" that is followed by the "lowest dejection" (102), a reaction presumably due to the contrast between the life depicted in these books and his own miserable state—a typically

Romantic response to the disparity between ideals and reality. Pinocchio has little use for books, especially those employed in the schoolroom. If reading Milton, Plutarch, and others leads the Creature to ask such fundamental metaphysical and ontological questions as, "Who was I? What was I? Whence did I come? What was my destination?" (102), Pinocchio is more concerned with satisfying his immediate, material desires.

Spatially and geographically too, the two humanoids inhabit very different worlds. The Creature crosses vast spaces under extreme climate conditions. Pinocchio remains entirely within the narrow confines of small-town and rural Tuscany. The contrast of these natural worlds is echoed by the contrast of social worlds: in *Frankenstein*, we have English and continental society in the first decades of the nineteenth century; in *Pinocchio*, the society of Florence and rural Tuscany in the closing decades of the century. This difference is evident in the treatment of social institutions, especially the educational system. Attending school is one of Pinocchio's first projects, but he never completes it; in the end he learns to read and write on his own. The Creature manages to garner a solid education for himself. By the conclusion of Shelley's book, he is in many ways Victor Frankenstein's intellectual equal. While both Pinocchio and the Creature learn independently, Shelley's book seems to assume that education is suitable and natural for everyone, even for such an unnatural being as the Creature. But if Collodi repeatedly stresses the value of education, its utility as preparation for survival in a difficult and sometimes dangerous world receives at best skeptical treatment—certainly not the hopeful attitude toward education expressed by Mary Shelley.[2]

These different perspectives on learning are a consequence of how these two authors view society, especially in terms of the class struggle. Although both Shelley and Collodi were progressive thinkers in the context of their times, Shelley considers social issues from the perspective of an establishment from which she has distanced herself but that is still her point of departure in the formulation of many of her views. Toward the beginning of her novel, for instance, she describes a particularly happy moment in Frankenstein's life, when even "the peasants were dancing" (52). No peasants dance in *Pinocchio*. The agricultural workers who appear in Collodi's book belong to a "hard and pitiless" world (Asor Rosa 596), and the puppet's contacts with peasants are generally painful rather than jolly.

The characters in *Frankenstein* are almost exclusively well-off, educated, middle-class professionals or intellectuals whom we seldom see working for a living. Despite their present status as subsistence farmers, for example, the Laceys are in reality prosperous and cultured people temporarily in exile and forced to earn their living in this unaccustomed fashion. In *Pinocchio*, almost everyone works, many at the slippery margins of a difficult economy.[3] Only a few characters seem reasonably well-off. In the description of the city of Catchafool in chapter 18, Collodi satirizes the victims and victimizers of the new Italian capitalist economy in his descriptions of the disenfranchised and impoverished aristocrats as pheasants and peacocks without their tails and roosters without their combs, the rising new social class of the period as strutting predators.

Despite their many differences, the two novels have a unifying similarity. Both the Creature and Pinocchio represent repressed aspects of their readers' identities: that we could be the Creature frightens us; that we have been Pinocchio leaves us with a fond memory tinged with regret. As we recognize these hidden aspects of ourselves, we identify with the books' central characters, not with the books' overt messages. It is this recognition that accounts for the enduring fascination of *Frankenstein* and *Pinocchio*.

NOTES

[1] In this regard, see Meirieu, who thinks that the Creature might have grown up quite differently had Victor Frankenstein only attended more to his education.

[2] For the complex history of how newly united Italy developed national standards for education, see the excellent and thorough study by Bacigalupi and Fossati.

[3] The theme of unemployment is as important in *Pinocchio* as it was in the Italy when it was written. It is stated many times in the book that those who do not work and are not old or sick can look forward only to jail or the poorhouse rather than a normal life. Yet Collodi must have been aware of the enormous waves of emigration to the Americas and elsewhere during this period. Most of those who made the dangerous and unpleasant journey out of Italy were neither infirm nor old but ready and able to work, as they quickly demonstrated in the new countries to which they traveled.

Collodi and Ariosto: Episodic Misadventures in *Pinocchio*

Dennis Looney

Carlo Collodi was familiar with the work of Ludovico Ariosto (1474–1533), the Renaissance poet best known for his romance epic poem *Orlando Furioso*. In this essay I explore the intertextual relation between *Pinocchio* and Ariosto's work. In addition to several clear points of contact, aspects of Collodi's narrative design suggest that the nineteenth-century author may have learned a trick or two from his Renaissance predecessor. The serialized narrative of the thirty-six chapters of *Pinocchio* in certain essential ways resembles the narrative of *Orlando Furioso*.[1] Pinocchio is a puppet on a mission to become a boy—specifically, a good boy—somewhat like the knights in Ariosto's *Furioso* on their various quests in search of objects (e.g., weapons, horses, lovers) that will enhance them. To bring closure to a narrative built around the theme of the quest means ultimately to satisfy the quest. Ariosto's knights do not always find what they are looking for and in some cases suffer accordingly, but the principal quests that motivate his narrative are fulfilled by the poem's end. Pinocchio, too, eventually accomplishes his mission with his magical, moralistic transformation into a human being at the very end. That this transformation comes only after much delay brings me to the subtitle of my essay: "Episodic Misadventures in *Pinocchio*."

I take the phrase "episodic misadventures" from the fine analysis of Nicolas J. Perella:

> This motif [Pinocchio's rebirth from the belly of the Great Shark], then, allows Collodi to hasten to the happy ending of a story that, because it is built on episodic misadventures and the hero's proneness to fall into them, could otherwise have gone on indefinitely. ("Essay" [*Avventure*] 23)

Pinocchio's progress from puppet to boy is repeatedly interrupted by episodes that stall his transformation. Collodi depicts his character's life as a literal journey through a magical landscape full of enticing detours; it is also a metaphoric journey from the woodshop floor to boyhood, with many rites of passage along the way. These various escapades or misadventures enable the puppet to see the vices and virtues of the world as if he were a kind of pilgrim. From this experience he learns, eventually, to tell the difference between right and wrong. In generic terms Pinocchio moves from romance to epic or, one could say more specifically, from random and miscellaneous adventures to a quest that he succeeds in fulfilling.

The different nature of these two parts of *Pinocchio* has its origin in the serialized composition of the work. I know of no reflections by Collodi on the genre

of his book, but the title he chose and the versions of the title he used are significant. When he began publishing the serialized installments in 1881, he entitled
the ongoing story *La storia di un burattino* ("Story of a Puppet"). When he resumed publication with what would become chapter 16 of the larger narrative,
he named the continuation *Le avventure di Pinocchio* (*The Adventures of Pinocchio*). For the book-length publication that came out in 1883, immediately after the serial ended, he combined the two titles: *Le avventure di Pinocchio: Storia di un burattino*. Each of the main terms in these versions, "adventures" and
"story," has generic implications. The plural "adventures" suggests the multisto-
ried, open-ended narrative design of romance, in which the hero haphazardly
zigzags from one encounter to another, veering off the course that would take
him where his quest directs him. In fact, *aventure* in the French chivalric tradition is a technical term to describe the knight's endless and fruitless motion
driven by chance (Zatti 39). The singular noun *storia*, on the other hand, suggests
that the conglomeration of episodes does eventually yield a unified narrative. At
least there is enough unity that one can speak of the story of the puppet. In the
juxtaposition suggested by the title, "story" (one might also translate it "history")
assumes the generic burden of epic with its suggestion of narrative closure. For
Collodi, Ariosto provided an example, I believe, of how to balance the contrast-
ing requirements of these different genres.

There are two main nodes of Ariostan influence in *Pinocchio*: one between
chapters 15 and 16, where Collodi stopped and then resumed the narrative at the
juncture between *Pinocchio 1* and *Pinocchio 2*, at what I call the Ariostan hinge;[2]
the other is in the famous episode of Pinocchio in the belly of the Shark.[3]

We should not be surprised to detect Ariosto's influence at the juncture of the
two parts of the narrative. If Collodi learned anything about narrative construction from the *Furioso*, he learned how to begin and end sections. As an author
embarking on a serialized project, he found in Ariosto's cantos a handbook of
ways to end and resume a story. Ariosto is a master of opening and ending cantos
as well as of splicing different story lines into one another in the middle of cantos. At the end of a typical canto the narrator alludes to his feigned courtly setting and audience, claiming to need a break in order to rest his voice—for example, "Not more, My Lord, not more of this canto, for I am already hoarse
and wish to rest myself a little" (*Furioso* 14.134). Another, rather risqué, example
comes at the end of canto 10, where Ruggiero, eager to possess the naked Angelica before him, cannot get his armor off quickly enough. The narrator mis-
chievously breaks in on the scene of frustrated arousal. Although there is nothing quite so malicious in Collodi's design, he does enjoy teasing his reader with
suspenseful interruptions in his serialized narrative.

Each chapter opens with a brief summary of the sort one finds in many editions of the *Furioso*. At the opening of the prose after the introductory summary,
Collodi often plants a hook to link to the end of the previous chapter. For example, chapter 2 ends, ". . . se ne tornò zoppicando a casa" (94; "he hobbled on

home" [95]), and chapter 3 begins "La casa di Geppetto" (96; "Geppetto's home" [97]). A more complex link is how the narrator concludes chapter 3 and resumes the story in chapter 4 to emphasize the bond between the audience and him. "What happened afterward is so strange a story that it is hardly to be believed; but I will tell you about it in the following chapters" (105) is followed by, "So, children, I will tell you that . . ." (107), and the narration is off and running again. Chapter 5 opens with a typical "Intanto" (112; "In the meantime" [113]), somewhat like the cliché from westerns, "Meanwhile, back at the ranch." When the author is developing two story lines at once, "in the meantime" is needed.

In the fairy-tale discourse of *Pinocchio*, Collodi often feigns an orality that, whatever its other functions, also reminds one of Ariosto's pretending to recite his poem to the members of the Estense court. The narrator may use adverbs like "here" and "there," as if to point out a specific item to a watching audience (Lavinio 267–68). He will often link paragraphs with a word or phrase. The first paragraph of chapter 5 ends with, ". . . Pinocchio felt a little pang in his stomach that very much resembled a twinge of appetite." The second begins, "But a child's appetite grows fast . . ." (113). The phrase "The Talking Cricket was right . . ." is repeated almost verbatim near the end of that chapter: "The Talking Cricket was really right, then . . ." (113, 117). This pretense of orality is balanced with references to the world of print and manuscript culture. There are, of course, many references to books, since key turns in the plot revolve around Pinocchio's revulsion to book learning. There is an unexpected comparison when Pinocchio first enters the belly of the Shark: "All around him there was total darkness, so deep and black a darkness that he felt as if he had gone headfirst into a full inkwell" (419). Ariosto similarly moves from the realm of pretended orality to one in which writing rules, as when he comments on Astolfo, "[F]or I must attend to a great duke who calls to me and signals from a distance and prays that I will not leave him in my pen" (*Furioso* 15.9). Collodi's tone and posture as a literary storyteller are strikingly similar to Ariosto's.

In addition to the Ariostan touches that inform Collodi's narrative design, the first half of *Pinocchio* contains a verbal clue that signals the importance of Ariosto for Collodi. The first half of the Ariostan hinge is conspicuously marked by the prepositional phrase "in qua e in là" ("here and there," "back and forth"), used to describe how Pinocchio's body dangles in the wind when he is left for dead by the two assassins (186). Donald Carne-Ross has brilliantly pointed out that this phrase ("qua e là") is Ariosto's signature for the theme of the quest ([1976] 201–02). The phrase, or versions of it, turns up repeatedly at crucial points throughout the *Furioso*. Collodi does the same at crucial moments in his narrative. It is as if he were giving his scene at the end of chapter 15 an Ariostan imprint. The phrase also occurs at the beginning of chapter 24, when Pinocchio searches for Geppetto, and it recurs on his quest to find his father: in Perella's Italian text, see pages 268, 274, 318, 346, 364 (where the puppet looks for the voice of his conscience), and 414.[4]

In chapter 16 the Fairy, who has been brought into the work to save and revive

Pinocchio, summons her faithful servant to fetch the puppet from the tree where he was left dangling. The Fairy's servant is a poodle who is able to walk on his hind legs "just exactly as if he were a man" (193). The Poodle comes dressed as a coachman wearing the finest livery imaginable. After this introduction, one does not know quite what to expect next, when the Fairy commands him to get to work in terse, idiomatic Italian, "Su da bravo, Medoro!" (194). "Quick, my good Medoro," translates Perella (195); Ann Lawson Lucas renders it, "Come here, good boy Medoro!" (50). The dog's name is taken straight from Ariosto's *Furioso*.

In Ariosto, Medoro is a lowly Saracen infantryman with whom Angelica, the princess of Cathay and the object of desire of many of the Christian and Arab knights, falls in love. Angelica finds him wounded on the battlefield and nurses him back to health. Medoro memorializes their love by composing a Petrarchan poem in Arabic, which he writes on the walls of the grotto where the couple consummates their love. The poem says that Medoro has now been where no man was before. Orlando's discovery of the grotto and its telltale poem sends Orlando spiraling off into madness. The disgrace is not just that Angelica has taken up with another man but also that she has taken up with a nobody, a man of lower station. Lawrence Rhu notes that with the etymological echoes of Medoro's name "Ariosto explicitly signals his representative mediocrity. Medoro stands for the *aurea mediocritas* (golden mean) . . ." (79).

Collodi's casual allusion to a character in Ariosto's *Furioso* suggests much more than appears at first glance; it raises the theme of social mobility and the overcoming of class barriers. In Ariosto's poem the mediocre Medoro wins the biggest and most aristocratic prize of all. Collodi and other nineteenth-century authors similarly make the social standing of their characters and social mobility an issue in their work. Collodi's narrative becomes a lesson on the possibility of climbing the social ladder, of rising above one's station. For Ariosto's Medoro, blind luck and love do the trick, although he does exhibit a certain nobility in his desire to protect and then bury his leader, Cloridano. For Pinocchio (and all his young readers), Collodi stresses repeatedly that the key to social success is through education.

Collodi's Medoro retrieves Pinocchio so that the Fairy can tend to him—a crucial task, inasmuch as it resuscitates the flagging narrative, which had ended with chapter 15. Medoro links the two parts of the work into a unified whole. But if we examine the parallels that Collodi establishes with his allusion to Ariosto's narrative, we discover that the Fairy is to Angelica (who nurses Medoro back to health) as Pinocchio is to Ariosto's Medoro. Collodi's dog does not really have a counterpart in Ariosto's poem. The dog's function, a coachman no less, is to invite the reader to explore the connection in more detail. That is, the dog, bringing together the two parts of the narrative, enables the reader to perceive that an Ariostan hinge holds them together.

The episode of Pinocchio in the belly of the sea creature is the most famous Ariostan allusion in *Pinocchio*. Several critics have discussed it (see Frosini;

Gilbert). Some focus on the importance of *Moby-Dick* as a source (Campa; Colombo; Dusi). Incorporating a passage from Ariosto's relatively obscure, fragmentary piece the *Cinque canti* and privileging the Ariostan source by allowing it to be the literary space in which Pinocchio is reunited with Geppetto, Collodi positions himself at the cutting edge of literary historical scholarship in his day. The *Cinque canti* had recently been published in Florence in an important edition edited by Filippo-Luigi Polidori in 1857, at the time of the flourishing of scholarship on Ariosto in the mid-nineteenth century. Vittorio Frosini argues that Collodi knew the *Cinque canti* in this edition (71–72). Readers interested in an outline of this parallel between Collodi and Ariosto should consult Allan Gilbert's succinct piece. Typically for Ariosto, the scene in question, from his *Cinque canti* 4, itself has many sources. Ariosto's version of the man in the belly of the beast—for Ariosto it is unambiguously a whale and not a shark, as Collodi describes it—is modeled on a similar scene in Lucian's *True History*, the title of which Collodi cleverly inserts at the beginning of chapter 34.[5] We observe Collodi imitating Ariosto, who in turn is imitating Lucian. Collodi also knew the Lucianic source (Gannon). And both Collodi and Ariosto (and perhaps Lucian too) knew of the biblical story of Jonah in the belly of the great fish, the typological Old Testament version of Christ between death and resurrection.

We first hear of the terrible beast of the sea from the civilized and kind dolphin who answers Pinocchio's questions about Geppetto in chapter 24. An ungrammatical construction, atypical in Collodi's economical prose, calls attention to Pinocchio's anxiety: "Gli è il più babbo buono del mondo . . ." (272; "Oh, he's the best father in the world" [273]). The sign of heightened anxiety lies in the word order. In Italian, syntax requires that "best" follow "father," but Collodi splices the words to great comical effect, as if he were saying in English, "he is the most father good in the world." In the next clause, Pinocchio's syntax returns to normal.

Pinocchio wonders what has become of his father lost at sea in a boat not unlike the thematic "boat of romance" familiar to readers of romance (Quint 248–53). The dolphin then mentions the Shark. The Shark is the narrative device that sets in motion the reconciliation of father and son and the eventual transformation of puppet into boy. The beginning of the story's end resounds in these lines.

It may be helpful at this point to emerge from the belly of the beast briefly to consider in more detail the genre of Collodi's shipwreck narrative. Pinocchio's interactions with the Shark follow a specific kind of tale that was wildly popular in the second half of the nineteenth century. In his useful annotated bibliography, Kevin Carpenter outlines the constituent elements of the island adventure tale or, as it is often called after Defoe's *Robinson Crusoe*, the Robinsonade. In this subgenre of the novel and distant cousin of the romance, the protagonist usually experiences a dangerous arrival on an island; an encounter, often a confrontation, with the locals; exploration of the new island home; and a heroic return, with treasure, to the mother country. Variations of these four moments occur in the episode of Pinocchio in the Shark's belly, which marks the beginning of the end of the book's narrative.

Typically a protagonist washes ashore after a shipwreck, but Pinocchio lands on his desert island, as it were, when the Shark swallows him, as it did Geppetto before him. Once inside, Pinocchio encounters one of the locals, a philosophical tuna who tries to console him and advises him to resign himself to his fate. Pinocchio, noticing a glimmer in the distance, sets out to explore his new surroundings and discovers none other than his long-lost father, isolated deep in the belly of the beast. After their joyful reunion, Pinocchio cleverly plans their escape. One might conclude that Geppetto, riding on Pinocchio's back as he swims through the sea at night, is the treasure the puppet takes home with him. Or one could argue that the transformation of the puppet into a boy once they are safely home is the intangible treasure Pinocchio now possesses. Predictably, subsequent authors extended Pinocchio's islandlike adventures. Lucas refers to an unidentified work that highlights "Pinocchio Robinson with fur cap on desert isle" (Introduction viii).

I conclude with an admittedly more tenuous connection between *Pinocchio* and Ariosto. As the Renaissance poet dispenses with the character of Angelica deep in the poem, he challenges future writers to resume her story and finish it to their liking (*Furioso* 30.16). Many, in particular Spanish playwrights of the late Renaissance, responded to that call. Collodi does not challenge future authors to develop any section of his narrative, but the nature of this serialized medley of tales is such that many epigones do pick up where he leaves off. Why not append one more adventure to a book whose title puts "adventure" in the plural? Tommaso Catani writes of Pinocchio's extended visit to the moon, *Pinocchio nella luna* (1924). Eugenio Cherubini follows the puppet to Africa in *Pinocchio in Africa* in 1913, at a moment in Italy's national history when the dream of planting colonies in Africa was becoming palpably real. In subsequent works of other authors, our puppet travels to Rome, Vesuvius, China, Alaska, the North Pole, and Purgatory! Collodi ends his adventures with that ultimate transformation from puppet to boy, but one can imagine in some later phase of Pinocchio's spiritual growth a further change of the sort that Dante tries to describe with the neologism *trasumanar* as he first travels from Purgatory into the realm of Paradise: "passing beyond the human" (*Paradiso* 1.70). Once the puppet becomes human, what can stop him from going further in the rich literary traditions of romance and epic, secular and Christian, to which Collodi is so beholden?

NOTES

[1] See Perella on the publication of *Pinocchio* (Collodi, *Avventure/Adventures* 483); see Dedola's comments (153–56).

[2] D'Angelo, following Garroni, makes this helpful distinction between *Pinocchio 1* and *2*: the former consists of chapters 1–15, the latter of chapters 16–36. The reader without Italian can benefit from the four graphic figures the author uses to help visualize his points about Collodi's narrative design (78–82).

[3] For a list of other possible points of comparison, from the minute to the grand, see Negri, especially 441–43. Bàrberi-Squarotti also reviews some of the links between *Pinocchio* and Ariosto's writings in the broader context of narrative design. More generally, Perella suggests that Ariosto's blend of fantasy and realism is essential to understanding Collodi's art ("Essay" [*Avventure*] 58).

[4] This list of examples of the phrase is not exhaustive.

[5] "'Volete sapere tutta la vera storia? . . .' Quel buon pasticcione del compratore, curioso di conoscere la vera storia, gli sciolse subito il nodo della fune . . ." (408; "'[D]o you want to know the whole story? . . .' That fine oaf of a buyer, being curious to know the true story, quickly undid the knot in the rope . . ." [409]). Collodi's Italian repeats "the true story," with its Lucianic echoes. Another clever touch in this passage points to the sophistication of Collodi's art. The author puns on one of the most typical phrases for narrative construction and resolution, "untying the knot." The buyer unties the literal knot, which prompts Pinocchio to untie the narrative knot—that is, to tell his story.

Pinocchio and Italian Literary History

Michael Sherberg

Pinocchio's road to fame in Italy does not lack for potholes. While a fellow Tuscan, Giuseppe Prezzolini, could write in 1923 that *Le avventure di Pinocchio* is a key for understanding Italian culture,[1] many critics over the decades have given only a passing nod to Collodi's masterpiece. Some of the earliest attestations of the novel fail to highlight its importance: as Ornella Castellani Pollidori points out, in his preface to *Note gaie* in 1892 Giuseppe Rigutini lists the *Avventure* indiscriminately with Collodi's other works. Even Collodi's great friend Ferdinando Martini named Giannettino and Minuzzolo, protagonists of Collodi's schoolbooks, in an 1894 profile of the author, leaving out Pinocchio altogether (Castellani Pollidori xviin). The novel's instantaneous popularity with children appears not to have convinced the Italian intelligentsia of its value.

A dismissive attitude toward the novel characterizes many of the various histories of Italian literature that sprout like mushrooms from Italy's academic humus. One of the earliest examples, Vittorio Ferrari's *Letteratura italiana moderna e contemporanea (1748–1903)*, names some six hundred authors in the period studied, with the striking exception of Collodi. Edmondo De Amicis receives three pages, but with only the briefest mention of his great novel for children, *Cuore*. Collodi will subsequently make his way into literary historiography; but in competition with Alessandro Manzoni's *I promessi sposi* and Giovanni Verga's *I Malavoglia* to characterize the Italian *Ottocento*, *Pinocchio* generally loses. In his *Disegno storico della letteratura italiana*, first published in 1949, Natalino Sapegno grants *Pinocchio* two sentences, judging it superior to *Cuore*. In Giuseppe Petronio's *L'attività letteraria in Italia*, first published in 1963, Collodi earns barely a mention in a subsection devoted to Mario Pratesi and Renato Fucini. Petronio does judge *Pinocchio* positively, however, calling it

> [un] modello di narrazione asciutta e linda, senza sbavature sentimentali e senza facili moralismi, apparentemente abbandonata tutta al piacere dell'invenzione immaginosa e, diremmo oggi, surrealistica, in realtà tutta controllata da un vigile senso del concreto e del reale.   (749–50)

> a model of dry and pretty narration, without sentimental droolings and without easy moralisms, apparently wholly abandoned to the pleasure of imaginative and, we would say today, surrealistic invention, in reality wholly controlled by a vigilant sense of the concrete and the real.

Worthy of mention and contemporary to Petronio's history is Renato Bertacchini's essay on Collodi, published in 1962 in Marzorati's series *Letteratura italiana: I minori* ("Carlo Collodi"). While this series clearly seeks to give critical space to authors whose works tend to vanish from the pages of the more synthetic histories such as those mentioned above, Bertacchini's essay has the specific merit of seeing *Pinocchio* not as idiosyncratic but consistent with Collodi's journalistic career:

> Decidersi a un taglio netto tra il Collodi di *Pinocchio* e il Collodi precedente, e per *Pinocchio* perdersi dietro elementi di giudizio distaccati dall'opera, da un loro concreto storico motivarsi sull'esperienza delle prove minori, divagare infine sopra piani etici, culturali, politici, diversi da quelli in cui storicamente possono essere fermentate le *Avventure di un burattino* [sic], questo comporta, secondo noi, il rischio di compromettere l'intelligenza unitaria, organica, dello stesso capolavoro.   (2822–23)

> To choose in one fell swoop between the Collodi of *Pinocchio* and the earlier Collodi, and in the case of *Pinocchio* to get lost behind elements of judgment that are detached from the work, from their concrete historical motivation in the experience of the lesser efforts, to ramble finally among ethical, cultural, political planes that differ from those on which the *Avventure di un burattino* could historically have fermented, carries, we believe, the risk of compromising the unitary, organic intelligence of the masterpiece itself.

Bertacchini does not develop his argument at length, but his essay is one of a handful of critical works that examine the novel in the broader context of Collodi's career.

Only in more recent histories, which reflect the novel's established status as a classic, do Collodi and *Pinocchio* receive their full due. Giulio Ferroni dedicates four pages to the novel in his *Storia della letteratura italiana*, noting, in an ironic reversal of earlier trends, that because of the multitude of readings that by now cluster the critical landscape,

> [l]a grazia e l'intensità di questo capolavoro rischiano di rimanere schiacciate sotto il peso di tante e tali interpretazioni, sotto cosí serie responsabilità: ma il fatto stesso che queste interpretazioni siano possibili mostra l'inesauribile ricchezza inventiva e strutturale dell'opera.   (443)

> [t]he grace and intensity of this masterpiece risk ending up crushed under the weight of so many and such interpretations, under such serious responsibilities: but the very fact that these interpretations are possible demonstrates the inexhaustible inventive and structural richness of the work.

Beyond being a key to understanding Italy, as Prezzolini claimed, Collodi's novel thus is also something of a key to understanding the attitudes of the Italian intellectual class toward great works of literature that do not conform to the standards of the canon. Within the parameters of the Italian literary experience in the decades that bookend the Unification, when Giosuè Carducci, Vicenzo Monti, Giacomo Leopardi, Ugo Foscolo, and Manzoni receive the greatest attention,[2] Collodi does not write literature. His novel's rampant success does not suffice for entry into a canon predicated on seriousness and a sense of national purpose.

To be fair, along the way critics have examined *Pinocchio* with a sympathetic and often insightful eye. In 1921, Pietro Pancrazi wrote a lovely, nostalgic essay about rereading the novel over the years. His nostalgia is twofold: first, a wistfulness for a childhood long past, memories of which return each time he reads the novel; second, the sense of another Italy, "la piccola Italia onesta di Re Umberto" ("Elogio" 235; "the little honest Italy of King Umberto"), now lost as the storm clouds of Fascism gather on the horizon. At the other end of the Fascist experience, Antonio Baldini wrote a similarly nostalgic essay, "La ragion politica di *Pinocchio*," which however drew the opposite conclusion. Instead of locating the novel in a specific historical moment, Baldini focuses on the timelessness of Collodi's Tuscany: "È la Toscana vuotata di storia, vale a dire guarita in eterno da ogni commozione e turbamento e mondata d'ogni spirito di competizione politica" (123; "It is Tuscany emptied of history, in other words healed forever of every commotion and disturbance and stripped of every spirit of political competition"). The two essays are instructive, for beyond demonstrating the way in which *Pinocchio* came to be entwined in the history of Fascism, they disclose the novel's unique ability to give comfort. Both Pancrazi and Baldini testify to some degree of pain and find in the novel an analgesic, either in its evocation of a better time or in its evasion of history altogether.

In the last thirty years or so, Pancrazi's and Baldini's affirmation of the novel as a serious work for adults has generated the many and varied readings that Ferroni fears might bury it. More serious interest has treated Collodi's novel as a work of literature, understanding it both as a novel for children and as an object of serious research and appreciation for adults. Central to that effort, despite the debates that arose around it, has been Castellani Pollidori's critical edition, with accompanying essays about the language and structure of the novel. While much of her detailed philological research does not lend itself to the American college classroom, her work, as well as that of others, can find beneficial application on our shores.

For an American audience the most important work of the Italian philologists concerns the novel as a material artifact. Whether in Italian or in English, modern editions of the novel belie its serialized origin in the *Giornale per i bambini*, a children's magazine that first appeared on 7 July 1881 and continued publication for several years, eventually under the direction of Collodi himself. Castellani Pollidori unwittingly abets this tendency to obscure the novel's origin by basing her edition on the text of the last edition of the novel to appear in Collodi's lifetime (published in Florence by Bemporad in 1890) rather than on the serialized installments, which contain significant textual variants. But reading *Pinocchio* today as a novel, one should not neglect its first, adventurous form.

Much of the Italian criticism of *Pinocchio* deals with the unique parturition not just of the puppet but of the novel as well. Its serialized appearance, the irregularity of its production, the famous hiatus separating the *Storia di un burattino* from its sequel or continuation, depending on one's point of view, are well-known aspects of its production. Indeed, unlike a novel that first appears as a single unit between hard covers, *Pinocchio* allows its readers to study it in fieri, as if they were standing behind Collodi's shoulders as he wrote. Equally important is its movement from the ephemeral *Giornale per i bambini* to a none-too-stable form as a finished novel. Not only does the text itself change, so does the experience of reading it. Until Collodi published his definitive final chapter, in which Pinocchio awakens as a little boy, readers had no idea for how long installments would continue to appear. Collodi had teased them in a couple of ways: first, by apparently killing the puppet and then reviving him; second, by producing the chapters on an irregular basis, so that one could never be sure when or whether another chapter would appear. Readers of the book, on the other hand, know that they have before them a complete work with a beginning, middle, and end. They therefore cannot approach the text with the same anxiety of anticipation as did its earlier readers.

The sporadic appearance of installments in the *Giornale*, coupled with their pauses, raises another point. Readers tend to think of the serialized novel as something produced sequentially, when in fact one can only assign a *terminus ante quem* for the composition of each chapter, the date of publication. But order of publication does not necessarily reflect order of composition. In this context, Collodi's silences assume new significance. During the nearly four months separating chapter 15 from chapter 16, he likely worked on chapters 16–23 in an undisclosed order. In like manner the six weeks separating chapter 23 from chapter 24 may have involved work on chapters 24–29, and at some point during the almost six months separating chapter 29 from chapter 30 he began work on the concluding chapters. Each hiatus is accompanied by a moment of high narrative tension: chapter 15 ends with Pinocchio's hanging, chapter 23 with Pinocchio's underwater disappearance, and chapter 29 with the foretold stalling of his conversion into a *ragazzo perbene* ("proper boy"). The first two cases in particular represent potential moments of closure. Pinocchio's hanging has received the most commentary in this regard, but his disappearance under the waves is equally ominous—had Collodi never written another word, Pinocchio would simply have vanished, awaiting perhaps the pen of another to tell what became of him. The novel form, which elides the chronology of composition, tends also to obscure the significance of such moments; but attention to the novel's serialized origin highlights them.

To the extent that our experience of the novel *qua* novel has eclipsed its earlier incarnation, little attention has been paid to the material context in which it first appeared. Writers about *Pinocchio* regularly invoke the *Giornale per i bambini*, but the critical literature contains little about this magazine. A weekly, the

Giornale eclectically mixed nonfiction, prose stories, poetry, and short plays, with many translations from English and French. Its editor, Ferdinando Martini, had intuited along with Horace that the useful and the delightful are best served up together. Indeed, at the end of the first year he declared that his magazine would continue to *dilettare istruendo*, "delight by instructing," without recourse to *la boria pedagogica*, "pedagogical vanity." The first issue contains, for example, "Un viaggetto per la casa," by Rigutini, a grammar and vocabulary story with certain words (diminutives, metaphors, metaphoric verbs, etc.) in italics. Some articles cover such topics as the physics and mechanics of the telephone and how cookies are manufactured. With clear nationalistic intent the *Giornale* includes an article by Guido Mazzoni, "Qui c'è la nostra Italia," published 1 December 1881, which explains why young Italians should love their country.

La storia di un burattino, specifically chapters 1 and 2, follows as the second feature in the first issue, a placement that is anything but casual. The first piece, by Martini himself, is entitled "Come andò" ("How It Happened"), and explains the magazine's birth through a story about reading, history, and vocabulary building. Several children of various ages—the oldest, Carlo, has completed the *quarto elementare* or fourth grade—are sharing a story about Spurius Cassius; the group includes both active readers and a preliterate audience. At one point some of the children get angry at the use of the word *insigne*, "great" or "famous," which they do not understand. Consulting the dictionary, they happen upon *casta*, "chaste," which they take for a dirty word. One of the children, Mariuccia, offended by what their foray into the dictionary has led to, exclaims, "se è un libro che la dobbiamo leggere noi, bisognerebbe che ci mettessero delle parole che le intendiamo, o se non bisognerebbe ce la spiegassero" (1–2; "if it is a book that we must read, then they should put words in it that we understand, or else they should explain them to us"). Two other children then rebel against reading history and lobby for a *novella*, suggesting familiar titles like "Puss in Boots." An exasperated Michele mocks them, so the two go off to read by themselves.

The conversation then turns to a generalized complaint that stories become boring after a couple of readings. Mariuccia recalls that the previous summer at the baths some American children had magazines that arrived in the mail every week. They remember all the wonderful features, including "il teatro dei burattini," the puppet theater. The father explains that he cannot buy this publication for them, because it does not exist in Italy. The children ask why not, and the father stammers, "Perchè perchè . . . il perchè non lo so nemmeno io" (2; "Because because . . . I really don't know why not"). Martini then identifies himself as the father who asked why such publications exist for children in America, England, and France but not in Italy and who decided to address this problem.

Certain elements of the narrative suggest that Martini wrote it after having read Collodi's first two chapters, as a sort of pendant to the *Storia di un burattino*. Besides the reference to the puppet theater and the expressed sense of frustration that children do not have regular access to new reading material, there is a brief exchange in which the children parody the stereotypical openings of stories. After the two youngsters insist on hearing a *novella* instead of the Spurius Cassius history, Michele responds by beginning a story: "C'era una volta un re . . ." ("Once upon a time there was a king"). Carlo then continues, "Che aveva tre figluole" ("who had three daughters"), and Mariuccia adds, "La più piccina si chiamava Rosetta" ("the youngest was named Rosetta"). The children then chime in together, "E era bella come un occhio di sole" ("And she was beautiful like a sunbeam"). The choral conclusion suggests that they know this incipit only too well, to the point of boredom (1).

In this context Collodi's own opening springs to mind:

> C'era una volta . . .
> —Un re!—diranno subito i miei piccoli lettori.
> —No, ragazzi, avete sbagliato. C'era una volta un pezzo di legno.
>
> (82)

> Once upon a time, there was . . .
> "A King!" my little readers will say right away.
> No children, you are wrong. Once upon a time there was a piece of wood.
>
> (83)

Collodi's adjective *subito* ("suddenly") acquires unexpected value, suggesting the sort of reflexive intuition of narrative formulas that these sophisticated little readers display. His refusal to tell a conventional story about a king accompanies a dramatic tonal drop, from the children's automatic invocation of a king to the disconcerting presence of a piece of wood.[3] The novelty of Collodi's shift in protagonist, which suggests that something as simple as an uncarved piece of wood can be the stuff of a satisfying tale, suggests just how bored and desperate these young readers are. It also discloses instantly an aspect of Collodi's novel that makes it a classic: the subtle ironies. For while the piece of wood may substitute for the king as protagonist of the tale, these first sentences also leave open the possibility of an identity between the king and the piece of wood, suggesting a reading of the novel as political allegory or, more specifically, as a critique of the young Italian monarchy.

Martini's brief narrative, coupled with the opening of Collodi's masterpiece, thus serves to demonstrate in yet another way how that part of the critical history that marginalized *Pinocchio* missed an important point. Literary histories are by their very nature prescriptive enterprises: they mean to tell their readers what to read and what to value. To some degree they assume a naive audience; their respectful tone in fact masks an underlying condescension. The same sort of paternalism informs the relation between the literary culture for children and its products. When Martini's alter ego exclaims that he cannot explain why Italy does not supply the sort of children's magazines that circulate elsewhere, he takes aim at a publishing industry that confines the acceptable choices for children in narrow boundaries. By mocking the standard formulas, the children vociferously reclaim the right to be their own arbiters of quality.

In this context Collodi's novel realizes its full subversive power. Pinocchio himself, as Collodi makes clear in the metaliterary play with which he opens the narrative, reflects the textual ideal of an older generation: he is invented in order to be functional, exploitable, and profitable. By refusing to conform to this ideal, the puppet comes to personify a broader rebellion against the poverty of an exhausted literary tradition. His faux deaths at the hands of assassins or the sea suggest the difficulty that the new will encounter as it forges a path through the thicket of the old. But the novel's ending, in which Pinocchio realizes his dream to become a *ragazzo perbene*, need not be read as a sign of conformist defeat. Rather, it marks the puppet's entry into the mainstream, a passage from a place of marginality, the magazine, to a place of legitimacy, the novel, in which endures the image of Pinocchio not as *ragazzo perbene* but as rebel. In other words, the narrative accurately reflects the novel's trajectory in literary history, the ambiguities of embrace and diffidence that have marked its reception, not just among children but among adults as well. Appearing as it does at a propitious moment, following the birth of the new Italy, *Pinocchio* announces the need for a new literary culture—a culture that it helps generate.

NOTES

All English translations supplied in this essay, except those from Perella's bilingual edition of Collodi's *Avventure/Adventures*, are mine.

[1] "Pinocchio è la pietra d'assaggio degli stranieri. Chi capisce la bellezza di Pinocchio, capisce l'Italia" (184; "Pinocchio is the gauge [touchstone] for foreigners. Those who understand the beauty of Pinocchio, understand Italy").

[2] The exception that proves the rule, in Ferrari's volume, is Verga, mentioned for his plays and later for his novels, though dismissively: "Nel romanzo del Verga l'ambiente, sempre siciliano, è vigorosamente dipinto, men chiari e spiccati son forse i singoli personaggi; lo stile è nervosa, a scatti, a reticenze, la forma deliberatamente ricca di dialettismi di costrutto e di parola" (347–48; "In Verga's novel the setting, always Sicilian, is vigorously painted, while the individual characters are perhaps less clear and distinct; the style is nervous, jerky, reticent, the form deliberately rich with dialect, both in syntactical constructions and words"). The emphasis on the Sicilian quality of Verga's writings marks him as a marginal writer of faint regard. Collodi would appear to have a similar defect, not for being overabundantly Tuscan but for writing outside a different mainstream, that of adults.

[3] Adopting Frye's categories, the drop corresponds to a shift from the high mimetic mode, in which the hero is a leader, to the ironic mode, in which the hero displays inferior power or intelligence (34). Redoubling the irony is the fact that Pinocchio's power and intelligence may not be inferior to our own after all.

Pinocchio between Symbols and Archetypes

Rossana Dedola

Thanks to its use of the formula "C'era una volta" (82; "Once upon a time, there was" [83]), the incipit of *Le avventure di Pinocchio* would seem to begin in the absolute time of the fable. Yet here, as is said at once, the king typical of the fable is missing. The protagonist is a piece of ordinary wood, of the type used to light fires and warm rooms, which appears by chance in the workshop of an old wood-carver. If we pay attention to the story's initial situation—following the suggestion of Jungian analytic psychology, which in the interpretation of fables attributes great importance to the initial situation and compares it with the *lysis*, the conclusion to which the developing events lead—we realize at once that the dimension of royalty is missing. It will be necessary to see, following the story, to what solution this initial lack will lead.

The story of Pinocchio can be read as a process of initiation. Geppetto, who brings Pinocchio to life, not only carves him but also teaches him to walk. The ability to walk on one's own two feet is the first act toward separation and autonomy, but the search for autonomy and the attempt to separate, from the first pages in the novel, are exaggerated beyond measure. Just as soon as he has been carved, Pinocchio finds the door open and escapes; a carabiniere who grabs him by the nose ends his flight (ch. 3). The frustrated search for freedom is followed by an extreme remedy that involves not Pinocchio but Geppetto. It is for the wood-carver that the prison door opens, in order to enclose him in the extremely limited space of a cell. The exaggerated openness of Pinocchio contrasts with imprisonment for Geppetto.

Yet it is precisely by modeling the puppet and then making beautiful new feet for him (ch. 8) that the old parent reveals himself as an artist of genius. Pinocchio receives life from Geppetto, but the wood-carver's talent, which would otherwise remain hidden, thanks to his puppet acquires space, revealing a power that one would not have suspected. The initiation of the little Pinocchio is intimately connected with his creator.

Following Pinocchio's misadventures, we realize that the puppet does not succeed in making his lived experiences his own: they slide past him or pass through his body, as if he were a sieve that can hold nothing. At the same time, he cannot resist temptation, passing from one desire to the next and getting continually in trouble. He is quick to repent, but his repentence is superficial, and only at the moment of danger does he recall the warnings of his father or of the Cricket. He tells whomever he meets what has happened to him; he cannot hold onto what he receives (the spelling book [ch. 9], the gold coins [chs. 12 and 19]); he cannot stop himself; he does not reflect on what has happened to him; he always repeats the same mistakes; he allows himself to be persuaded and is easily influenced. Moreover, he does not know how to nourish himself, as the scene of the omelette and the chick that flies out the window demonstrates (ch. 5). That he is too open to the outside is seen in his encounter with the Cat and the Fox. Notwithstanding their repeated deceits, he continues to consider them both good people (ch. 12).

But Pinocchio, at least in the first scenes, is not alone. The modest Geppetto is always with him. Geppetto has an attitude of closure in the face of reality. He may imagine traveling around the world but shows no great spirit of adventure; he has no ambition, content with his fantasies and his life of poverty. The symbol of his situation is the painted fireplace with the painted pot of beans that boils happily in an empty, cold little house, lacking even the smallest trace of food (97).

Opposed to omnipotent childhood—the excessive openness, the total availability, and the temporariness of the child—is impotent old age, an old man closed up in himself. We compare the infantile puppet and the ancient puppeteer, two male figures who represent the extremes of human existence. What is missing is the adult male. If we think about the novel's conclusion, in which Pinocchio and Geppetto reunite after a long separation, we can say that the movement begun by the initial lack goes precisely in the direction of adulthood.

That impetus will in fact lead to events that only seem to lose their way in the labyrinth of error and repetition. Actually they are directed at this lack that must be filled. The son (child) will act as a father (adult) to his old father. The process will reach this solution-conclusion.

But the initiation into manhood can be realized only after the confrontation with what is absent at the beginning: the feminine. Then Pinocchio can emerge from the blocked condition of the puppet and enter the process that will bring him to the adult dimension. The feminine, though it changes in appearance, will remain constant and help the puppet in his often dramatic encounter with the powerful, voracious, destructive masculine: Fire-Eater, the fisherman, the peasant, the little man, the circus manager, and so on.

The beautiful Little Girl with blue hair is the first female figure that appears in the novel, and she shows at once that she has something in common with Pinocchio: she appears as a doll, she speaks without moving her lips, and her little voice seems to come from the other world: the Little Girl awaits the bier that will carry her away (183, 185). The child soul, sister of Pinocchio (213), is dead. From now on, he cannot be a child; the omnipotent dimension of childhood is abandoned. The apparition reveals that Pinocchio may not turn back. Immediately thereafter the assassins capture him and hang him from a branch of the Great Oak. It would seem therefore that the unbridled instincts, divided from consciousness, the assassins Cat and Fox, lead to paralysis and suffocation. In this tree, Pinocchio dies and is reborn.

The Little Girl does not help Pinocchio; she does not let him into the little white house. She replies to his openness, his availability, as in the meeting with the Cat and the Fox, with closure, leaving him in the hands of the assassins. Is this refusal an act of cruelty, as many have said? Or is it a test, which, leading to pain, pushes Pinocchio along the road of initiation?

Suspended in air on the Great Oak, Pinocchio cannot move; he cannot go forward or turn back; he is forced into passivity. The narrative makes a sharp turn: *Storia di un burattino*, the first version of the novel, ends, and the *Avventure di Pinocchio* begins. In this new beginning, Pinocchio has returned to the woods, to the mother-tree. The Little Girl will not help him. Or perhaps, by not coming to his assistance, she is in fact helping him: he must experience solitude and abandonment.

By putting the word "end" at this point in the story, the scene of the hanging, the author chose to leave the puppet hanging forever from the tree of death. In starting to write again, Collodi transforms the tragedy into a new beginning. This symbolic shift allows us to understand the great power of destruction and rebirth that is tied to the maternal archetype represented by the tree. If the son cannot grow as an autonomous personality, he will remain forever dependent on the mother, the eternal object of his dedication.

The beautiful Little Girl, transformed into a fairy, not only saves Pinocchio but also makes him confront what seems completely missing in him: the ability to change. Over the course of the novel, the Fairy will be transformed into a beautiful lady, the kindly woman of the Island of Busy Bees (ch. 24), and will even become a powerful dream figure in the final apparition in Pinocchio's dream. The "good" Fairy has lived in the woods for a thousand years (191); she is therefore older than Geppetto yet still a child. At the same time she is the lady of the trees and the plants, the lady of the animals, the great goddess. The goddess-fairy becomes Pinocchio's spiritual guide; from the moment he is freed from the Great Oak, he is under her protection, even if the Fairy never intervenes to deliver him from suffering, error, or fear. Like a solicitous mother, she is patient; she puts up with his many requests when he does not want to take his medicine; she even adjusts his pillow and, to make him happy, closes the door to the room. But the door that she closes suddenly opens, and four black rabbits enter, carrying a little coffin on their shoulders (205). The suddenness with which death appears, frightening the sick little one, shows how life and death do not oppose each other but end up touching.

In the Fairy's house Pinocchio confronts the ambivalence of life; he swallows his medicine, which is bitter but restores his health. While taking care of him, the Fairy does not hold him back, does not indicate the road that he must travel in order to become a human being; she lets him go, to find the path by himself. His adventures will not be a simple repetition, an empty back-and-forth movement as before; now he will learn something new from each experience, from each regression. The vicious circle that led him to repeat the sterile movement of flight and return has been broken, and he will proceed along a spiral that does not close on itself, to reach new goals.

Pinocchio learns a lesson of great importance from the Fairy, one that Geppetto could not give him: the way to grow up. Pinocchio asks her how she managed to grow, and she responds that only "proper" children can grow (283, 285). For the first time, serving almost as a mirror to him, the Fairy shows him that he is not empty: he has a good heart, therefore change is possible.

A relationship of consanguinity ties the Fairy to Pinocchio, a maternal bond that does not constrain him but shows him how to walk the true path ("vera strada" [286]). Note that the Fairy does not say "right" but "true" path: one follows it by obeying not external laws but one's own heart. He is under her benevolent eye; her maternal presence, which serves as a guide to change, is reinforced through the second part of the novel, leading up to her final appearance in a dream. The dream expresses the feeling of being accepted for what one is and not because one conforms to an imposed model of obedience and good behavior.

> Then he went to bed and fell asleep. And while he slept, he dreamed that he saw the Fairy, all smiling and beautiful, who gave him a kiss and said:
> "Well done, Pinocchio! Because of your good heart I forgive you all the mischief you've done up to now. . . .   (457)

When Pinocchio awakens and looks in the mirror, he sees reflected there the new image of him, "a handsome boy with chestnut brown hair and light blue eyes, and with a festive air about him that made him seem as happy as a holiday" (459). Geppetto too is transformed: he is healthy, sprightly, in good humor and fully active, seen designing "a beautiful picture frame richly decorated with leaves, flowers, and little heads of various animals" (459). The conclusion to which the initial thrust arrives is therefore the transformation not only of the child but also of the old man.

Facing the old wooden Pinocchio, propped up in a chair and now immobi-
lized in the abandoned pose of the marionette, the new Pinocchio says good-bye
to his old identity and to the readers: "How funny I was when I was a puppet!
And how glad I am now that I've become a proper boy!" (461). The final ellipsis
in the Italian text (460) links up with the initial sentence, which announced the
exceptional nature of the fable that was about to be narrated: "Once upon a time,
there was . . ." (83).

Pinocchio-Picaro / Pinocchio-Parzival

Carlo Testa

Modern Italy was made (unified, that is), rather quickly and to some extent un-expectedly, between 1859 and 1861. Alluding to the immense cultural and eco-nomic heterogeneity of a country that had been politically divided for about thir-teen centuries, the politician Massimo D'Azeglio thereupon famously quipped that, after Italy had been made, the next challenge was "to make Italians."[1] It is to some degree in this context that we need to read Carlo Collodi's abundant ped-agogical production, which stretches far beyond *Pinocchio*. Even a cursory look at his work suggests that Collodi does not simply write for children—he writes for *Italian* children in fieri. And this is precisely what makes *Pinocchio* stand out in the history of the novel of education. His other educational works assume the (fictional) preexistence of his young protagonists, but *Pinocchio* does not: in *Pi-nocchio*, he proceeds to an eerily literal concretization of D'Azeglio's metaphor by making an archetypal Italian, quite literally, ex nihilo.

Pinocchio is unique also because its author provides mixed, open-ended sig-nals about the very project of education he is attempting to drum into the pup-pet's (and the readers') wooden heads. Collodi makes much of the *ordo mundi* of post-Unification Italy to which he is trying to convert Pinocchio, but he is also deeply ambivalent about it. *Pinocchio* is not merely an artistic fairy tale (a *Kunst-märchen*); it is, more exactly, the old-age fairy tale of an elderly man who lives in post-Romantic melancholy for the depressing reason that the cherished, wished-for woman of his early dreams (in this case, Italy) has materialized, when all is said and done, as old and ugly.

Framed in the context of the European bildungsroman, Collodi's puppet story reminds us from many different angles about one and the same basic dif-ficulty: that Italy's literary tradition in the nineteenth (and twentieth) century is haunted by a recurrent inability to depict the successful—or, for that matter, even failed—insertion of young people in a structured, multilayered modern so-ciety. Rarely, if at all, can one find a young outsider trained or guided by a men-tor to develop, through apprenticeship and maturation, skills that will enable the outsider to become integrated in a reasonably market-minded society.[2] The rea-sons for this insufficiency, particularly in the nineteenth century, are clearly to be found in contemporary Italian society. In stark contrast to France and England, and a somewhat more nuanced contrast to Germany and Russia, backward, ru-ral, capital-starved, politically fragmented Italy did not possess the *capital* nec-essary for ambitious projects of that kind. Italy did not have London or Paris—and it did not have the money, lifeblood of any market economy, to produce a symbolic form that would correspond to those more modern social conditions. Hence the need for an Italian equivalent of, for example, Balzac's *Old Goriot*,

Goethe's *Wilhelm Meister*, or Goncharov's *Oblomov* to function at a figurative level rather than at a representational one.

In what follows I offer a reading of *Pinocchio* as a (problematic) specimen of the tradition of the novel of education. I then approach it as a (no less atypical) representative in the lineage of literature of enlightenment. Here too I discuss aspects that make this masterpiece of post-Romantic disillusionment a highly self-contradictory text and yet—or, perhaps, precisely therefore—also an exemplarily open one, able to accept and invite endless rewritings.

Pinocchio the Dropout

> "Have you an incurable illness?"
> "Yes, Father."
> "Ah, we're coming to it," said the priest. "And what is it?"
> "Poverty."
>
> —Balzac, *Lost Illusions*

How do young nineteenth-century arrivistes jump on the stagecoach of capitalism?

Stagecoaches come in many shapes and sizes; but even more varied are the reasons for boarding them. One typical (indeed, archetypal) way of catching the stagecoach of modernity is that described in Balzac's *Lost Illusions*, part 1 (*The Two Poets* [1837]). Accompanied by David, his brother-in-law, Lucien goes to an unspecified junction north of Mansle where he has arranged to board the barouche of Mme de Bargeton, his almost-but-not-quite lover, as she deserts the provinces for a dizzying new life in Paris. At dawn, when the massive vehicle emerges from darkness, the two young men say farewell. Lucien disappears in Mme de Bargeton's coach, while, replete with well-founded misgivings, David climbs back into his shabby trap: "His heart was heavy as he drove away, for he had horrible presentiments of the fate in store for Lucien in Paris" (148).

Lost Illusions, a novel almost quintessentially representative of the European bildungsroman, upholds certain realistic conventions: Lucien, an unsurpassed arriviste, goes to Paris to test his mettle in the only arena that really matters in his time and place, hoping to find there—in whichever sequence—fame, fortune, and fond females. Expecting those pleasures, he unhesitatingly accepts the capitalistic logic of the society that surrounds him, without (as yet) grasping the full meaning of the monetization of all spiritual values and the reification of people's abilities entailed by that logic.

Moving in the opposite direction, one reaches the sun-drenched, slow-moving, rural backwater of a southern province. There, forty-six years later, Pinocchio is just about to hop onto the carriage headed for a true land of Cockaigne:

At last the wagon arrived; and it arrived without making the slightest noise, because its wheels were swathed in rags and tow.

It was drawn by twelve pairs of donkeys, all of the same size, but with different colored coats.

Some were ashen grey, some white, others were speckled in the manner of pepper-and-salt, and others had wide stripes of yellow and blue.

But the most curious thing of all was this: those twelve pairs, that is, the twenty-four donkeys, instead of being shod like other draft animals or beasts of burden, had men's high-shoes of white leather on their feet. . . .

All [the] boys were charmed by him as soon as they saw [the coachman] and fought with one another in getting up into his wagon so as to be taken by him to that true land of heart's desire known on the geographical map by the seductive name of Funland. (357, 359)

In Collodi the implications are entirely different from those in Balzac: Pinocchio's climbing on the stagecoach does not mean any endorsement of the mechanisms of capitalistic exploitation, accumulation, or exchange. Pinocchio is not a social climber, bent on obtaining pleasure through the manipulation of resources, people, and skills; he is here a visceral, instinctive consumer. To him, hedonism comes first; instant gratification is the only kind there is.

One might be tempted to conclude that the examination of the chronotope of the stagecoach leads us neatly to oppose a standard, canonical form of bildungsroman—Balzac's—to Collodi's substandard, subcanonical one. There is some truth to this view, but things are not so clear-cut.

First, the dynamics between delayed, or sublimated, utility and immediate fulfillment is far from obvious in Balzac, as the asymmetrical friendship between Lucien and Vautrin (Jacques Collin) abundantly shows in the *Comédie humaine*. Second, and conversely (to stay closer to the village of Collodi, from which Carlo Lorenzini took his pseudonym), in *Pinocchio* capitalism, ignored by the puppet's wishful thinking, ultimately makes a grandiose comeback—in and by the actions of the evil man who drives and owns the stagecoach. The short man's intentions are brutally, bestially capitalistic: after the runaway children, stultified by a long stay in Funland, turn into jackasses, he sells them for their skins. Balzac's novels of education may explore the cruelty of the world, but as far as ruthlessness goes, Pinocchio's experience of capitalism hardly lags behind.

In Collodi's novel, the puppet's education as a citizen, a consumer of services, and in general an actor in a capitalistic system is full-fledged and altogether explicit; but it is expressed figuratively. Unlike Lucien's, Pinocchio's hell does not receive an easily identifiable name on a map, because in the Italy of those times Lucca, Firenze, even Roma simply would not work, as Paris does. To hold together at all, the nineteenth-century Italian bildungsroman must be rewritten in the anagogic mode: only through fantasy can it become *real*.[3]

A novel of trial is not ipso facto a novel of education; we justly consider a litmus test of the bildungsroman the presence of rationalization alongside the painful facts. Otherwise the adventure novel or picaresque novel is a more appropriate category.[4] Pinocchio does not rationalize his experiences at all. In terms of a common Buddhist conceptualization, he is a bottomless pot. He does not retain experience; he remains ever none the wiser. True, the good-for-nothing is uninterested in success, in exerting power over others; he is not an arriviste. In other words, he is clean, pure. Or is he? In one area at least, the puppet does strive and with a truly Faustian knack—for a parasitic role in society. Pinocchio has no idea that there cannot be any such thing as a free lunch; in 1881, he still has not read his Marx and does not know that all of society's wealth is derived—directly, indirectly, or very indirectly—from the extraction of surplus value (*Mehrwert*) from the proletarians of the world. But, one may reply, Pinocchio is illiterate! Well, exactly. We should not confuse cause with effect: quite possibly he does not want to read precisely because he does not want to learn uncomfortable truths about his marginal, good-for-nothing position.

Decidedly, Pinocchio is a *homo superfluus* who cannot—will not—envisage a transition to awareness: to self-awareness and, least of all, social awareness. For this refusal, he will pay a price: we may ignore our context, but our context never ignores *us*. "He that can forget, is cured," wrote Friedrich Nietzsche in 1882, but it seems doubtful that he was thinking of *Pinocchio* (*Joyful Wisdom* 14). Pinocchio's social superfluousness, his good-for-nothing-ness, spins parasitically on itself; the potential for education is there, but Pinocchio is ever beside that point. In the perspective of the wished-for making of Italians, such behavior is not a good omen for the citizenry of a new country, seeking a new social contract after 1,300 years of split existence. It is an excellent omen, instead, for any glib-talking short man coming along to promise everyone a free ride to Funland. Pinocchio does not meddle with politics–but the glib, short politician meddles with him.

When we read *Pinocchio* through the analytic grid of the bildungsroman, one feature stands out: the profusion of potential helpers and mentors, characters who guide Pinocchio, advise him, give him succor, transport him, rescue him, and so forth. Most of these are animals—in fact, wise animals, who can be considered emanations of the good principle embodied by the Fairy. But only two have a canonical role, to give Pinocchio the well-defined, black-or-white ethical alternatives typical of the bildungsroman tradition: the Cricket and Lucignolo.

A humane animal, the Cricket tries to impart some (starkly conservative) judgment on the rebellious puppet but is hammered to death for his efforts. His calling the puppet a blockhead—*"testa di legno"* (110; "wooden head" [111])— is factually correct but unlikely to help much. His resilient shadow reappears to warn Pinocchio against the financial advice offered by the Cat and the Fox; and he is resurrected, in flesh and blood, as one of the doctors witnessing Pinocchio's return from the dead. The reader is surprised that Pinocchio kills his mentor only to find him alive and well a few episodes later.

Such extremes are unheard of in mainstream novels of education. In *Old Goriot*, for example, Rastignac controls his instinctive antipathy for Vautrin and does not think of killing him; eventually he comes to treasure the convict's experience, plundering his mind for every scrap of information he can on societal practices. Different literary genres employ different symbolisms, but the issue of conflict remains: in *Pinocchio*, the Cricket is always out of the pedagogical game, and he never has a serious chance to influence the puppet's behavior.[5]

As for Lucignolo, he is of course the Luciferian mentor.[6] He is the mentor *ad infima*, who leads Pinocchio onto the proverbially easy, downward-sloping path of sloth and who—just like Pinocchio—ultimately must pay dearly for his choice of instant gratification. Were he only that, however, Lucignolo would be yet another avatar of the antihero in the densely packed gallery of moralizing literature. But Collodi strikes gold in sketching Lucignolo's persona by showing a direct causality between the gullible mentor's acceptance of mendacious political promises and his brutal exploitation by the very forces that circulated those pie-in-the-sky fables.

Lucignolo's failure to see through the lies of the great master of the entertainment industry[7] makes him not only a victim (as is Pinocchio) but, worse, a further unwitting propagandist for the thickset driver's smooth talk. On this point one can unreservedly admire Collodi for turning a dry parenetic argument from precapitalistic times into one sharply pertinent—albeit through the artistic fairy-tale form—to the mercantile logic of modernity, the logic of capitalistic exploitation. In other words, to the wavering extent that *Pinocchio* upholds the mentoring patterns built into the bildungsroman model, the novel becomes less about the need to interact meaningfully with an enlightened guide than about the need to be, from the outset, able to choose between competing mentors. Yet, as Pinocchio's blunder shows, ignorance rarely leads to good choices—which, of course, is just the reason why the short-bodied strongman in Funland tightly seals education out of his cheerful republic.

Education stresses personal responsibility; ignorance is traditionally linked to a preference for magic. It is hardly surprising, then, that literarily Lucignolo's and Pinocchio's plight in Funland smacks of the pact with the devil. A vague commitment to the coachman leads to front-end enjoyment of the promised service and eventually brings about tail-end retribution (paid for at a usurious rate). All this is sprinkled and seasoned by the pseudo logic of a demonically subverted discourse.

Does Collodi's *Pinocchio* thus include a Faustian compact? To a large extent, yes, mutatis mutandis—that is to say, taking into account the fact that Pinocchio's misfortunes in Funland are written and encoded as comedy rather than tragedy. And how does the hard-pressed hero save his (asinine) skin in the end? Here, too, a *Faust*-like, unexpected turnaround happens. Just as Goethe has recourse to divine grace—it is through grace, not merely on a technicality, that Faust is eventually rescued from hell—so the Fairy's gratuitous intervention reverses

Pinocchio's fortunes—at least on the two occasions when the hapless miscreant is forced to kiss dear life good-bye.

Another place in Collodi's novel touches the devil's sphere: Pinocchio's interaction with those other egregious representatives of seduction by faulty speech, the Cat and the Fox. A different variant of demonic deal making operates here: at stake is not the full-fledged alienation of one's being but rather, folklore-like, the reckless acceptance of commerce with impostors who promise truly devilish rates of return. However, unlike the devil of folklore, usually left empty-handed by such transactions, in their dealings with Pinocchio the Cat and the Fox come out on top. The numerous administrative and financial scandals of unified Italy represented as many excellent reasons for Collodi to nourish such deep-seated skepticism toward the new economic-industrial system that, after the Unification, came roaring through his beloved Tuscan countryside. The good old pre-Italian times might well have been times of gnawing hunger; but at least values were reliable during that golden age. Hence Collodi's ambivalence about any *Bildung* aimed at perfecting one's dealings with the dawning economic system: why should we bother training ourselves to deal with this?[8]

There is, in Collodi's worldview, a better alternative to pedagogy: enlightenment. Enlightenment, or something resembling it, is aimed for in *Pinocchio* but in a manner that steers clear of capitalistic patterns of behavior—away from modernity, taking more traditional paths.

Pinocchio the Compassionate

> "Uncle, what is it that troubles you?"
>
> —Wolfram, *Parzival*

Parzival is a youth of royal birth, incomparably handsome appearance, innate grace—and he has all the extended Grail family behind him. At first sight, therefore, no one would seem more remote from him than the quasi-picaro Pinocchio. The ligneous rascal has all the traits of the outsider about him; it is precisely his nature as an outsider that allows him to become a vehicle for questioning the society that Collodi describes.[9] But there is one immediately recognizable feature that Collodi's picaro and Wolfram von Eschenbach's holy fool share: an initially irresponsible attitude toward the mother.

Wolfram's Parzival wants nothing more than to become a knight at King Arthur's court. He badgers his mother for a horse and suitable attire. The distressed Herzeloyde deliberately responds to this request with laughably inadequate equipment, in the hope that her only son's clownish appearance will cause his peers to dissuade him from the dangerous profession to which he is attracted (strophes 126 and 127). Once the young man has obtained the minimum wherewithal, he ambles away (strophe 128) and for the longest time gives no thought to his mother's sorrow over his departure.

Laughingstock of civilized, courtly-courteous society though he is, Parzival soon shows a manly belligerence sufficient to make many others suffer unjustly. His odyssey of ineptitude reaches its climax at the sumptuous ceremony of the Grail's presentation on Munsalvaesche, to which fate has led him. Here he fails to ask the sympathetic question that would have supernaturally released the ailing King Anfortas from his long-standing affliction. Only after countless more vicissitudes does Parzival finally learn (from his uncle, Trevrizent) about the suffering his rashness has caused. Among the many victims are Anfortas and, more poignantly, Herzeloyde, who "died because of you . . . . Your mother, for her faithful love of you, died the instant after you parted from her" ([trans. Mustard and Passage] 255; strophe 476).

Pinocchio, too, has undertaken an errancy that entirely neglects the distress experienced by his mother figure, the Fairy. The occasional flash of awareness notwithstanding, his first, inchoate *prise de conscience* that the Fairy might have any feelings at all occurs as late as chapter 23, when he learns that she has "died of grief" because she was—as her tombstone rather melodramatically, even vindictively, advertises—"abandoned by her little brother [*sic*] Pinocchio" (257). Just as the sense of guilt will never abandon Parzival after the sobering realization of his past faults, so Pinocchio too, albeit at the opposite end of the social scale, will never forget the Fairy (when he bothers to think, that is).

For both heroes, the hope of atoning for the sorrow caused to beloved people by clumsiness (Wolfram's *tumpheit* [261; strophe 488, line 15]) is, in the final part of their respective *aventiures* (a term explicitly used on 233; strophe 433, line 7 and following lines), inextricably linked to—one could argue, identical with—the wish to transform their minds and to attain a higher level of spiritual awareness. In Pinocchio, that metamorphosis seems to take a banal turn toward the petit bourgeois or even the philistine; but given the constraints imposed by sheer logic on Collodi's novel, for a higher-plane Pinocchio there is no other place but human status to look to. Being crowned Grail King is, after all, easier for wayward royals than for proletarian puppets—in Collodi's Italy or anywhere else.

Both *Parzival* and *Pinocchio* revolve around not one but two cycles of education. The first is a lay education to the way of the world; the second embraces all aspects that can be subsumed under the category of the spiritual. In Wolfram, the first realm is the knightly one; the second, the divine. The two obey sharply distinct logics, as Parzival must so painfully learn. In Collodi, the first realm is that of the secular bildungsroman, concerned with the hero's relation to the capitalistic society around him; the second, in the absence of any properly defined religion, is the development of Pinocchio's emotions in a manner befitting an aspiring human being. True enough, this development is intermittent; but the puppet's comically simple *intermittences du cœur*[10] toward the Fairy are necessary and serious and quite adequate to the logic governing the mind in which they occur. Pinocchio loves her, takes her fate to heart, and is eventually rewarded.

This logic is not a transcendent one; nothing could be more incompatible with Pinocchio's universe than a Fairy who would duplicate, in latter-day version,

Beatrice's role in the *Divine Comedy*. Yet, Dante the pilgrim and Pinocchio have something in common: both ardently desire (from a certain point onward, at any rate) to transcend their status, and both find guides willing to help them do so. Because of the weak development of her civic and social institutions, Italy was historically inept (comparatively, anyway) at producing great novels of education; but over the centuries Italy certainly produced major narratives of enlightenment, at least two. One cannot ignore the fact that in both the *Divine Comedy* and *Pinocchio* a dead woman assumes the decisive role of protective psychopomp.

So Pinocchio, by story's end, feels compassion toward his ever well-meaning "Virgin Fairy." But what of the other parental figure in the novel, his putative father, Joseph/Geppetto?

The same feelings of *Mitleid* appear here: cruelly indifferent at first, Pinocchio gradually notices the sufferings Geppetto incurs on his account. The recognition is again belated: not until late in the text does he reminisce about his *povero babbo*—his "poor father" or, as Italian allows, his "late father" (264, 265). By no coincidence, this sorrow is triggered in the same chapter as that about the Fairy, when Pinocchio stumbles on the Fairy's tombstone. It seems as though the author himself has fortuitously happened upon the symbolic valences of the father's hypothetical death and is drawn to delve into their narrative implications.

If the Fairy's death by grief is a relatively brief affair, relegated to less than a page and quickly forgotten by Pinocchio because of an interposed animal's good services, Geppetto's Jonah-like ordeal in the bowels of the Shark is the object of an elaborate mise-en-scène covering a chapter and a half. Furthermore, the staging of the father's near-death experience takes place with a full accompaniment of realistic details that, after a long coexistence with fairy-tale narrative devices, slap the reader with the full force of an episode torn from Balzac or Defoe.

After returning home with Geppetto, Pinocchio begins to work for the benefit of his father. This fact is in itself so astounding as just about to obliterate Pinocchio's motivations in the reader's attention. But, leaving aside any incredulous amusement in seeing Pinocchio drip with sweat "from head to foot" (451), let us focus on the one truly substantial point regarding Pinocchio's about-face. When he comes across the Cricket one more time, he exclaims, "[D]ear Cricket! . . . throw a mallet at me now, too [*scilicet*, in symmetrical revenge]; but have pity on my poor father" (447). "Pity" is not a sufficiently strong rendering of "pietà" (446). The Italian *pietà* is a direct descendant of Latin *pietas*, and it means "piety" as well as "pity": while English possesses two distinct, specialized alternatives, in Italian the same term covers both senses. Pinocchio thus exhorts compassion toward a fellow human being's suffering.

The rest of Pinocchio's exertions occur without much rationalizing; he simply makes, with great zeal, sacrifice after sacrifice to help his two parental figures. But a collateral incident reinforces the translation slip about *pietà* just mentioned: despite bearing Lucignolo a grudge for his earlier, incompetent recommendation of a nice little trip to Funland, when Pinocchio sees his metamorphosed friend agonize and then die before his very eyes, he exclaims, "Oh! povero Lucignolo!," and bursts into tears (450). By every indication, his heart is now open to a sentiment heretofore unknown to his careless behavior: sympathy. It is thanks to this new feeling that his efforts and renunciations pile up, as do the fruits of his labor.

This change leads us to the double paradox that is central to Pinocchio's story and controls his painful transmutation from picaro figure to Parzival figure. First: so long as Pinocchio refuses to acknowledge his ignorance, he not only fails to obtain the desired success but also falls back into an exploited condition. But as soon as he allows compassion to rule him, he starts to understand how little he knows about the real world. As a consequence he finds an interest, even pleasure, in actively fighting his inferiority. Second: so long as Pinocchio rejects physical exertion and insists on his right to instant gratification of his instincts, he relapses into the humiliating enslavement to matter that permeates the animal state. But as soon as he allows compassion to conquer his mind, the animal state becomes no burden for him; through his relentless work in the most humiliating circumstances, he embraces that state with enthusiasm and joy.

In other words, compassion for another human being is just the conversion (i.e., U-turn) that gives Pinocchio access to the human condition. Unlike Lucignolo, he finally accepts for the sake of someone else the animalization he stubbornly opposed when acting in his own name. It is his selfless embracing of animalization that eventually allows him to transfigure his previous animal self into a properly humane being. The story of how Pinocchio pays back his father for debts incurred is the story of an immanent, secular redemption (the Latin derivation of *redeem* is "payback") if ever there was one. Parzival, had he been reincarnated as a nineteenth-century puppet, would not have been ashamed.

But isn't the "proper boy," the well-behaved *ragazzino perbene* (461, 460), a petit bourgeois anticlimax to Pinocchio's adventurous mind-set? Of course; and one quakes at the thought of what the cheerful chap might become in a world that bestows the title of "respectable people" ("galantuomini," as the Cat and the Fox call themselves in chapter 18 [214]) on characters like the Cat and the Fox. Yes, the human condition amounts to a state of suffering and exploitation in a thoroughly cynical world; but Pinocchio's fairy tale tells us that there is no reason that condition should be tackled from a three-foot-tall position of inferiority. At least the new Pinocchio can hope to face the world with the resources available to all adults . . . the present and the future ones.

NOTES

This essay is part of a broader project on *Pinocchio* and the European novel on which I am currently working. I wish to thank Daniela Boccassini for reading this text and providing me with much useful criticism and insight.

¹ A good recent discussion of D'Azeglio's dictum is contained in Banti 203–05.

² For the sake of simplicity, I am using an abstract general pattern that most definitions of a bildungsroman would be likely to endorse.

³ This principle also seems to apply to what is usually considered Italy's most important nineteenth-century novel, Manzoni's *I promessi sposi*, which narrates neither the nineteenth century nor, for that matter, Italy proper.

⁴ Today's standard theoretical treatment of the adventure novel and the picaresque novel can be found in Bakhtin's *The Dialogic Imagination*. In a different critical mode, Bjornson remains among the best and most commendable works in English.

⁵ It is on reading passages such as those involving the Cricket that I most appreciate Jone Gaillard's vigorous and original essay.

⁶ Because the *-ignolo* ending has a diminutive connotation, the literal meanings of *Lucignolo* are "tiny Lucifer" and, accessorily, "tiny light bearer." Rendering the name in English as Lampwick focuses on the second, sacrificing what is probably the more interesting half of the scale of mental associations evoked by the boy's Italian name.

⁷ A splendidly archetypal Berlusconian figure, of course.

⁸ In Roberto Benigni and Vincenzo Cerami's film *Pinocchio* (2002), the Cat and Fox's speech is characterized by a heavy Milanese accent—in the Italian context, an eloquent way to underline the new, capitalistic component in the behavior of Collodi's animals. Today's main Italian stock exchange is located in Milan, as are the headquarters of the most important financial institutions—and of Berlusconi's empire.

⁹ Such questioning is the main textual function of the picaro since time immemorial. See Bakhtin, *Dialogic Imagination*, esp. 158–67, 400–22.

¹⁰ "Les intermittences du cœur" is a key concept in Marcel Proust's multivolume novel cycle *À la recherce du temps perdu* (1913–27).

The Hero's Journey in Collodi's *Pinocchio*

Jacqueline L. Gmuca and Lorinda B. Cohoon

Almost every student knows Pinocchio, ever popular through the Disney version, first released in 1940: how his nose grows when he lies, how Jiminy Cricket is his conscience, and how above all he wishes to be a human boy. Pinocchio remains a cultural icon, a lovable, cute character whose wish "upon a star" to become human is just as strong as Geppetto's yearning for a son. With these expectations, students understandably feel dismay when they read the novel. Discussing *Pinocchio* in undergraduate courses on children's literature thus poses fascinating problems. An undisputed classic that explores essential questions of what it means to be a child, a boy, an adult, and even more broadly a human being, its picaresque plot (Heins 202), reflections of conventions from the *commedia dell'arte* (Lucas, "Enquiring Mind" 164), and sharp departures from Disney's animated version (students often see the film as the original version of the story) present particular difficulties for the contemporary reader.

In our children's literature courses, required of preservice teachers on the elementary level, we decided to guide students in an exploration of how Pinocchio and his deeds reflect the journey of the archetypal hero, a universal journey termed the monomyth by Joseph Campbell (30). In his seminal work *Hero with a Thousand Faces*, Campbell posits that the hero figure, whether male or female, progresses through three stages: separation from the known and familiar, initiation through tests and trials, and finally a return to the world left behind in which the hero brings a transformed self as well as an elixir to transform others.

While the monomyth theory has been influential and supported by numerous examples from world mythologies, Campbell's work, as well as the mythic and archetypal approaches on which it is centered, has been validly criticized for its sexism and claims to universality. Post-structuralist and feminist approaches critique mythic criticism for its denial of individual differences in terms of both the particular author of the text and the distinctiveness of the "national identity" from which the work springs (Jones and Watkins 8). Yet David Russell notes that Campbell's "work is particularly useful for a study of the great childhood tales taken from the folk tradition. And these are the tales that most significantly influenced Collodi" (204–05). In fact, Russell concludes that *Pinocchio*'s popularity is a direct result of its incorporation of the monomyth: "Pinocchio has not been loved so long by children because he has good advice for them or sets them a good example. Perhaps he has so readily captured our imagination because he is imbued with the qualities of the great mythic hero . . ." (204).

On first inspection, the stages of the hero's journey appear easy to identify, but they quickly become complicated. In the departure stage, Pinocchio embraces the call to adventure when he succumbs to the music of the puppet show on his way to school. His elaborate fantasy of quickly learning how to read and write evaporates as he desperately sells his primer for a ticket to see the marionettes. It can be argued that he encounters the guardian of the first threshold in the form of Fire-Eater, the showman who almost ends his life by throwing him into the fire to cook his supper (147). Fire-Eater, a reversal of the fire-breathing dragon that battles many a hero in Campbell's examples, is won over with both tears and courage. Pinocchio's cries for mercy prompt the showman's pity and decision to spare his life, but when the showman turns to Harlequin as his fuel, Pinocchio bravely volunteers to sacrifice himself to save his friend. Fire-Eater, moved by Pinocchio's bravery, spares Harlequin's life as well (155). At this point, in the victory over the "dragon," Pinocchio may be seen as crossing the first threshold, about to enter the second stage of initiation.

In Campbell's theory, the first threshold is not passed until the old self dies and the new is reborn, an event that Campbell associates with a descent into some form of death. In his diagram, he lists multiple forms through which this descent may occur—through "brother-battle . . . dismemberment, crucifixion, Abduction, Night-sea journey, Wonder journey, Whale's belly" (245). Most of these crossings do occur in *Pinocchio*, not solely in the departure stage but throughout the initiation and return as well. In fact, the dismemberment occurs before the call to adventure, when Pinocchio burns his feet off, falling asleep too near to the fire (ch. 6). Pinocchio's crucifixion occurs during the initiation stage, when he is hanged by the assassins (ch. 15). Calling out to Geppetto to save him, he echoes Christ's words on the cross in a direct allusion to the Crucifixion (189).

As Pinocchio embarks on the adventures and temptations that compose the stage of initiation, he is helped by a number of characters. During this part of his journey, he faces a number of trials as he is almost killed by the assassins, chained up as a watchdog (ch. 21), imprisoned for being cheated by the Cat and the Fox (ch. 19), transformed into a donkey (ch. 31), and almost drowned for his hide when he becomes lame (ch. 33).

Throughout all these near deaths, the blue-haired Fairy is his greatest aid. When he is hanged by the assassins and left for dead, it is the Fairy who rescues him, calls in the physicians, and brings him back to life with her sugar-sweetened medicine. When she asks him about the location of the four gold coins, he begins to lie, and with each lie his nose grows longer and longer (209, 211). As a phallic symbol (see Rosenthal, "Alice" 488), Pinocchio's lengthening nose suggests another parallel to the hero's initiation stage: the meeting with the goddess, a prelude to a sacred marriage. Although Russell does not give credence to such an interpretation (208), Pinocchio's nose, the Fairy's laughter, and her emphasis on assuming the role of sister suggest, at this point of the plot, that the relationship between Pinocchio and her has assumed a sexual dimension. The suggestion of emerging sexuality falls away when Pinocchio once again separates from the Fairy. When they are reunited, she is figured as a mother who offers guidance and tests of worthiness. In the ultimate act of motherhood, she finally becomes the agent for Pinocchio's transformation into boyhood.

According to Campbell, the hero's nadir also includes the "ego-shattering" confrontation with the father (131). In this terrifying encounter, the hero must believe in the father's mercy (130) and attain a state of oneness with a being who seems determined to destroy him. For Pinocchio, such "atonement" (which Campbell rewrites as "at-one-ment" [130]) occurs during his return stage, in the belly of the Shark, where he and Geppetto are reunited. Geppetto assumes the role of devourer in the opening scenes of the novel when he picks up Pinocchio by his neck, declaring, "Let's go straight home. And when we're home, you can be sure that we'll settle our accounts!" (105). In the next scene between Geppetto and Pinocchio, Geppetto is a totally different person: a father full of unconditional love, happy to give Pinocchio the three pears he brought home for his own breakfast (127). Perhaps Pinocchio's "at-one-ment," then, is a matter not so much of being destroyed (he has met death many times) as of being united in selfless love, a love embodied in Geppetto's constant sacrifices for his son. Appropriately, after this reunion-union, Geppetto's and Pinocchio's roles are reversed. They escape from the Shark's mouth. The puppet saves the man as Pinocchio swims with Geppetto on his back; then both are towed to safety by the Tuna (ch. 36).

It should be noted that the end point of their return fulfills not the circular pattern identified by Campbell but a linear one, found so often in works of children's literature (McGillis 53), as the two reach not Geppetto's home but a beautiful cottage given by the Fairy to the Talking Cricket. Pinocchio's apotheosis, his transformation from wood to flesh, finally occurs during this return, but not without the elixir of his love for both Geppetto and the Fairy. Having disdained work throughout the novel, Pinocchio willingly slaves as a donkey to turn the gardener's windlass in order to earn milk for his father. He labors in his spare time to make baskets for extra money and teaches himself to read and write. Finally, he takes the last step. Hearing that the Fairy is alive but ill and penniless, Pinocchio without one thought gives the shillings he has saved for new clothes to help her. That night, she visits him in his dreams to confide that "[b]oys who take loving care of their parents when they are sick and in need always deserve a great deal of praise and love . . ." (457). By the next morning, Pinocchio's apotheosis is complete—he has attained his boon, his transformation into a real live boy.

Pinocchio's resonance across times and cultures suggests that this story of a wooden puppet who becomes a boy speaks to readers on a mythic level, about the human condition as well as life's quests for control over daily physical circumstances and needs for food, shelter, and connection with other human beings. We thought that the mythic approach would prompt our students to trace the socialization and emotional growth of a wooden puppet who finds out what it means to be human. We also hoped that our students would apply the pattern to other texts during the semester. To what extent would students find these stages of Campbell's monomyth and their complexities in *Pinocchio*? Would they ultimately feel that viewing the novel in terms of the hero's journey had value for them? These two questions guided our study of students' reactions to and analyses of *Pinocchio*.

Our teaching strategy was built on the idea that because of the structure of the hero's journey, the use of mythic criticism would provide a scaffold for students' initial explorations of this text. Campbell's pattern can be easily introduced, and graphics from *Hero with a Thousand Faces* or other variations can be used to help students grasp the concepts. Students can then examine Pinocchio's quests and his status as a hero in the light of other mythic heroes who, unlike Pinocchio, are often adult, extremely talented, and more than human. Pinocchio is only a wooden puppet, with little knowledge of the laws of the world in which he finds himself, yet he still ventures on a quest for humanity that comes into conflict with his ongoing desires for food, clothing, and pleasure. We felt that the mythic criticism approach would help students discuss and build connections to a text that seems remote from their tastes and ways of life. Not only did a number of students find the novel to be boring and difficult "to get into," but many also found the story confusing with the disappearance, transformation, and reappearance of key characters. We hoped that focusing on the monomyth would answer such reading difficulties as well as encourage students to consider other heroes and their journeys.

In follow-up class discussions, students noted that the novel traces a number of monomyths. Each journey has a didactic function to illustrate the cost of greed, deception, and laziness: the Fox loses his tail and becomes old, the Cat goes blind, and Lampwick dies from his exceedingly hard work as a donkey.

The journeys of Geppetto and the Fairy assume additional significance, for without Pinocchio's quest theirs would remain unfulfilled. Geppetto, who behaves like a childish puppet himself in the scuffle and name-calling exchange with Master Cherry, attempts to be a creator; he partially fulfills this role when he uses the special log to make Pinocchio. But he quickly abandons his plan to exhibit Pinocchio for money and instead undertakes his own journey, to become a father.

The Fairy undertakes a parallel journey. Throughout the novel, she assumes multiple guises that include supernatural (the ghost of a child [ch. 15]), human (the woman at the well [ch. 24]), and animal (snail and goat [chs. 29 and 34]) forms, but ultimately she needs Pinocchio's devotion and vulnerability to breathe life into her own motherhood. The accomplishment of motherhood is central to the novel. Jessica Espinoza, one of our students, concurs: "[t]he fairy does grow into a woman and becomes a mother figure for Pinocchio as the book progresses." Espinoza's reading of the Fairy's transformation extends Lois Rostow Kuznets's suggestion that parental uses of toys and children work out desires for godlike, transformative, or creative power (6–7). The mythic implications of *Pinocchio* suggest that childhood itself has the power to transform others and that the child gods created by the desires of parent figures must be both given freedom and restrained in order to prevent disaster, maintain order, and accomplish growth.

Approaching the teaching of *Pinocchio* through mythic criticism and exploring the nature of the archetypes and monomyth hold several advantages for today's students, many of whom are underprepared for literary studies. All too often students taking courses in writing about literature or introductory literature surveys are unfamiliar with the journey pattern, and this lack of familiarity makes it difficult for them to comprehend plot events and language in epics such as *The Odyssey* or *Beowulf*. By introducing first- and second-year university students to the monomyth through a study of *Pinocchio*, professors can engage them in discussions of events and characters that reduce the anxiety of struggling to read what may be perceived as esoteric, complex works. For preservice teachers, this approach reinforces the effectiveness of teaching strategies that are student-centered, collaborative, and holistic. It demonstrates that models are only starting points, not ends in themselves. Perhaps the most compelling reason to use mythic criticism to approach *Pinocchio* is that this method affords unique insights into the structure of the text while it offers a pleasurable and intellectually rigorous way to question what it means to be human.

Our experiment with teaching *Pinocchio* in college-level literature classrooms showed us that mythic criticism can prompt serious inquiry into patterns that inform literature. Our students noticed that the hero's quest was not only for a material reward but also for the transformation that comes from self-testing, discovery, and sacrifice. Without prompting, they applied the journey model to other texts, including Pam Muñoz Ryan's *Esperanza Rising* and folktales from Virginia Hamilton's *The People Could Fly*. They were also able to critique the model by noting which characters were given opportunities to undertake adventures. They expanded the model beyond the main character and asked questions about the Fairy and the Fox and the Cat. Others used their increased familiarity with the text to begin explorations of parenting in *Pinocchio* and inquiries into the judicial system in Italy.

We believe that this approach was useful and would recommend it as one among many strategies to try in the classroom. Our students were able to use the approach to think critically about the text and the model. Since they can work together to critique and adapt the monomyth, the approach offers preservice educators experience with the kinds of thinking skills necessary to resist formulaic strategies and worksheet-driven curricula, which they will encounter in the schools when they begin teaching. In addition to deepening discussions of Pinocchio's humanity, the mythic approach provides students with an excellent starting point for exploring other ways to read a text. Instead of simply recalling an instructor's analysis of a text and overview of a critical theory, through their work with the mythic approach to *Pinocchio*, they became participants in both the struggle and joy of critical inquiry.

"I'm a Real Boy!": Consciousness of the Breath of Life and Origin Myth in the Course Literature of Childhood

Holly Blackford

With exquisite vitality and a rare combination of regular roguishness, impassioned impetuousness, and visceral vulnerability, Pinocchio distills the essence of childhood. Although Collodi's *Adventures of Pinocchio* can be understood as a form of bildungsroman (Wunderlich and Morrissey, *Pinocchio* 9), arguably a child's journey to adulthood (Cech 172), the reader's journey through the text resembles an antibildungsroman. We experience the pleasure of sheer repetition (Wunderlich and Morrissey, *Pinocchio* 203) as the child puppet continually proves that he is incorrigible. We know that he is a real boy from the beginning, but one cannot begin life with self-consciousness, which is a product of looking back on oneself.

The episodic, picaresque structure of *The Adventures of Pinocchio* complicates the picture of child development in the way that my students, mostly in the education program, have become accustomed to seeing it. Accustomed to thinking of childhood as a sequence of learning stages, described in the developmental models of Sigmund Freud, Jean Piaget, and Erik Erikson, they harbor the cherished belief that a fixed sequence of development *is* childhood. But having students work through and discuss each episode of *Pinocchio* teaches future teachers that a child's everyday experience is as much one of not learning and making progress as it is a journey toward a conclusive metamorphosis, which, in *Pinocchio*, involves the puppet's final performance of compassion or conformity, depending on your point of view (Perella, "Essay" [*Italica*]; Rosenthal, "Alice"). The adventures themselves define Pinocchio's "zigzag progress toward rebirth as a human being" (Rosenthal 488), imitating the much more chaotic structures of real children's lives.

Stelio Cro describes the structure of Pinocchio's progress in terms of "dialectic" cycles of learning, forgetting, and learning, involving cycles of loss and redemption based on the father's love (107). Indeed, the parental response to Pinocchio in the text guides our response. Geppetto and the Fairy continually become frustrated by the child, but they also unconditionally love and forgive him, moved by his vitality and passionate feeling. The text teaches us to prefer a parental rather than educational view of the child: to love, unconditionally and passionately, the vitality of the child; to wonder at the adaptability and heartiness of the wooden child, despite continual abuses and deaths; to wonder at the child's incredible resistance to cultural expectations; to know that children will return to their roots and that childhood will pass.

The form of *Pinocchio* works against the theme of growing up: the passionate expressions of Pinocchio's good heart are short-lived as Pinocchio sets off to do one thing and persuades himself or is persuaded by others to do quite another. His growth and metamorphosis at the end are rather sudden and eliminate the perpetual child-rogue that we have appreciated in the repetitious journeys.

The inspiration for my course, Literature of Childhood, comes from many quarters. Lois Kuznets's book *When Toys Come Alive* explores the existential questions of toys as they come to life and worry about autonomy, abandonment, their real status, their challenge to the creator, and their potential for being loved. In a philosophical book on what makes human beings human, Willard Gaylin uses Adam and Eve and Pinocchio as metaphors for freedom and choice, feelings, sexuality, dependency, work, conscience, and love. A conference paper by June Cummins compares Christina Rossetti's *Goblin Market* and Beatrix Potter's *Tale of Peter Rabbit*, both of which display cycles of temptation and redemption in a personal genesis. I was inspired also by my recognition, in *Out of this World*, of Pygmalion motifs surrounding so many child-appreciated stories, even including popular teen films such as *She's All That* and *Weird Science*. Teens are experiencing accelerated metamorphoses in a self-conscious way, exemplified best by the changing perceptions of Annie in Jamaica Kincaid's *Annie John*, read later in the course.

The opening of *Pinocchio* articulates the importance of form and the oral quality of the narrative, which positions the reader as a listener in the manner of the fairy tale or folktale and which involves direct address to the child reader. This opening announces both its roots in the fairy tale and its difference from the fairy tale: "Once upon a time there was . . . 'A king!' my little readers will say right away. No, children, you are wrong. Once upon a time there was a piece of wood" (83). Collodi ironizes the fairy tale and invokes wood as the reality principle (Perella, "Essay" [*Italica*] 18, 36). By focusing on a common yet spirited piece of wood, he calls Pinocchio's fate into question. The text does not promise redemption, just as there is no guarantee of riches as a reward to our everyman hero. The teller's voice continually asserts itself as the artistic (and secular) shaper of the tale ("I don't know how it happened," "you can imagine," "you must know," etc.). Moreover, the author explains some occurrences but not others— it is a mystery, for example, how the puppets in the theater recognize Pinocchio (143). As with the fairy tale, the reader is continually left with a sense of wonder yet must follow the restless pace of the adventures.

As Maria Nikolejeva points out, young children's literature follows the rhythms of mythic rather than linear time. The serialized form of *Pinocchio* renders a particular sense of iterative time reminiscent of Genesis, which is also organized by mythical time. Initiated by God's creation of an innocent man-child in his own image, *Pinocchio* thus repeats God's frustration as his created children become independent and challenge the power of the creator. Even as God destroys what his children have done, he always gives them another chance to be worthy of the life given them. Time in *Pinocchio* is precultural and solidly preadolescent.

The role of the Fairy in the book's repetition suggests an ongoing opportunity for the female principle of a real rebirth. Her presence is even more remarkable than Geppetto's, because he is absent during many of the adventures. The Fairy is not a deus ex machina figure but central to the book's repetitious structure and rhythm. Her active role in offering forgiveness and the chance to be good symbolizes the missing mother in patriarchal creation stories. Some critics object to the view of the Fairy as a restored spiritual mother like the Virgin Mary (Wunderlich and Morrissey, *Pinocchio* 7), because Pinocchio is solidly a secular hero. I agree with Nicolas Perella that the comparison is reasonable as long as the departure from religious allegory is understood as well ("Essay" [*Italica*] 19). My students were particularly intrigued by the Fairy's ability to command animals as she intervenes in the story, sometimes overtly, sometimes covertly. If she commands the creatures that often help Pinocchio at the last minute, it seems logical to suspect her presence in diverse animals, such as the Cricket, that are linked to Pinocchio's moral conversion. Cro in particular emphasizes the figure of the Cricket and tries to separate him from the Fairy, but my students were struck by the possibility of the Fairy as the moral conscience that speaks through various figures. They were also intrigued by her transformation from domestic symbol, contained by her home, to a dead woman free to rove anywhere, continually forgive and love, and bring about the moral reformation of Pinocchio with her final test through the Snail.

Pinocchio's structure makes several arguments about growth and development:

> Growing up is a continual cycle of believing in human goodness and then measuring the actual behavior of the self against goodness.
>
> One should never give up hope that a child or a parent will turn out well.
>
> While most children's books depict a fall from innocence to a vantage point of experience, Collodi's *Pinocchio* offers a more realistic vision of the gradual process of self-consciousness, for Pinocchio increasingly reflects on his decisions, even when he makes selfish or unwise ones.
>
> No matter how troublesome parenting is, we feel compelled to create and nurture children, because they are the vital force that organizes a social community, bringing the dead (the Fairy, the swallowed Geppetto) to life.
>
> Children should have the freedom to make mistakes and still be passionately loved.
>
> Imperfection is the very condition of humanity.
>
> The puppet represents an accurate vision of boyhood, perhaps even a cultural ideal. Some critics, such as M. L. Rosenthal, see him as the embodiment of conflict in every human self: the desire for freedom from social constraint and the desire to be a responsible human being ("Hidden *Pinocchio*" 60). My class agreed but only partially; they preferred to think of Pinocchio as the male self reluctant to take up adult responsibilities. Thus Geppetto and Pinocchio resemble each

other. My class believed that girls would not have to work quite so hard at learning empathy and respect for those who love them.

The class disagreed on the issue of why Pinocchio is rewarded with reality. Keeping structure foremost in their minds, they found goodness to be relative to a specific community. What is good for the Fairy or Geppetto will not necessarily win acceptance by peers. Thus the adventures allow Pinocchio to test the water of various communities and learn what each expects of him. He moves through various peer groups (puppets, thieves, boys), which define him in various ways. Any figure that moves in more than one circle is, by definition, liminal (Turner). Being a real boy thus depends on the setting, and the structure of the serialized novel makes that dependence apparent. Lying is really learning what to say to which inquirer, the text argues.

The episodic structure thus gives meaning to the final metamorphosis of the puppet into a real boy-man. Some of my students found the ending false, for issues are not resolved. The image of the discarded puppet horrified them, and they saw no precedent for it in metamorphosis traditions. But many preferred (sought) a more unified whole and thus focused on the symmetry of the opening and ending. For example, the father is not only restored and allowed to prosper, but he is once again an artistic craftsman, working on new products rather than fixing the body of his child. In this reading, both art and life are resurrected. Geppetto has also changed. Like Pinocchio, he learned patience in the "full inkwell" (419) of the Shark's belly. Pinocchio's final act, involving a coat, mirrors Geppetto's first white lie. As Gaylin asserts, it is not an accident that Geppetto sells his coat for Pinocchio's alphabet book at the beginning, veiling his sacrifice in a way that Pinocchio perfectly understands (135), and that Pinocchio gives up buying a coat for the Fairy, after which he lies to his father in the same touching and tactful manner (457). He becomes the laborer and provider that none of his family ever could—reformed by considering others, accepting responsibilities, and deserving the mother's love. This message does not diminish the importance of the picaresque resistance to learning that the reader has enjoyed, but the thematic symmetry gives the work its unity: the ending returns to the opening's suggestion of a true fairy tale, in which love conquers all.

In the final actions, the reader gets the sense that growing up means identifying more with adults in a community than with children, puppets, or scoundrels promising miracles. Pinocchio's new status is signified by the fact that to become an adult is to become an entirely different species. Only in looking back can one see the species one was. This idea was once a common predevelopmental model: "At the end of the last century, childhood was still considered a radically different world from that of the adult. In order to bridge the gap, the child had to be trained like an animal, controlled in every particular like a puppet" (Apostolidès 77). My class was not sure which model was more appropriate, developmental sequence or sudden coming of age, metamorphosis. Both have problems.

My class believed that both Geppetto and Pinocchio need to pass through the belly of the Shark for cleansing. This surprising assertion seemed to come from their resistance to violence. Geppetto's introduction to the reader, for example, occurs in the context of ridiculous violence (ch. 2). Many of my students struggled to tolerate the ironic violence and cruel world of *Pinocchio*, but some said that they would teach this text only to high schoolers or that they could not imagine teaching it at all. Pinocchio's vision of life, Perella argues, is that of the "human being as a puppet created by a Master Puppeteer" ("Essay" [*Italica*] 31), which we are encouraged to regard with ironic distance. The narrator asserts his voice and addresses his reader in order to create distance from Pinocchio and to establish a relationship between himself and the reader as laughing co-puppeteers. We discussed the fact that fables are supposed to be horrible and hyperbolic. The parable of the golden ass in the center of the work, when boys turn into donkeys, certainly demonstrates the warning style of the fable in a way that announces itself as metaphor: "In *Pinocchio* Collodi has fulfilled the classic metaphor of Pico della Mirandola as explained in the *De hominis dignatitate*, that man, by his free will, can elevate himself above the angels or descend below the beast" (Cro 91). At the end, Pinocchio finds it funny to see his eerie discarded puppet self from afar (461). His transformation into a real boy gives him the privilege of joining the vantage point of the narrator-reader-puppeteer. He can view the poor boy's condition with satisfied irony.

The students' distaste for violence and death reveals that they are American students, after all. They object not to the violence per se but to the comic treatment of it. They are products of the psychological model of self and childhood, the liberal subject of the mind invented in the nineteenth century and predominant in the twentieth. They want Pinocchio to have a self-conscious angst about his life, which the form and nature of the book do not allow and which its premodernist nature does not allow. It is important for students of children's literature to read works published before the dominion of Freud over childhood! They see the psychological, alienated self as so natural that they are surprised to learn about the recent historical development of adolescence and the adolescent novel. *Pinocchio* does not have adolescent angst, and my students have had little critical exposure to irony.

To confront this problem, a close comparison between versions of Geppetto in Collodi's novel and film adaptations was helpful. Drew Carey's television version, *Geppetto*, spoofs the Fairy and makes the implicit argument that Pinocchio's transformation results from Geppetto's transformation into a responsible, loving father. Students liked the transformation in Steve Barron's film version, *The Adventures of Pinocchio* (1996), because the boy looks wooden and becomes real at the "death" of his father. Saving his father was a good theme of family reification, they asserted. They successfully critiqued the Disney film with the help of Jack Zipes's observations ("Toward a Theory"). All immediately felt the absence of Collodi's fresh, vivid style and *Pinocchio*'s harsh, cruel world. Suddenly they saw that the story lost something when the comic narrator and style were altered.

Comparing Collodi's novel and the Disney film is particularly instructive for students; it turns a critical lens against American visions of childhood.

It is useful also to examine *Toy Story*, because it displays the kind of humor and irony with which one views Pinocchio's story of genuine problems. The comic characters include the two main male toys, Woody and Buzz Lightyear, but the female toy, Jesse, does not enjoy their autonomy and cannot entertain a comic perspective on her role in the life of toys. Viewing her story brought about a discussion of the earnestness and abandonment of the Fairy in *Pinocchio*, the consequences of gender and authentic love. In his discussion of teaching *Pinocchio* to young children, Herbert Kohl asserts the problem of Pinocchio as "the good bad boy" (see also Perella, "Essay" [*Italica*] 7; Kuznets 70–71; Fiedler 471–511) and asks whether girls can behave like Pinocchio (97–99). If Pinocchio looks back on his discarded puppet self and thinks it funny, Jesse of *Toy Story 2* looks back on her abandoned self with posttraumatic stress. None of the other female characters in the texts we read held an ironic perspective on developmental issues. Is growing up in a violent world ever regarded as a picaresque adventure by women?

The question of gender ran through our discussions and course, as indeed it must in any children's literature course. All literature of childhood involves the study of the foundational orientation of the human subject to being a boy or a girl and the parental style of men and women. *Pinocchio* is solidly patriarchal. The good mother is not physically present in the family; she is a pure fairy, an ephemeral being who appears everywhere and yet nowhere. She is beyond the fallibility of the human male characters, rather like the Christian perfect mother who is immaculate, without an earthly, birthing body. Pinocchio's redemption comes not by his actions alone but also by the goodness of women. Boys enjoy independence in the text, the freedom to do as they please, even to death, as the death of Lampwick shows. Despite Pinocchio's behavior, the Fairy judges him good at heart. She hovers between a powerful goddess figure and a real character linked with responsibility, nurturing, and domestic stability. I presented Perella's suggestions about the Fairy's middle-class ideology and the conflict between her vision of growth and the working-class vision, centered on the role of school and played out in the fact that Pinocchio's parents will never meet because they occupy different spheres. I also shared with the class Perella's ideas about the cruelty of the Fairy's pedagogy (26)—her constant threats of death, for example. There was lively debate about whether she was cruel or the stereotype of a female nurturer, irresolvable by the text.

This debate was useful in setting up the readings that followed *Pinocchio*: Christina Rossetti's "Goblin Market," in which a female character sacrifices and heals another girl who encounters the evils of patriarchy and temptation; Frances Hodgson Burnett's *The Secret Garden*, in which Mary becomes and replaces the mother to heal patriarchy and bring about a reconciliation between father and son; Shel Silverstein's *The Giving Tree*, in which the mother tree continually sacrifices herself for "the boy," who repeatedly abuses her, a sacrifice that we are asked to believe makes her happy; and Laura Ingalls Wilder's *Little House in the Big Woods*, in which a girl's tiniest actions are considered rebellion and strictly punished. Are there opportunities to be a "good bad girl?" There are not. In "Goblin Market," Laura's bad-girl behavior is redeemed by Lizzie's good-girl behavior. In *The Secret Garden*, Mary changes herself (with a lower-class Pan figure) in the mother's abandoned garden, ultimately transforming a sick family to a healthy, patriarchal, landowning one. These female metamorphoses are not funny. They do not indulge in the comic burlesque as Pinocchio or his American counterparts, Huck Finn and Tom Sawyer, do (Rosenthal, "Alice" 488–89; Lucas, "Enquiring Mind" 164–66).

That Pinocchio's first instinct is to laugh in the darkest hours of making a complete ass of himself does not suggest cold-heartedness; Pinocchio is truly moved by the death of Lampwick and the earlier death or deaths of the Fairy. But laughing one moment and crying the next, begging for forgiveness and love one moment and rejecting the grace of others the next, reflects a kind of humor that my class firmly believed was infantile—appreciated by children and, curiously, adult men. Men, they argued, like scatological humor à la *South Park*. Why they find such behavior acceptable in today's society and not in Geppetto is beyond me. The point, however, is that the students felt that certain types of humor—and coping with disturbing issues through comedy—were related to gender.

Ultimately, we had to contradict ourselves to gain a full appreciation of *Pinocchio*. We broke down the text's roots, structures, themes, and arguments about developing (or not developing) to explain the universality of the puppet-child, and then we placed him squarely in a deconstructive framework. Perhaps it is his liminality that in the end allows him so perfectly to bridge a specific vision of gender, class, and nation with a universal and particularly vivid sense of human development. At any rate, *Pinocchio* is an approach to teaching, as much as my course was an approach to teaching the parable of the puppet son.

A Field of Miracles: *Pinocchio* and Italian Children's Literature

Maria Truglio

This essay offers strategies for presenting Carlo Collodi's *Le avventure di Pinocchio* to undergraduate students of Italian literature and culture in the context of a course on children's literature in Italy. The course, which spans the period from Unification to the present day, devotes approximately three weeks to Collodi's text. Many of the suggestions, I believe, can be adapted to other class contexts. The seminar addresses two overarching questions: What does *Italian* mean? What does *childhood* mean? Collodi's *Pinocchio*, which recounts the arduous process of a boy's formation, explicitly engages the second question and allows readers to investigate how the text constructs the category of childhood (see Sadler; see esp. Knoepflmacher; A. Richardson). Written in the immediate post-Unification period, a time in which the issue of national identity emerged with particular urgency, the text invites us to consider if and how it participates in the project of "making Italians" (Massimo D'Azeglio, qtd. in Perella, "Essay" [*Avventure*] 43). We approach *Pinocchio* after a study of Luigi Capuana's fables and follow it with Edmondo De Amicis's *Cuore*. Thus we are able to study three nearly contemporary works from three markedly different regions of the newly created Italy: Sicily, Tuscany, and Piedmont. Students are assigned relevant chapters from Harry Hearder's *Italy: A Short History* to help them become familiar with the broad political developments of the period, while I provide brief lectures on aspects of Italy's social and cultural landscape.[1]

The class work on *Pinocchio* focuses on locating and discussing proverbs, biblical allusions, and depictions of utopias. I ask students to enumerate themes, images, and concerns that seem to stand out. Because of the wide circulation of this tale in American culture through Disney's animated movie and other film and print adaptations, not surprisingly students notice most of all the text's differences from their expectations as readers familiar with other versions. Indeed, these points of reference and contrast serve our inquiry well, since the aspects of the text that undergo deletion or mutation in the newer versions are often those that most forcefully mark the original text's engagement with its specific cultural and historic moment. Themes such as violence, food, mother, father, and education (and, of course, the intersections of these themes and images) typically emerge as elements for further investigation. This preliminary list of topics helps maintain coherence while not precluding unexpected paths of inquiry.

The theme of education, in particular the text's portrayal of formal schooling, demonstrates the book's immersion in and dialogue with its historical moment. Students learn about the educational reform efforts and the push for increased literacy undertaken by Italy's newly established constitutional monarchy.

Discussion includes such topics as the funding allocated for the construction of schools throughout the peninsula, laws regarding compulsory education, and the publication of Francesco De Sanctis's *Storia della letteratura italiana*. In Collodi's original audience were children born after 1870—in other words, the very first Italians. Those whose families had the education and income necessary to be able to read and subscribe to the *Giornale per i bambini* were, as statistics regarding literacy indicate, in the privileged minority.[2] The class considers whether Geppetto's "carv[ing] and shap[ing]" of the wood into his puppet (97), and the subsequent education of this recalcitrant imp, suggest the daunting task of shaping this first generation of children into good Italian citizens. Students also consider how the book's overt messages may be undermined by other elements. An analysis of its references to education indicates that the overt and the implicit messages contradict each other. The story clearly advocates conformity to the demands of formal schooling, learning to read and write, and appreciating the sacrifices of those who provide the opportunities and means of this education. Yet Pinocchio's reluctance to conform seems to be at the heart of the book's charm and enduring appeal, creating a tension between his impish energy and the adults' guiding wisdom.

To pursue this issue, students peruse the text for various lessons that are delivered in proverb-like form. The Talking Cricket, Geppetto, the Fairy, and other adult figures in the text offer seemingly endless advice and guidance to Pinocchio, in pithy adages. After culling several such quotations and noting the specific context of each, we consider their form. These lessons have two qualities that serve their didactic purpose. Their succinctness lends itself to easy memorization, and Pinocchio does seem to remember, sometimes verbatim, the lessons delivered in this fashion. Often a sentiment is repeated, and indeed many of the proverbs on our list are variations (ad nauseum) on a theme. Repetition, too, helps memory. But students do not fail to point out that consistently Pinocchio remembers these lessons only after he has experienced the consequences of ignoring them.

I encourage the students not to shy away from the possibility that the book may be self-contradictory. While it clearly advocates deference to the wisdom that adults confer on children and that is encapsulated and passed on in these proverbs, it also dramatizes the futility of trying to teach by words. Further, it implies that children do not benefit from the experiences of previous generations, that they learn only from their own experiences.

I ask the students to step back from the details and think about the overall structure of the story. The plot itself is grounded in repetition, mirroring the repetition of the lessons that seem never to be heeded. This repetition, students point out, allows the listening or reading child to be reminded of the story's lessons. But at the same time it calls into question the efficacy of its own didactic enterprise. Is the whole book doomed to the fate of the many proverbs it contains?

We also discuss the content of the proverbs. Almost all the tidbits of wisdom meant for Pinocchio's consumption concern food. The Italian text confronts the reader with preoccupations that are far more material and immediate than the concerns of the American version (i.e., Disney's) with the abstract concepts of honesty and goodness. Far from an etiquette book on refined table manners, the story deals with the acquisition of nourishment on the most primitive level, or, as Pinocchio succinctly phrases it, how to eat without being eaten (271; "one can eat without danger of being eaten?"). The rules he must learn to accept revolve around the merciless equation of production and consumption. A close analysis reveals the preoccupation with property and its boundaries and with the related concept of appropriateness, or equality, on both sides of the production-consumption equation. Note, for example, Collodi's use of the terms "proprie mani" and "propria testa" (226; "own hands" and "own brains" [227]) and "appropriare" (240; "appropriating" [241]). The book brings its privileged audience into contact with a world of limited resources, a world from which it is otherwise shielded. But while exposing bourgeois children to the reality of poverty, the text softens the blow by suggesting that such destitution results, as in the case of the hardheaded Pinocchio, from a refusal to work.

Death, the ultimate consequence of trying to cheat the production-consumption cycle, appears in a stark and at times gothic fashion throughout the book. The scene of Pinocchio's hanging startles even those readers familiar with Capuana's gruesome fables. The Fairy's eerie first appearance at the window of a haunted house and her macabre proclamation, through lips that hardly move, "I am dead, too" (183), are direct echoes of contemporary Italian gothic writings.[3] Students are often surprised by these elements: how could young readers be exposed to such harsh realities at such a tender age? This surprise reveals certain assumptions about childhood that we can now recognize as culturally specific, at least in part. Collodi's text does not foster the notion that children are innocent and fragile and need to be shielded from poverty, violence, deceit, and death. Far from trying to protect the child, the text strives to thrust the child into contact with them. Indeed, the equation of childhood and innocence was debunked from the very moment of Pinocchio's creation. We thus begin to understand that different historical and economic contexts produce different evaluations of what childhood is and should be.

If childhood itself is not a rigid and universal category, then what a "good child" (specifically, a "good boy") entails must not be considered self-evident. A useful way to examine this question, particularly given the influence of Catholicism in Italian culture, is to locate various episodes of the text that resonate with biblical passages. Some students point to Pinocchio's hanging (188–89) as an echo of Christ's Crucifixion (Mark 15.33–38; Matt. 27.45–52) and to the episode of the Shark (424–37) as a retelling of the story of Jonah. These episodes, which invoke archetypes of death and rebirth, clearly prefigure the ultimate death of the puppet and birth of the real boy. But what is at stake in the evocations of

Scripture passages? Are these allusions evidence that the text carries a religious, a Christian, moral?

The two memorable episodes mentioned above and their biblical antecedents can be supplemented by two additional episodes. But in them, *Pinocchio* gives a message that is antithetical to the Christian moral. Geppetto at least three times worries aloud that, "So many things can happen!" (127, 129). His conviction that one must be always concerned with obtaining nourishment and with planning for the future contrasts with Christ's calling on his disciples to contemplate the birds. Such creatures "do not sow or reap or gather into barns; yet your heavenly Father feeds them" (*New Jerusalem Bible*, Matt. 6.25–34). Pinocchio's final confrontation with his old adversaries, the Cat and the Fox, offers a second point of contrast. The deceitful pair have "fallen into the most abject misery" (443), yet their condition elicits no pity from the puppet. Instead of compassion, Pinocchio offers proverbs, in order to make clear to them (and to the readers) that their current poverty reflects the inevitable workings of justice. Rather than the begged-for alms, he hurls at the Cat and Fox a smug, "Stolen money brings no gain," and, "The devil's grain yields naught but chaff" (443, 445). Here he generates rather than receives the preachy proverbs, marking his imminent transformation into a *ragazzo perbene*. The scene, inasmuch as it advocates a commensurate kind of justice, seems at odds with Christ's injunctions to provide charity even to one's enemy and to embody a generosity that transcends commensurability (Matt. 6.38–42).

These confrontations with analogous Gospel lessons underscore the nature of Collodi's enterprise as secular and civic. While I would not suggest that Collodi's text is anti-Catholic (though of course students are free to argue for such an interpretation), the book does seem less concerned with the moral goodness of the individual soul than with the call for civic responsibility and playing one's role in the social machine. Pinocchio's assimilation into society is achieved when his body literally becomes part of the mechanism that draws water in order to cultivate plants. Pinocchio must actively participate in the production of what he hopes to consume. Turning the windlass requires that he walk in circles, curbing his earlier impulse to run off and run away (449). The triumph of his assimilation offers a vision of a new, homogeneous Italy: hardworking, secular, and bourgeois.

The biblical account of the Garden of Eden and its role as a possible source for the depiction of the *Campo dei miracoli* ("Field of Miracles" [165]) opens the path for a discussion of utopia. Collodi's utopias include the Field of Miracles and Funland. Funland's status as "no-place" is reinforced by the ironic identification of its name "known on the geographical map" (359). More than simple places of fun and entertainment, these utopias are expanses where the laws of production and consumption, and the conservation of matter and energy, do not apply. In these privileged realms one can eat without working, and food grows without cultivation. In this regard the belly of the Shark becomes a kind of dystopia: an enclosed, prisonlike space offering limited resources and the ever-looming threat of death. The cavern emerges not as the maternal womb (itself a kind of utopia) but as a somewhat exaggerated rendition of the actual adult world. In opposition, the utopian spaces that must be abandoned are metaphors for childhood, seen not as a fragile innocence to be protected and kept blind to harsh realities but as a privileged freedom operating outside the circle of production and consumption, unfettered by the chain of social obligation that links citizens together (see Nodelman, esp. 11). The tale figures the utopia of childhood as a miraculous yet dangerous and threatening space that unfortunately must be renounced for one to enter the security of adult Italian society. At the end, the now lifeless wooden puppet not only remains but is mocked by the new, "real" Pinocchio; the scene emphasizes not so much conversion or transformation as a definitive rejection and expulsion of the former self.

My pedagogical approach to *Pinocchio* thus stresses the internal tension of the book—what Nicolas Perella terms "a dramatic tension between a desire for freedom and a need for order" ("Essay" [*Avventure*] 37)—in the light of its historical moment. This emphasis encourages (friendly) class debate. Some students will insist on the story's praise of playfulness and subversion of authority (citing, for example, the fish's disgust after having consumed the schoolbooks [303]); others may argue for a more conservative reading that highlights the book's call for restraint and conformity. Such discussions hone the students' critical reading and thinking skills, obliging them to sustain their opinions with evidence from the text and to construct persuasive arguments. At the same time, we are able to appreciate literature, children's included, as a discourse that can accommodate ambivalences and multiple perspectives.

NOTES

[1] A useful source for this topic is Kertzer and Barbagli.

[2] On literacy in the post-Unification era, see B. Richardson, esp. 64–65; on the socioeconomic landscape of this period, see Bull, esp. 38–40.

[3] See Tarchetti ("Composition VI," from *Disjecta*). Here, the speaker meets his beloved, at her request, in a cemetery. When he asks her why she has chosen such a space for their encounter, she replies, "Io son morta . . . e tu nol sai" (2: 453; "I am dead . . . and you do not know it" [my trans.]). She goes on to invite her lover to lie in the tomb with her. A similar gothic moment appears in Pascoli's "La tessitrice" (*Canti di Castelvecchio*), which depicts a woman weaving her own shroud and informing her beloved that she is dead (507). These connections go somewhat beyond the scope of a children's literature seminar but may be of interest to those teaching *Pinocchio* in other contexts.

The Short-Legged Fairy: Reading and Teaching *Pinocchio* as a Feminist

Cristina Mazzoni

Lying can be an adaptation to dominant ways of knowing or a means of challenging them; one can lie to avoid conflict or to present an alternative epistemology. These strategies are found at the personal, the pedagogical, and the political levels. In *Pinocchio* there are two kinds of lies, and it is the Fairy who explains the difference: "There are lies with short legs, and lies with long noses" (211). Her distinction has by now become proverbial in Italy, thanks to that most memorable image of Collodi's tale: Pinocchio's growing nose. But we may ask about the first type of lie, the short-legged one. The Fairy mentions it, even lists it first, but Pinocchio's lies are manifested on his face, not in his limbs. Where are the short-legged lies in this book, whom do they characterize, and how do they contribute to a feminist reading of the novel?

One can lie verbally as well as with body language, so let us consider an enchanted, deceptive, and fairly short-legged animal—a blue-haired female goat whose bleating lies, located halfway between body and language, incarnate the Fairy's pedagogy of mendacity: "While he was swimming along aimlessly, Pinocchio saw a rock that seemed made of white marble there in the middle of the sea, and on top of the rock a pretty little She-Goat who was bleating tenderly and beckoning him to come near" (415). Liberated by the Fairy's fish from his asinine bodily envelope, Pinocchio flees by water and sees and hears, on a rock as white as the Fairy's house, a magic animal in whom he recognizes, thanks to the incongruous color of her hair, his beloved Fairy, because "[t]he most curious thing of all was that the pretty Goat's hair . . . was all blue—but such a radiant blue that it very much recalled the hair of the beautiful Little Girl." She calls out to him, warning him of the dangerous Shark: "'Hurry, Pinocchio, for mercy's sake!' the pretty little Goat bleated loudly" (417). She even holds out "her little hoofs to help him out of the sea" (419), but her short legs are useless: he is swallowed.

"The Fairy of land and sea, of birds and fish, knows too many things, governs too much for this scene to be read literally" (Manganelli 183). Indeed, from a literal perspective, the scene does not make sense, fraught as it is with contradictions. The Goat-Fairy calls Pinocchio to herself like a siren her sailors—does she not know a monster is near? Throughout the book she commands the animals—is she powerless to stop the Shark? Omniscient about Pinocchio's affairs, she must know that Geppetto is in the monster's belly—why does she try to pull Pinocchio away from his father? Ever an intermediary, unstable character, her role as mother brings her near Pinocchio in his time of danger, even as her pedagogical sternness refuses to diminish the pain of his learning: he must enter the belly of the Shark in order to find his father and, eventually, his human self; there is no easier way. Sent by the Fairy, the little fish had physically eaten away his donkey body; the encounter within the big fish, orchestrated by the same magic being, will divest him of his wooden body.

The reader cannot help but wonder what this Fairy is: helper or enchantress, metaphor or archetype, alter ego or mother figure. In a book famous for its mendacious long-nosed protagonist, there is also the question of whether her long skirts hide short legs—whether the Fairy's lies, that is, are the short-legged kind to Pinocchio's long-nosed ones.

Pinocchio tells the story of a male puppet made by a man and surrounded by boys and middle-aged and elderly men. The puppet will someday become one of these boys and eventually, it is assumed, grow into one of these men. Funland is a place emblematic of this masculine society: "Its population was made up entirely of boys" (367). Few female humans are found in Collodi's book: Pinocchio encounters a "little old lady" by the beach (265; perhaps an incarnation of the Fairy), and among the circus audience, enjoying his donkey tricks, there are "girls and boys of all ages" (395). The Fairy first appears at the end of chapter 15: she is a dead little girl with blue hair. In the first version of the book (1881), this chapter was the last one, and the Fairy's role was minor. A feminist reading of *Pinocchio* will inevitably focus on the blue-haired Fairy as the only female of relevance in the book. Additionally, a feminist reader may explore questions of identity in the ambiguous figure of Pinocchio as he relates to the Fairy: how we come to be who we are, socially and psychologically, and how this process is expressed in literary terms. Lastly, in studying a book like *Pinocchio*, which explicitly presents itself as being about teaching and learning, a discussion on the objectives and methods of feminist pedagogy can be rewardingly developed: how we read, learn, and teach; how Pinocchio and the Fairy, in particular, do these things; how they can be done in a feminist way; and what the place of lying and ambiguity might be in pedagogical and feminist practices.

Whether or not the half-truths the Fairy utters and the deceptions in which she is involved can be considered lies depends on what we make of her as a character. In the many decades since its publication, numerous scholars trained in a variety of disciplines have interpreted *Pinocchio* and thus created the field humorously referred to as "Pinocchiology" (Stone 329). Each of these perspectives can provide the basis for a feminist classroom discussion of Collodi's masterpiece, thus introducing students to the polyphony of literary criticism in general and of its feminist possibilities in particular. A literary-historical examination of the genesis of the book, for example, makes us wonder what is earned by Collodi's continuation of the book beyond the fifteenth chapter and how Pinocchio's actions and decisions afterward differ from those of the first part, where there was no Fairy to guide (and perhaps misguide) him. In the second, longer part, she assumes an active narrative role. Structuralism asks to what extent the blue-haired Fairy fits in the tradition of fairy tales. Collodi's fairy is *sui generis*, pushing Pinocchio away from herself and into the real world instead of enchanting him into her bed. She plays the role of sister and mother rather than the traditionally more fairylike role of lover; her behavior defies the genre and perhaps the gender limitations this genre imposes.

The complex themes of sexuality and reproduction are central to a feminist reading of Collodi's tale. A sociohistorical perspective can illuminate differences in Geppetto's and the Fairy's class and gender roles. In chapter 17, her comfortably furnished house contrasts with his bare one. Pinocchio too can live in such posh surroundings (and at the end of the novel, he does), if he heeds her advice in chapter 25: everyone has the duty to work lest they contract the "horrible disease" that is idleness (287). The Fairy embodies the middle-class work ethic, in opposition to Geppetto's beggary; she is a stern educator as much as a generous giver. In the novel the two foster parents never meet—they literally live worlds apart. This narrative choice might say something about the Fairy's position as mother and as woman, that she is unnecessary, perhaps even deleterious, to the now-adult human being who has acquired his identity thanks to her mediation.

The Fairy's loss of position can be interpreted from both a social and a psychoanalytic perspective. Geppetto's paternity embodies a maternal dimension, but the Fairy also relishes the role of single parent, raising Pinocchio without a father. The differences between Pinocchio's two parent figures are not only socioeconomic and behavioral; more radically, they are sexual, and psychoanalytic tools can be helpful in understanding the complex family dynamic at work in the Geppetto-Fairy-Pinocchio triangle. While living with Geppetto, Pinocchio often must seek his own (scant) food, while with the Fairy his oral drives are all amply satisfied. In chapter 29, for instance, she plans a breakfast for Pinocchio and his friends consisting of "two hundred cups of *caffè-e-latte* and four hundred buns buttered on the inside and on the outside" (343). From a Freudian standpoint, Pinocchio is for the blue-haired Fairy "a child-phallus" whom she makes "the pampered center of a world structured around oral drives" (Apostolidès 78). In Jungian terms, she is an alimentary Goddess, the archetypal Great Mother, representing the unconscious forces of nature that he needs to reconcile with the Father as the structuring principle of social and psychological order (Grassi 91–92).

In addition to structuralist, sociohistorical, and psychoanalytic readings, the blue-haired Fairy plays an important role in religious interpretations of the tale: she has been seen as an incarnation of Isis, the mistress of animals and transformations (Zolla 166–167). According to a popular Christian interpretation, based on the acquisition by the puppet, in chapter 36, of humanity as his true nature, Pinocchio is Everyman, and the Fairy—blue like the color of Mary's mantle but especially, like Mary, different from all other creatures—is a multivalent figure of redemption and salvation. She is the Virgin Mary, coredeemer and, like the Fairy, sister and mother to her only son; she is Sophia and Providentia, God's wisdom and providence; she is Christ the redeemer; she is the Church, principle of renewal and vehicle of salvation (Biffi, *"Mistero"* 41–48, 74–76).

The sea scene, during which Pinocchio swims in vain toward the bleating blue Goat, can be read from each of these perspectives. Transformed into an animal, the Fairy plays the role of helper delineated by structuralism. As Pinocchio's primary educator, his social mother, the Goat facilitates, through her failed rescue, his physical reunion with his father, the true head of any traditional family. As an object of desire toward which Pinocchio swims, the Goat brings both life and death: after fulfilling Pinocchio's oral drives, she now lets him be the object of the Shark's. Like Mary at the cross, the Goat is present at Pinocchio's necessary suffering, and, like Christ and the Church, she ensures her protégé's eventual salvation—though not before a symbolic, Jonah-like death.

Although a changing being, Pinocchio does not become a boy until the book's end. He remains throughout his adventures an in-between creature, at once inanimate as the wood that makes him and animate as the boy he wants to be. He easily slips into the behavior or form of an animal: he does the work of a dog, is mistaken for a fish, and gets changed into a donkey. Equally hybrid is the Fairy, Pinocchio's sister for a time, creature of forest and town, child and adult at once, alive and dead, human and inhuman both. She takes the appearance of an animal and orders animal servants around—the Snail, the Poodle, the Pigeon, to name just three. If Pinocchio's transformations are a figure for adolescence and the attainment of individuality, then, *pace* theories of sexual difference, the self-dignity Pinocchio achieves is a figure of human growth and change, both male and female. But that growth comes at a cost and with a loss.

Pinocchio, like his readers, is puzzled by the puppet body he has cast off ("How funny I was when I was a puppet!" [461]). Equally puzzling is the Fairy's disappearance at the end. He last sees her in the flesh as a goat; then he sends her money while she is sick in the hospital; and finally she appears to him in a dream and transforms him into a boy. As his sister, the Fairy is his female other ("you shall be my little brother, and I your good little sister" [213]), because she is the only other character to undergo the process of change as maturation: "When you left me, I was a little girl, and now you find me a woman, such a grown-up woman that I could almost be your mother" (283). She is Pinocchio's only model of change as growth, and in the end, paradoxically, such change corresponds to a narrative disappearance: the puppet is as inanimate as the Fairy is unreachable. They are both gone.

The final transformation of the puppet into a boy makes of this story a bildungsroman, a novel of education; as such, and because of the recurrent didactic moments throughout the book, *Pinocchio* is about learning and about teaching. The book encourages the interpretation and necessary deconstruction of the world and its words, since for Collodi growing up "requires not only learning self-discipline but also learning to discriminate whom to trust and whom not to, learning to reciprocate others' caring, and discovering when and why truth-telling is important" (Card 63). Through the Fairy, the theorist of lying as well as an expert in its practice, and through other enchanted beings,

Pinocchio teaches the importance of reading the world correctly, of not letting oneself be duped by its liars and of lying when one must. Not all lies are bad: Geppetto lies when he tells Pinocchio that he sold his coat because he was too warm (135); Pinocchio must lie and claim to be a criminal in order to get out of jail (231). And though Pinocchio's nose grows four times, only two of those times does he lie, and he lies on other occasions without nasal consequences. The didacticism of Collodi's novel is ambiguous; its invitation to social conformity is persistently interrupted by the pleasure of playfulness, by an awareness of the centrality of conflict and struggle to the process of growing up, and by a biting criticism of schools and of organized teaching and learning in general.

Thus the Fairy's short-legged lies are the most complex of all: she claims to be dead when Pinocchio first meets her ("I am dead too" [183]); she pretends to die of grief because of Pinocchio's abandonment and informs him of his role in her demise (257); she masquerades as a bourgeois woman in the Island of the Busy Bees and denies her true identity (283). Short-legged as they are, these lies, though not immediately self-indicting as the long-nosed ones, do not go far, and Pinocchio quickly discovers the truth. Then there is the Goat scene. A goat in the middle of the sea is as incongruous as the color of the Fairy's hair. Surely the Fairy could have picked a more helpful animal to turn into—a sea animal, for example, would have flippers or fins instead of spindly legs ill-suited for swimming or rescuing. It does not seem that she really wants to be helpful, but rather that she is lying with her body and with her bleating.

In a kindergarten classroom, the reading of Collodi's *Pinocchio* "raises the issue of boys' mischief, the role of girls in the world of adventure and troublemaking, and loyalty to the family" (Kohl 99). The lessons in a college-level classroom will be similar and different at once. Is Pinocchio's mischief uniquely boyish? What is the role of the Fairy in his adventures? What does the very concept of family entail in the ideology of this book? Self-reflectively, it might be said that Pinocchio, like a feminist student, must learn through experience rather than through books. Just as in Collodi's book "true maturity is a function of individual insight which cannot be learned except through personal experience and reflection" (Heisig 28), so also does feminist pedagogy place "a high value on subjective experience as a route to understanding our lives and the lives of others" (Bell, Morrow, and Tastsoglou 23). What are the teaching and learning lessons that feminists can find in *Pinocchio*? What is, first of all, the slippery border between reality and the imagination, between lying and telling the truth? In some cases this distinction may be obvious—money, after all, does not grow on trees: the reader knows this, if Pinocchio at first does not. But sometimes distinguishing between truth and falsehood requires sophisticated skills: the blue-haired Fairy is a practiced user of didactic deception, of lies "flavored with pedagogy" (Manganelli 91). Her power over Pinocchio is parental, economic, intellectual, and physical. Students and teachers might discuss the relation between power and teaching, between power and learning, and how it affects every pedagogical approach, whether self-consciously or not. In order to develop this question, it is helpful to go back to some teaching moments in Collodi's text.

Though the Fairy is the only female character of any importance in the text, Italian is a grammatically gendered language, so the many animals that crowd Collodi's book are all necessarily male or female. Thus, the Fox, "la Volpe," is female, and the Cat, "il Gatto," is male; the martens that Pinocchio captures while in his canine disguise are "le faine," and, talkative females that they are, they wake the sleeping puppet "with their chatter" (253). Closer to the Fairy, as her mouthpieces or even (the reader is led to wonder) her incarnations, are three other female beasts: "la Lucciola" (240), the "dear little Firefly" who teaches Pinocchio, caught in an animal trap, about the wrongness of stealing ("Hunger, my boy, is not a good reason for appropriating what is not ours" [241]); "la Marmottina" (376), "a pretty little Marmot" (373) and the only female resident of Funland, who instructs the donkey-eared Pinocchio about the effects of laziness, the dangers of bad companions, and the futility of regret ("all lazy boys . . . must end up sooner or later by turning into little jackasses" [377]); and "la Lumaca" (336), the Snail with the "little lighted lamp on her head" (335), who is reminiscent of the Firefly and whose talk of the Fairy's sleep ties her to the marmot (a hibernator and an icon of sleep in the European tradition).

The Snail, insistently didactic, is the Fairy's closest associate and the most passive-aggressive of the lot. Unlike the other two, she has few words of wisdom for Pinocchio and little verbal pedagogy; her lessons are practical, experiential. She inflicts frustration through her slowness, which is intentional more than proverbial—she is quite fast when it comes to helping the Fairy in the last chapter, when the Snail "darted off like a lizard in the torrid days of August" (457). She also frustrates by presenting the famished Pinocchio with bread, a roast chicken, and four apricots—made, respectively, of chalk, cardboard, and alabaster (341). Barely illuminating as a firefly, mostly sleeping as a marmot, excruciatingly slow as a snail, the Fairy's female teaching assistants resemble the positive male animals in function (the Cricket, the White Blackbird, and the Parrot) yet differ from them in their proverbial weakness—of light, wakefulness, or speed. Among them, it is the Snail that claims primary importance, not only because, unlike most other teaching animals, male or female, she appears more than once but especially because, like the Fairy, she lies, deceives, and teaches with actions more than with words.

The Snail's feminist pedagogy, as we might call it, is not averse to didactic lies, and the teaching by experience she incarnates and enforces proves more effective than Geppetto's or the Cricket's verbiage. Their traditional, word-centered pedagogy is more easily destabilized by the act of lying—itself an activity that is usually verbal. But the slowness the Snail manifests to Pinocchio is a lie, a metaphor for the short legs that she, a gastropod, does not have; the food she gives to him is a lie, hard and inedible however desirable it looks; and the story about the Fairy in the hospital, like the earlier one about the Fairy sleeping, is also probably a lie: how is the reader supposed to believe it? That the Fairy is hospitalized and in need of Pinocchio's financial assistance is the last pedagogical lie in the book, intended to give Pinocchio a final opportunity to forget the selfish puppet and assume the body of a good boy. Pedagogically, it works: he learns and changes. But we don't know how his new identity will turn out for Pinocchio, as the Fairy's words have not always been truthful. That his life as a boy will be better than his life as a puppet might well be the Fairy's last lie. The legs of this lie may be short, but Pinocchio, once again, trips on them all the same.

Talking (with) Animals: *Pinocchio* and Dialogicity

Nancy Canepa

The world of Carlo Collodi's *The Adventures of Pinocchio* is overrun with animals, which in number and variety far surpass the human characters of the novel. One scholar has counted five hundred mentions of animals, ranging from figures of speech to cooked food to actual characters. These are, for the most part, animals that could have been found in Collodi's agrarian Tuscany, either in the courtyard or the wild; many talk, a few are enchanted, and others appear in their natural guise (Ferretti 215). Although some perform narratological functions necessary to advance the plot, just as many are metaliterary markers of the diverse axes (realistic and fantastic) and traditions (the fairy tale and the beast fable, among others) that merge in *Pinocchio*. Analysis of these animals thus elucidates the wider intertextual dialogues at play in the novel and helps us better understand Collodi's ambivalent moral and pedagogical vision.

As children's literature came of age in the nineteenth century, animals that act like humans—"creatures that can recreate, flatter, and repudiate the human wish that we are not alone" (Sale 98)—were becoming a standard of this new genre. In *Pinocchio* we find animals of Aesopian extraction that represent precise social types and serve the end of Collodi's satire of contemporary life by often appearing in realistic situations, such as in Pinocchio's encounters with institutions. We find proselytizers like the Talking Cricket and his alter egos, also descending from the moralizing fable. And finally, we find more fantastically drawn animals that typically play the part of helpers or antagonists in the fairy-tale mode. The promotion of an idealizing marvelous dimension in which adventures steer Pinocchio to the classic happily ever after of fairy tales is constantly undermined by the realization that the sought-after place "where one can eat without running the risk of being eaten" (Cro 104) does not, in the end, exist.

Many of the animal helpers—falcon, poodle, mice, rabbits, woodpeckers, and so on—serve Pinocchio's head magic helper, the Fairy, and appear when she first does, at the time of Pinocchio's revival from hanging (chs. 15–17). Some recall characters and episodes from the French fairy tales that Collodi translated. The coach sent to retrieve Pinocchio from his hanging place, for example, is drawn by mice, the same animals that are transformed into the horses that pull Cinderella's golden coach. Its whimsical elegance would have certainly appealed to Charles Perrault, as would that of its driver, the impeccable poodle Medoro.

Other animal helpers result from a more personal interpretation of the fairy-tale mode. Although the Pigeon that in chapter 23 flies Pinocchio to the sea to find Geppetto evokes magical birds of folklore and mythology, there is an earthy interlude in its marvelous flight, when both Pinocchio and bird succumb to their bodily needs (hunger and thirst) and make a stop at a dovecote, where Pinocchio stuffs himself with vetch and learns again that "Hunger knows neither fancies nor delicacies!" (263). In chapter 24 Pinocchio is beached on an island in the middle of the sea and encounters a dolphin, an animal since antiquity associated with the rescue of the drowning or shipwrecked. Pinocchio seems to appeal to his authority when he asks if "there are any villages on this island where one can eat without danger of being eaten" (271). The Dolphin directs him to the town of the Busy Bees, but not before he tells him, with a touch of the same subtle cruelty that colors many of the Fairy's actions, that Geppetto has probably been eaten by the great Shark. The Dolphin's intervention does enable Pinocchio to meet the Fairy again, but the puppet's reception in Busy-Bee Town is none too pleasant, for he finds there an ethic that does not mesh with his own. In chapter 29, we meet a snail whose help is driven by an even clearer moral imperative. In a comic sequence in which Pinocchio returns to the Fairy's house, starving, on a cold and rainy night, the Snail (the Fairy's servant), faithful to her physiological nature, makes him wait half a day as she travels from floor to floor. Even when the door finally opens and she offers the distraught Pinocchio a tray of food, it turns out to be fake: plaster bread, a cardboard chicken, and apricots of alabaster.

Significantly, the only animals whose good deeds are devoid of any pedagogical end are those who reward Pinocchio for his kind heart: the mastiff Alidoro is transformed from a police dog and Pinocchio's pursuer to his savior after he himself is saved from drowning by the puppet (chs. 27–28), and the philosophical Tuna saves Pinocchio and Geppetto after Pinocchio shows him the way out of the Shark's mouth (ch. 36). These creatures interpret the grateful animal motif common in folklore and especially fairy tales and are among the few characters in the book who appear to recognize the power of solidarity to effect real change.

Collodi explicitly parodies the fairy-tale tradition in his representation of antagonistic creatures. The Serpent that Pinocchio encounters on his way home to the Fairy descends from a long line of snakes and dragons that embody evil and dissimulation and are consistently vanquished by heroes of mythology, epic, legend, and fairy tale. But right from its description we note a certain comic debasement of this tradition, in the transference from head to lower body—and in the domestication—of one of the iconic traits of the dragon, its breathing fire: "It had green skin, fiery eyes, and a pointed tail that *smoked like a chimney stack*" (235; emphasis added). Without a trace of heroism Pinocchio attempts to skirt this obstacle altogether by slipping past the Serpent as it lies motionless, but when it suddenly opens its eyes and springs up, he is frightened so badly that he trips and ends up with his head in the mud.

> At the sight of that upside-down puppet frantically kicking his heels, the Serpent was seized with such a fit of laughter that he laughed and laughed and laughed until, from the strain of too much laughing, he burst a blood vessel in his chest; and then he really died.   (239)

Pinocchio overcomes his obstacle without actually doing anything, and the Serpent dies of a heart attack before getting a chance to prove his evilness; the very categories of hero and villain are thus put into question.

A similar comic lowering marks the character of the puppet master Mangiafoco (Fire-Eater), who, though technically a human being, distinctly reminds us of the ogres of both Giambattista Basile and Perrault. But whereas the ogre of Perrault's "Tom Thumb," for example, devours his mutton half raw, which in turn stimulates his appetite for the flesh of Tom Thumb and his siblings, Mangiafoco complains that his mutton is too underdone to be edible and makes plans to use Pinocchio to stoke his fire. His role as monster is seriously undermined when, as Pinocchio is screaming, "I don't want to die, no, I don't want to die!" (149), he begins to sneeze, takes pity on Pinocchio, and ultimately sends him on his way with a gift of five gold coins.

Besides its many fairy-tale resonances, the episode of the great Shark that swallows Geppetto and Pinocchio has precedents in the biblical tale of Jonah and the whale, Lucian's *True History* (where an entire ship ends up in a whale's belly), and a scene from Ariosto's *Cinque canti* (which was not included in the *Furioso*) in which the hero, Ruggiero, is swallowed by a whale in whose belly he sees, from afar, an old man with a fishing net in one hand and a light in the other. But the Shark too is ultimately a caricature. First described in terms of a nineteenth-century urban reality curiously at odds with what should be his timeless monstrosity—"he is bigger than a five-story building, and has a horrible mouth so wide and deep that a whole railway train with its engine running could easily pass through it" (273)—it turns out that the Shark is not only very old but debilitated by severe asthma, heart palpitations, and sneezing fits that cause him to sleep with his mouth open, which facilitates Pinocchio and Geppetto's escape. Their escape, too, is a far cry from the acts of heroism usually involved in vanquishing a monster.

Together with fairy tales, the genres that we most associate with talking animals are the Aesopian fable and the beast epic, which result when "the primitive beast story, so widespread an element in folklore, . . . is shaped either to satiric or moral purpose" (J. Wight Duff, *A Literary History of Rome in the Silver Age*, qtd. in Phaedrus xvi). Collodi's use of animals for human caricature in the spirit of these genres is one of his great innovations. In Italy, the nineteenth century has been called the century of the fabulists because of the popularity of Aesop and especially the emergence of native-grown emulators of his tradition like Lorenzo Pignotti and Giovanni Battista Casti, who published *Gli animali parlanti* in 1802 (Frittelli 9). In Collodi's Tuscany, animal tales in their more archaic form were also present in oral tradition as short narratives usually intended for children and set in the familiar worlds of the village or countryside. Their talking animals served to deliver elementary moral teachings on what constituted vice and virtue (Ferretti 224, 232).

It has been noted that "Collodi's Aesopian sententiousness" is expressed, especially, in the "numerous warnings to the reckless marionette from the magical animal friends Pinocchio repeatedly fails to heed, the Talking Cricket above all" (Cambon 53–54). The Cricket first appears, and then is killed, in chapter 4, but he returns as a ghost in chapter 13, a doctor in chapter 16, and himself reborn in chapter 36. Throughout *Pinocchio*, a number of animals reiterate his message. In chapter 12, a White Blackbird attempts to warn Pinocchio of his questionable companions, the Cat and the Fox, and is immediately killed by the Cat. A Parrot informs Pinocchio he has been duped by the Cat and the Fox and chides him for his stupidity (ch. 19). A Firefly lectures Pinocchio for robbing grapes as Pinocchio writhes in a trap (ch. 21). In chapter 27, a Crab tries to convince Pinocchio and his classmates to desist from their fistfights and flying schoolbooks (305), and in Funland a Marmot confirms to Pinocchio that he has become a donkey and then scolds him for it (ch. 32). Taken together, these animals create the choral voice of a collective superego that preaches an ethic of work, family, moderation, and obedience—not only values stressed in many a child's education but also crucial requisites for the formation of responsible social subjects.

These animals also belong to the folkloric category of animals possessing magical wisdom—truth-telling animals, prophetic animals, wisdom-giving animals—and perform the fairy-tale function of interdiction, which may come as warning or advice and usually appears early in a narrative, when "one of the members of a family absents himself from home"; the typical violation of the interdiction moves the plot along (Propp 26–27). The Cricket first addresses Pinocchio, who has by chapter 4 already escaped from home and caused Geppetto to be imprisoned, with these words: "Woe to those children who disobey their parents and wilfully leave home. They will never come to any good in this world, and sooner or later they'll be bitterly sorry for it." When Pinocchio tells him that going to school is not part of his plans, the Cricket again warns him: "Poor little simpleton! Don't you know that if you do that, you'll grow up to be a perfect jackass and everyone will poke fun at you?" Pinocchio specifies that his chosen trade is "eating, drinking, sleeping, having fun, and living the life of a vagabond from morning to night," to which the Cricket replies: "everyone who follows that trade is bound to end up in the poorhouse or in prison" (109). The Cricket offers words of wisdom and prophecy, for Pinocchio will indeed become a jackass and frequent jail in the course of his adventures. The creature's admonitions result in his death by hammer and in Pinocchio's active disregard of his advice a few chapters later, when Pinocchio sells his schoolbooks for a ticket to the puppet theater (141).

Most of the animals that appear in *Pinocchio* have a long history of symbolic associations, and Collodi does not hesitate to play on these (see Sax 132). In particular, all the animals associated with the Cricket figure in popular or proverbial sayings, which may reduce their role as solemn pedagogues. The expression *avere il grillo* ("to have the crickets") means to suffer from nervousness to the point of obsession, practically the state to which Pinocchio is reduced by the Cricket's preaching. A *merlo* ("blackbird") is a foolish or naive person, appropriate for a bird who chooses to be self-righteous with a cat. A *pappagallo* ("parrot") repeats mechanically and mindlessly the words of others. *Vedere le lucciole* ("to see fireflies") means to feel great physical pain to the point of "seeing stars"; Pinocchio encounters the Firefly right after his foot gets caught in a trap. *Prendere un granchio* ("to catch or get a crab") is to be in error or deceived, which happens to Pinocchio when he disregards the Crab's words. And *pigliare o beccare una marmotta* ("to catch a groundhog") was an expression, at least in Collodi's time, meaning "to catch a cold from exposing oneself either to cold or to drafts";[1] the Marmot herself explains that Pinocchio is suffering from "jackass fever" (375).

Another set of animals illustrates the consequences of ignoring the Cricket. Pinocchio comes on the animals of the town Acchiappa-citrulli, or Catchafool, immediately before he arrives at the Field of Miracles in chapter 18. These animals—"mangy dogs yawning with hunger, fleeced sheep shivering with cold, . . . large butterflies no longer able to fly because they had sold their beautiful colored wings," and many others (219)—are victims of their own stupidity in allowing themselves to be duped, though their example will prove just as ineffectual to Pinocchio as the Cricket's warnings. The positive counterpart to Catchafool is Busy-Bee Town (ch. 24), a remote island inhabited by smugly industrious human beings.

The thieving martens of chapter 22 function as a different sort of exemplum. Guilty of cutting a deal with the now-defunct watchdog Melampo, in which they gave him one of the eight hens they stole every week from the farmyard in exchange for his promise not to squeal on them, the martens are turned in to the farmer by the new watchdog, Pinocchio, who condemns in them precisely the sort of systemic corruption of which he himself is often victim. Indeed, the martens' organized crime contrasts with Pinocchio's one-time, hunger-driven theft of a few grapes from the same farmer's vineyard only a few pages earlier, for which he pays with a painful trap on his feet, a severe lecture on private property, and the demotion to watchdog. The traditional association of the dog—especially the watchdog—with fidelity is also turned on its head in this episode; although he reports the martens, Pinocchio shows his loyalty to the disloyal dog by not saying a word about Melampo's role.

Pinocchio's degradation to a donkey, the ultimate icon of ignorance, stupidity, and laziness, literalizes the Cricket's prediction, in chapter 4, that he would grow up to be a "perfect jackass." Indeed, throughout his adventures Pinocchio fears that what society takes to be the defining characteristics of a good citizen—hard work and a sense of personal responsibility—will reduce him to a mere beast of burden. In chapter 24, for example, when asked to pull a cart, he exclaims, "I'll have you know that I've never been a jackass" (277). It is just, in the eyes of the offended, that his offenses will consistently lead to *contrapassi,* punishments that fit the crime, in which his refusal to lower himself to hard labor results in his be-ing treated like and finally turned into an animal.

A number of *Pinocchio*'s most memorable animals are forged even more clearly in the Aesopian mold. Playing the role of villains, the Cat and the Fox are consummate tricksters who appear more than any other animal of the book (in chs. 12–15, 18, and 36), first meeting up with Pinocchio as he heads back home to Geppetto with the five coins given to him by Fire-Eater. They seduce him with the story of the fabulous Field of Miracles (located in Dodoland); they pose as assassins and hang him in order to get the coins; and then, after Pinocchio has been rescued by the Fairy and is once again on his way back to Geppetto, they convince him to plant the coins, which, needless to say, results in the coins' dis-appearance. The Fox is a cross-cultural embodiment of wiliness, dissimulation, and perfidy, even if, as in the fables of Aesop and La Fontaine, foxes that consider themselves capable of outsmarting anyone are often made to pay for their pre-sumption (e.g., Aesop's "The Fox and the Dog" or "The Ass, the Fox, and the Lion"). *Pinocchio*'s Cat, who plays straight man to the Fox as he mechanically re-iterates his words, is himself an echo of more illustrious precursors. In Charles Perrault's "Puss in Boots" (another of the tales translated by Collodi), the cat takes center stage as an all-powerful, wheeling-dealing animal helper who is re-warded for his efforts by being made a great lord. Renard has a love-and-hate al-liance with a cat named Tibbert who is often more than his equal in craftiness. In La Fontaine's "The Cat and the Fox," of the two "frank furry-pawed schemers" the Cat proves himself the more clever (473).

When Pinocchio has begun his new, more responsible life, in the last chapter, the Fox and the Cat appear one last time, now truly down-and-out. But the pup-pet feels no pity for them, and the two con men pay for their success in the ear-lier chapters by being reduced to abjection. Appropriately, in this same chapter Pinocchio gets his wish of seeing his coins multiplied (though to a mere forty), when the Fairy gives him the magic gift of a purse full of gold (459). But that other subjects such as the Fox and the Cat, especially those who represent social institutions or professional categories, receive no such retribution suggests that in the world of *Pinocchio* justice is selective. Punishment depends not on coher-ent moral principles but, often, on how easily punishable one is, a truth that Pi-nocchio confronts over and over again. Figures like the Cat and the Fox are there-fore less social aberrations than exponents, at the lowest rung, of the self-interest and opportunism that are generally embraced by the inhabitants, both animal and human, of Pinocchio's world, in which there are no innocents.

In the portrayal of the doctors Owl and Raven (ch. 16) and of the gorilla judge (ch. 19), Collodi is at his most mordant. After Pinocchio's hanging, the Fairy con-sults with three doctors—the Owl, Raven, and Cricket—who are the comic an-tithesis of the rational diagnosticians they purport to be. The satire of the med-ical profession—or, more in general, of pompous fools who believe themselves to be wise men—has a long history, especially in theater. The ridiculous empty-headedness of Collodi's Owl and Raven also stands in ironic contrast to the traditional associations—prophecy and ill omen—of the two birds that play their part.[2] When asked for a simple description of Pinocchio's state, they offer conflicting diagnoses and persist in doing so even after the patient has resolved things himself. They not only hint at Collodi's views on rarefied learning and scientific authority but also illustrate his playfully deconstructive approach to traditional images and motifs.

The gorilla judge of chapter 19 is the representative of a similarly skewed judicial system. Introduced as "venerable for his advanced years and his white beard, but above all for his gold-rimmed spectacles without lenses, which he was obliged to wear all the time on account of an inflammation of the eyes that had been plaguing him for many years" (227), he listens sympathetically to Pinocchio's account of the theft of his coins by the Cat and Fox. Then, in an entirely original expression of blind justice, he has his two mastiff gendarmes take Pinocchio off to prison. Collodi here toys with the classic valence of the ape as a poor and often grotesque imitator and its use to figure the least noble aspects of human beings. The gorilla administers topsy-turvy justice, punishing the victim and vindicating the perpetrator.

If we step back and take a panoramic look at *The Adventures of Pinocchio*, its general contours are certainly those of the fairy tale. Pinocchio's miraculous transformation into a boy in chapter 36 is something that he and others have been aspiring to for a good part of the book, and it is necessary to make some sense of and justify all the trials the puppet has undergone. But the transformation is still quite modest compared with the usual fairy-tale finales of a lavish marriage or vast treasure, typical tropes for the progression toward the riches of mature life. Pinocchio becomes a boy or young adult, nothing more, and if we can talk at all of wish fulfillment, it consists in the simple rise from the destitution of Geppetto's threadbare existence to the respectable tableau of the end of the book, distinguished by familial obligations, hard work, and a few hours of self-schooling in the evenings. Even if this sort of metamorphosis had something marvelous about it for the audience of a nineteenth-century Italy, in which the middle class had yet to arrive, it is most certainly not the stuff of fairy tales.

At the end, then, in the dialogue between the fable's vision of a corrupt and imperfect real world and the fairy tale's utopian hope in the magic of something different, the first prevails. Most of the fairy-tale animals are situated in chapter 16, after Pinocchio's hanging, when Pinocchio is rescued by the Fairy. After overcoming the obstacle encountered in the preceding chapters (the Fox and Cat in the guise of assassins) and acquiring a magic benefactress, he may seem well on his way to reembarking on a classic fairy tale. Between his hanging and the final chapters—the bulk of the book—the animals that appear offer moral counsel, serve as cynical exempla or counterexempla, or parody classic antagonists of the fairy tale and epic traditions. Only in chapters 34–36 do some of the animal characters and narrative progression of the fairy tale return, in a mutation of narrative modalities and schemes that tends to accentuate more and more the marvelous, which substitutes itself for the metaphorical exasperation of discomfort, irritation, violence, misery, and disappointment that are dominant in the rest of the work.   (Bàrberi-Squarotti 97; my trans.)

The fairy tale serves as a palliative in the world of *Pinocchio*. By the enforced ending of chapter 36, Pinocchio has left behind his liminality as boyish puppet continually on the verge of being demoted to the animal state; he has also left behind his coterie of talking animals. Yet if in this new life, predictable and mundane, he will have no more encounters with smoking serpents or magic pigeons, it is difficult to picture that future without apish judges or vulpine wheeler-dealers or bulldoggish thugs—that is, without cruelty, deceit, or injustice.

NOTES

[1] These definitions are from the Rigutini and Fanfani dictionary, which is cited in Collodi, *Opere* 1015 n173.

[2] Both the Raven and the Owl were, in Greek mythology and religion, revered for their intelligence and prophetic powers; the first was sacred to Apollo, the second to Athena. For the Romans they were more often presagers of death, a role that they also assume in folklore.

Writing *Pinocchio*: Second Language Acquisition Theories Applied to an Advanced Italian Grammar and Composition Course

Laura Stallings

Collodi's *Pinocchio* is studied in the first of a two-course sequence in advanced grammar and composition at Washington University in Saint Louis. Improving reading and writing in Italian through the analysis of advanced grammar topics as well as through an introduction to prose analysis is the primary focus of this first course. The chosen literary theme is the representation of childhood in Italy in the late nineteenth and early twentieth centuries. The first half of the course is dedicated to short stories, the second to the reading and analysis of *Pinocchio*. This is the first novel our students read in its entirety, and it serves to introduce reading and writing as skills directed toward the creation of meaning and communication. This essay focuses on second-language writing based on the principles of second language acquisition using *Pinocchio* as the literary component.

Pinocchio is an ideal text for this undertaking, because it is both a novel and a didactic instrument. As children's literature, *Pinocchio* performs a dual role of entertaining and educating. The character of Pinocchio progresses in his learning of life's lessons from chapter to chapter, much as our students progress through the phases of learning to write. Given its theme of learning, *Pinocchio* is especially well suited to be used as pedagogical tool for the study of writing.

Creating an integrated writing component for the study of *Pinocchio* was my principal objective. Brenda Dyer has demonstrated that the integration of theory and pedagogy in second-language writing courses promotes general writing proficiency and improves academic composition. I chose to ground the writing component in a conceptual framework based on both sociocultural and second language acquisition theories with pedagogical applications that adhered to this framework.

As I designed the writing component for *Pinocchio*, L. S. Vygotsky's sociocultural perspective of language learning provided an ideal theoretical framework. Vygotsky calls for participation with one's environment. According to his theory of the zone of proximal development, students must use what knowledge they already have, coupled with suitable intervention from outside sources (sources of human contact), in order to learn.

Adding Stephen Krashen's input and conversation competence hypotheses, both components of his monitor theory, to Vygotsky's zone of proximal development was logical in the creation of the theoretical foundation for the *Pinocchio* writing component. Krashen's monitor theory has been a driving force in second language acquisition for the past two decades. It asserts that for language learning to take place, students must receive input that is slightly above their capabilities, represented as $i + 1$. The optimal method of presenting $i + 1$ is through interaction with one's environment, mainly through human contact.

Vygotsky and Krashen have each developed a similar premise in relation to social interaction. The zone of proximal development lies "between what students can already accomplish on their own and what they can accomplish only with appropriate help" (Zellermayer, Salomon, Globerson, and Givon 376). Krashen's input hypothesis, when merged with his conversational competence hypothesis, resembles Vygotsky's zone of proximal development in that Krashen too believes that foreign language students must be provided input that is comprehensible and just slightly above their level. He further states that social interaction provides for the development of conversational competence, much like the "appropriate help" called for in Vygotsky's theory. Each theory advocates, but does not limit itself to, meaningful input, social interaction, and practice as important processes in second language acquisition. These theories can be applied to *Pinocchio*. Throughout Collodi's novel, its protagonist is supplied with meaningful input in the form of advice, examples, or personal experience. Furthermore, he has ample social interaction as well as opportunity to practice what he is learning, exactly what Vygotsky and Krashen prescribe.

Student outcomes in foreign language writing courses often do not meet the expectations of either the instructor or the academic community. Frequently in second-language writing courses the pedagogy implemented to teach writing is not grounded in either theory or current research. (See Applebee 97–98 for a discussion of "the gap between educational theory and educational practice.") In creating an integrated writing component for the study of *Pinocchio*, I sought to bridge the gap between theory and practice so that students would be provided with more effective and meaningful writing strategies.

Three elements make up the pedagogical strategy implemented in the *Pinocchio* writing component: process writing, in-context grammar presentation, and the selective use of computer-assisted language learning. The combination of these three elements, varying from assignment to assignment, proved to be effective from a qualitative analysis viewpoint.

Process writing incorporates the premises of both sociocultural theory and monitor theory. Kimberly Koffolt and Sheryl Holt present the following list of benefits of process writing in the foreign language classroom. It encourages inexperienced nonnative writers to begin writing early; it provides feedback during the planning stage before students invest hours on writing a long draft without a focus; it allows nonnative writers to see models of other students' writing and samples of academic writing; it encourages feedback from peers about content, organization, and audience; it allows quieter students a chance to share their ideas verbally in a small-group setting; it provides a much less threatening (authoritative) audience in which students can fail in order to succeed in subsequent drafts.

Students of Advanced Italian Grammar and Composition arrive at the reading of *Pinocchio* at the midpoint of the semester, having already read a number of short stories on the theme of the representation of childhood in Italy. They have been writing about these short stories using the process writing system. What makes implementing process writing with a novel like *Pinocchio* so appealing is that the novel's length allows repeated rounds of writing in the same context, thus reinforcing its effectiveness. Students can approach the same work from different angles, all the while rethinking, renegotiating, and rewriting their ideas. In this way, writing is used as a real communication skill, not merely as a support skill. Students write three essays on *Pinocchio*. When comparing their first Pinocchio essay with their last, an exercise the class does together at the end of the semester, they are pleasantly surprised to see how much improvement they have made.

Here is a typical sequence of process writing for an essay:

1. The essay topic is announced.
2. Students do a prewriting exercise in which they brainstorm ideas and write freely on the topic.
3. Students work in small groups, sharing their freewriting exercise with one another and giving and receiving feedback. This informal peer-editing session helps them define and structure their ideas before writing their first draft.
4. Students write their first draft with peer and instructor comments in hand.
5. Students come together in either the same or a different small group, depending on the audience objective of the peer-editing session. In this formal session they present their first drafts. The instructor provides guiding questions to help address the content and organization of essays. (I strictly avoid student critique of grammar in order to keep the students on task to the writing itself. Vocabulary suggestions work well, however.)
6. Armed with feedback on their first draft, students write their final draft on the basis of peer editing and instructor commentary.

Following the process-writing format above, a typical assignment for the *Pinocchio* writing component could be the following:

1. The topic is given: Examine and comment on the nascent awareness of learning that Pinocchio feels when he says, "Jiminy Cricket was actually right! If I hadn't run away from home and if my papa were here, I wouldn't be starving right now!" [My trans. of Collodi, *Avventure/Adventures* 112, 114]
2. A freewriting exercise is assigned for homework. Students write 1–2 pages of brainstorming ideas.
3. During the next class meeting students gather in small groups where they present their freewriting; each reads the writing of each group member. The group proceeds to an informal peer-editing session, in which students make

general suggestions and help one another nail down the topics and formats of their first draft. The instructor provides individual feedback as well.

4. Students write their first draft on the basis of peer and instructor commentary.

5. A formal peer-editing session takes place. The same small groups reunite and review each other's first drafts. A series of guiding questions to help take students through the formal peer editing is provided by the instructor, but the students are free to address any aspect of each other's writing that they see fit to address. At this time, the instructor gives back his commentary of the first draft along with a grammar correction worksheet.

6. The final draft is written on the basis of step 5.

At an appropriate time during these steps the instructor calls the class together to examine and discuss their nascent awareness of the writing process as well as their understanding of what writing is (i.e., a vehicle for the creation of meaning). Finally, a comparison of Pinocchio's new-found awareness of learning and the students' new awareness of writing is made, and thus the connection between the literary and pedagogical components of *Pinocchio* is made as well.

A further objective was to make the writing experience authentic. Of the various elements of process writing listed above, peer editing confirms its instrumental role in providing the social input necessary to create authentic writing. Before I proceed to the peer-editing segment, it should be mentioned that peer editing takes place in a course only after there has been class time devoted to the discussion and practice of it—the how and why.

Peer editing, grounded in both Vygotsky's and Krashen's theories, allows for interaction, input, and exchange. Furthermore, it is student-centered; affords more opportunity to use both the verbal and written target language; increases self-confidence; and through interaction with fellow students and the text, it focuses on authentic audience (Tang and Tithecott). Authentic audience, in this instance, is classroom peers or the academic community (Reid). It provides student writers with a broader and more natural audience for which to write. It can be tedious and at times self-defeating to write for the instructor, an audience of one. Peer editing's use of the entire class, instructor included, provides a more natural and stimulating readership for the writer. Writing only for an instructor often ends up as a support skill rather than a communicative skill.

Another factor to consider in peer editing is that it allows informal writing to take place where it otherwise would not. The writing about writing that happens in peer review means that students practice writing informally about formal writing. The amount of writing that takes place increases, which means more writing practice than students would otherwise have.

There are numerous examples from *Pinocchio* that can be incorporated into essay topics that in turn can be related to different aspects of peer editing. For the purpose of this essay, I propose a general one. Because various characters throughout the novel give Pinocchio advice, the following topic could be assigned: Investigate the advice Pinocchio receives along his journey and consider why this advice is given and what he chooses to do with it. Students write their essay following the steps outlined above, but this time the instructor intervenes with an in-class discussion that connects peer editing to the advice Pinocchio receives. Both involve the exchange of ideas, suggestion giving, reflection, and human interaction.

Another segment of the process-writing sequence is a self-correction worksheet used between the first and final drafts—part of the instructor feedback noted in point 5 of a typical assignment. I developed a segment to fulfill the grammatical and structural analysis expected of the student essays as well as to create a more meaningful interaction with grammar. The segment examines grammar entirely in context, allowing for a more holistic and real analysis. There are two parts, a table that lists all the correction symbols with their accompanying descriptions and a correction worksheet.

The self-correction system seeks to place grammar in a meaningful context, and what can be more meaningful than one's own writing? I approach this exercise by reading through the students' first drafts and underlining the mistakes I find without marking them with a correction symbol. In their correction worksheet students must analyze each marked passage, name the type of error, and use the correct symbol.

The worksheet distinguishes between global and local errors and establishes their order of importance. Global errors interfere with understanding and prevent the reader from following the writer's message. Local errors distract the reader from the message but do not block comprehension. This correction system is highly adaptable. For example, one can easily narrow the focus to a few chosen grammatical features and use the worksheet to analyze only them. I do not allow students to correct for grammar during peer editing, for two reasons. First, they cannot always perform a competent grammar analysis and therefore might provide one another with incorrect information. Second, if they are allowed to correct grammar, they tend to focus their peer editing on this one factor alone and neglect making observations about the actual writing.

Grammar itself can link the literary and the pedagogical. Consider the following essay topic: Discuss the learning processes that Pinocchio goes through. Consider the different ways these "lessons of life" are given to him. Keep in mind his internal awareness and abilities and how he shows them to the reader.

At an appropriate point during the six writing stages for this essay, the instructor suggests that the different types of learning that Pinocchio goes through are related to the various strategies the class employs in learning how to write in Italian. The analysis of grammar in context is one of these strategies. For example, students might be asked to analyze the difference between gerund and infinitive use in a particular passage.

Peer editing in the *Pinocchio* writing component is implemented by two different methods, in-class and computer-assisted language-learning peer editing. I use entirely in-class peer editing for the first *Pinocchio* essay, a combination of

in-class and computer-assisted language-learning peer editing for the second essay, and the exclusive use of the computer for the third essay. The computer-
assisted design was managed either through e-mail or the discussion board of a
typical course-management software program. In-class peer editing can be oral,
written, or a combination of both. I normally use oral peer editing in the initial
feedback stage, when students comment on one another's freewriting. I reserve
written peer editing for the more formal process of critiquing the first draft.
In contrast, computer-assisted language-learning peer editing all takes place in
writing, although it may be in either synchronous or asynchronous time. A
threaded discussion-board session, for which all students are asked to be present, lends itself to a conversational format even if it is written. E-mail peer editing tends to be more formal, as there is no instantaneous back-and-forth banter.

I implement computer-assisted language-learning peer editing in addition
to in-class peer editing for several reasons. Nancy Sullivan and Ellen Pratt have
conducted a study that compares a computer-assisted writing classroom with a
traditional classroom. They found that the computer-assisted class improved significantly in all three measurements they tested: differences in attitudes toward
writing and writing apprehension, quality of writing, and nature of participation
and discourse. My students noticed a difference between their first and third *Pinocchio* essay, but I started using computer-assisted peer editing at the halfway
mark, so in this particular case one can make no conclusion about the efficacy of
computer-assisted language learning for peer editing. But such use of the computer agrees with the theories in the writing component's framework. The Su-
livan and Pratt study begins by quoting studies by Janet M. Eldred, Robert
Kaplan, Michael H. Long and Patricia Porter, and Mary McGroarty supporting
the view that, "The collaborative nature of networked computing fits well with
the social view of writing" (491). Similar findings are found in George Braine,
who investigated the differences in writing quality, writing improvement, and
quantity of teacher and student comments on student papers in a computer-
assisted foreign language writing classroom. He found positive outcomes in all
three areas of inquiry, but his most significant finding was that the length of comments during peer review in the computerized class averaged 480 words per
hundred minutes compared with 197 words per hundred minutes in the traditional writing class.

Braine's results regarding the quality and amount of teacher feedback provided to students in a computer-assisted language-learning environment are
promising. His study found that in this environment the instructor spent ten
minutes per student providing an average of 152 words in feedback compared to
an average of 148 words in feedback in sixteen minutes of writing in the traditional classroom. In my own experience I found similar results. In addition,
word-processing programs allow a manipulation of electronic text that is not possible with a hard-copy printout. I found that in an electronic medium I was more
creative and thorough in my comments. But using paper still has its advantages.

I believe that the combination of traditional and computer-assisted methods is best for satisfying student preferences. Some students are true techies; others are more comfortable with paper.

There are other indicators that computer-assisted language learning is beneficial in the foreign language writing classroom. Some hypothesize that it promotes a sense of group because it has an equalizing effect. One can see how such a sense is desirable in peer editing. The removal of attributes such as race, sex, and accent facilitates the interaction required to produce language learning. It can also be hypothesized, in conjunction with Koffolt and Holt's statements on process writing, that there is an equalizing effect on turn taking in brainstorming, peer editing, and feedback. That the network is in either synchronous or asynchronous time gives the most reticent student as much opportunity to participate as the most loquacious one.

One final observation about computer-assisted language learning is that it saves valuable class time toward the end of the semester, exactly the point at which I prescribe it. There are always many things to tie up then. Having the students do online peer editing frees up class time for addressing topics that are better dealt with in the classroom.

Process writing incorporates the theories of second language academic writing through its rigorous schema of brainstorming, prewriting, feedback, peer and instructor interaction, peer editing, revising, and the examining and critiquing of authentic work. One of the principal elements in process writing is peer editing, which is especially conducive to student interaction. For Ann Raimes the process approach fulfills more than any other the need to understand how a language is learned and how writing is produced. It creates an authentic audience. Through peer editing the writer must consider the reader's perspective, which in turn forces the writer to make the writing believable and real. I found process writing, situated in sociocultural and monitor theories, to be highly effective in the *Pinocchio* writing component. Process writing and *Pinocchio* are an especially effective duo in the Italian writing classroom, because they represent the teaming together of literature and pedagogy. *Pinocchio* is a story about initiation and metamorphosis. Its protagonist must go through the process of transformation in much the same way that the novice writer must go through and assimilate the process of writing. Thus the writing instructor has an excellent opportunity to marry literature and pedagogy in the classroom.

Pinocchio, a Puppet for All Seasons

Angela M. Jeannet

There is something curious about the puppet called Pinocchio: he has overshadowed his creator. Although born on paper, he lives in our world as an autonomous being. Naturally, Collodi had something to do with Pinocchio's birth; as a matter of fact, the novel can be read as an entirely transposed narration of his, and his world's, experiences. But most commentators, until about fifty years ago, focused on the character's life without wishing to know much about the middle-aged man who imagined him and wrote down his story.

The status of *The Adventures of Pinocchio* in the Italian tradition, from the 1880s until the major watershed marked by the late 1930s and 1940s, is well documented. The novel appeared at a crucial moment in Italian history and addressed problems facing a growing public, the so-called bourgeoisie. The anxieties of an emerging European country, the Kingdom of Italy, involved social, linguistic, and cultural dilemmas. Great difficulties faced the young nation, due to uneven economic development, profound social disparities, and a want of national cohesion reflected in the lack of a common spoken language. The well-to-do classes and the intellectuals yearned for a sense of national identity that had yet to be achieved. Tellingly, the period that led to Italian independence was given a highly significant name, Risorgimento, which alluded to another great season of Italian life, the *Rinascimento* or Renaissance, and carried a persistent reference to one of Italy's founding myths, the awaited return of ancient Rome's glory.

Universal literacy in a common written and spoken language was a major goal for the new nation. *The Adventures of Pinocchio* provided a text written for children, a novelty for the peninsula; indirectly, it addressed also an adult public; it spoke a language that was regional—Tuscan—but familiar to all educated people; and it spoke in a humorous, provocative way about life issues that the new society judged important, particularly in educating children.

Pinocchio's story emerged from a shared Italian experience, that of a rural society on the verge of change. Many commentators have remarked that landscapes are almost nonexistent in the novel. Quick, functional touches suffice, precisely because of the total identification between story and background—village, fields, woods, seashore. Description would be out of place. Yet Pinocchio's story escaped the narrow confines of the late-nineteenth-century village. The human landscape was what interested Collodi: each episode reveals personalities, beliefs, and existential choices. Herein lies the power of Collodi's work, its openness to rereadings. *Pinocchio* tells us that puppets and people alike understand life to be a discovery, a marvel, seldom easy, fraught with danger, and ultimately a solitary endeavor except for the presence of one or two loving but stern supporters. It proposes a sobering view of the world, which is most fortunately contradicted by the irrepressible vitality and very human resiliency that the protagonist exhibits throughout.

The Adventures of Pinocchio is a book of action; the puppet moves about continually, running, fleeing, jumping, swimming; he is a "champion of speed" (Gasparini, ch. 1). His playfulness and thirst for adventure elicit delight and admiration even as they clash with reality, a reality of penury, struggle, temptations, and illusions. The specter of death, a daily companion for Collodi's first readers, lends suspense to the story, and its chilling threat is a reminder of reality that only a bold imagination can mock and overturn. Drawn by Collodi in all its picturesque guises, the threat of near death acknowledges and exorcises the children's (and adults') very real separation anxiety. Life's lessons are harsh but surmountable; morality, in *Pinocchio*, is

> the possibility and opportunity to mend one's ways, not on the basis of an exterior moralism, but rather due to the individual's ethical redemption based on spontaneous motives, self-respect, and a sense of personal dignity.
> (Marcheschi xlviii)

The narration never stoops to the point of deluding its intended audience of young listeners by offering them a sugary vision of life; nor does it propose images or goals of impossible perfection. It is "never desperate, never without a solution" (Decollanz 179). It relies on comedy and irony and a fabulous imagination to reassert its conviction that life is, after all, worthwhile. "*Pinocchio* is not a consolatory, but rather a liberating, book," argues Marcheschi (lvi). Most important, Pinocchio's world is a universe of conflicting and coexisting opposites; good and bad are often mixed or undistinguishable. The novel brings children and grown-ups the most important news literature has to share, that of the existence of ambiguity.

One might assume that a book written for children under such special and complex circumstances would remain limited to its own times and territory of origin. Nothing is further from the truth. Richard Wunderlich and Thomas Morrissey, in their recent *Pinocchio Goes Postmodern*, have thoroughly documented the book's success in the English-speaking world, and most especially the United States. Pinocchio entered Great Britain in 1891, shortly after his Italian birth, and landed in the United States in 1892 (31). Well translated by Mary Alice Murray, the book at first had a checkered editorial history in the United States; nevertheless it met immediately with the public's favor. Its success led to subtle and not so subtle modifications to suit the pedagogical intentions of school and home: greater emphasis was placed on children's obedience, the need for school attendance, respect for authority, and the importance of order and toil.

But the late 1930s witnessed a fundamental transformation. The story, which had featured an irrepressibly undisciplined Pinocchio with the psychology of a child on the threshhold of adolescence, began featuring a naive little boy who engaged in mild and easily forgivable mischief; images of penury and harsh episodes were downplayed or eliminated. Wunderlich and Morrissey suggest that the atmosphere of the Depression induced writers and readers to opt for a sweetening of the stern vision that the original *Adventures* offered. The culmination of that change in Pinocchio's identity and background is represented by Walt Disney's acclaimed film, which is a perfect example of "intersemiotic" translation, the reading of a text through a different cultural filter and a different cultural medium (Jakobson, "On Linguistic Aspects").

Except for some elements, however fundamental, Disney's product is essentially a new text; "from the story by Collodi," as the credits say, something new was born. Disney and his team created a film for American audiences. Each detail proclaims its cultural matrix. Geppetto's house, located in a quaint Tyrolean-style village, is the quintessential image of comfortable simplicity. There is even a cake on the table, which astonishingly displaces the three most famous pears of world literature. No trace of the original Geppetto remains. Disney's Pinocchio is a little boy whose voice and behavior suggest an age range of seven to nine years. At "birth" he is a puppet on actual strings rather than the ornery, disrespectful piece of wood that had its own disruptive ideas about fun, freedom, and aspirations. Collodi's Pinocchio behaved more like a boy between nine and thirteen years of age; today we would call him a preteen. The Cricket acquires much more importance in the film. He is the story's narrator and witness and curiously embodies Pinocchio's conscience. He acquires the personality of the "common man"; he is garrulous and coarse, speaks and acts as an old-fashioned, and not too effective, city cop would have in the Norman Rockwell era. "I'll knock your block off," he warns as he threatens a fistfight, and his sayings are trite repetitions of everyday wisdom. He even creates clichés, such as the "Here we go again!" expression, which became famous many years later. At the end, he receives a gold medal, that fetishistic reminder of favorite school customs for American children and adults alike. He is just the type of character who would appeal to a naive audience.

Specific cultural obsessions are evident: the frequent emphasis on drinking as a transgression; the mild allusions to sexual seduction suggested in the most stereotyped way, therefore distanced and supposedly stripped of danger; and the amusing reference to leisure living as a "cure" that materializes as Pleasure Island, to which fake doctors direct poor little Pinocchio. Monstro, instead of being the shark-whale composite we find in Collodi, clearly carries some of the connotations of Moby Dick, a well-established presence in the collective American imagination whether by direct reading or indirect suggestion. Most important, in Disney

> the [characters'] assignment to the categories of good and evil is even. That evenness indicates that Pinocchio is placed in the middle of two forces that are equally balanced. The connotation of the characters is reinforced; they are one-dimensionally good or bad, and make the opposition between good and evil absolutely evident . . . . As for Pinocchio, he does not show any tension toward some objective. It is always someone else who decides for him.   (Annibaletto and Luchi 23–24)

In Ganna Ottevaere–van Praag's words, Disney "blends moral and spectacle . . . in a baroque delirium . . . there is no boring moralizing in Walt Disney, but he is so insipid!" (262–63).

What elements remain, then, of the original story? First of all, Disney borrows the original's passion for action. Like the novel, the film reveals the surprising and frightening merry-go-round of the world and chronicles the puppet's involvement in it. The best sequences, and the most disturbing, involve the transformation of Lampwick into a donkey and the storm at sea. Here the film attains true dramatic power. Lampwick, the hard-playing smoking and drinking companion of little Pinocchio, is already a teenager, faced with a metamorphosis filled with sexual undertones that the film suggests in a horrifying way. As for the Whale episode, the technical richness of the medium and Disney's fantasy transform the dramatic but reflexive moment of the original into a show of pyrotechnic beauty about marine life.

A second element reminds the viewer of Collodi's world: the remoteness of the feminine. Females are absent from Collodi and Disney, even as an imagined audience, except for the Fairy. In both works, her intervention ensures salvation, but she is not of the world, which is entirely masculine. Hers is an occasional and mythical presence. However, the sister-mother, who is a determinant character in the novel, becomes in the film a stereotypical beauty with golden hair and perfect make-up, consistent with the idealized image of woman in traditional

Hollywood, when the actresses were stars. Even Geppetto's flirtatious fish and the various dancing girls who appear in the film are empty icons, serial reproductions of the same femininity that can tease but has no warmth. In both texts Pinocchio's world includes no religious allusions. That absence is more surprising in Disney than in Collodi, who was fiercely secular; we can only wonder whether the Italian writer's universe exerted an influence on Disney in that area too.

Finally, both Collodi and Disney created works that address an audience of both children and adults. But again, Collodi's vision is filled with ambiguities, whereas Disney's narration is linear. Children, through the enchanting details of the film, are taught what it means to become acceptable members of their own society. Adults find in it a confirmation of traditional values and the pleasures of nostalgia. The popularity of the film and its worldwide diffusion testify not only to its artistic quality and the producers' commercial savvy but also—as with most Disney films—to a keen understanding of twentieth-century society's fears, hopes, and illusions. The authority of this new story is evident in its popular success and in the surprised reactions of contemporary American readers when they discover the original Italian.

Nostalgia is a very small part of the pleasure that today's Italians find in *The Adventures of Pinocchio*. Yet Collodi's book remains their "luogo della memoria" ("site of memory"), as Fernando Tempesti aptly wrote in a personal communication in 1994 (Letter). Many commentators and writers make clear why and how the book has retained its charm, and Pinocchio has acquired a new prominence in today's Italian-speaking world.

There is no doubt that Italian culture has changed profoundly in the last half century, rapidly incorporating new phenomena. Today more Italian children know Walt Disney's products than read the texts of Italian children's literature. But the ubiquitous wood reproductions of the marionette, displayed in stores everywhere, suggest a persistent engagement with that elusive character. More than twenty editions of the book are in print today. Recent biographies of the author reveal important aspects of his life, formation, and milieu. The novel itself has been manipulated, imitated, and rewritten. A term has been invented for such efforts; they are called *pinocchiate*. Since World War II, there have been numerous films and plays, made for the screen or television, which are more or less freely based on Collodi's major work. Scholarly analyses and illustrations by prominent artists have increased in number; they bring out more facets of the *Adventures* than the children's (supposedly) naive first encounters with Pinocchio ever did. Major writers provide evidence of the story's persisting resonance by quoting and borrowing from it. And from all the recent readings, new Pinocchios are born.

That *The Adventures of Pinocchio* lends itself to a plurality of readings is perhaps the most significant and attractive aspect of it for today's readers; the text has turned out to be truly open. Notwithstanding its author's unfathomable intentions and the expectations of the adults who bought the periodical and the book for their children over a century ago, what emerges now is a contradictory, intensely modern narrative. Contemporary critics have pointed to the irony, parody, and desecration of conventions, which are elements that should have made Pinocchio's *Adventures* an unlikely story for nineteenth-century children. Pinocchio's universe is an upside-down world (Bàrberi-Squarotti 89); Pinocchio is "different" (Boero and De Luca 55; Gagliardi 10); he is the antagonist by definition. Even when he conforms, reality becomes a delirium, an absurdity, as in the episode of Giangio the truck farmer (Boero and De Luca 56–57). Surprisingly, or perhaps not, Pinocchio's difference also suggests less positive observations: "[Pinocchio] is too different from the society around him not to provoke a negative reaction, or . . . society's attempt to domesticate him" (D'Angeli 157).

An important and telling development in Collodian criticism is the emergence of a topic that is central in most reflections on social issues in the last several decades: the crisis of the patriarchal family. A few years after Collodi, Luigi Pirandello explored that facet of social change with darker humor and more explicit awareness. In *The Adventures of Pinocchio* critics see the announcement of that crisis in the disjunction of Pinocchio's parental couple, which is hastened by the disruptive weight of poverty and a pervasive social restlessness. They argue that power is given to the sole female character, the Fairy; she embodies the figures of sister and mother, whose sacredness remains an important part of the Italian heritage. Those reflections lead in a direction that earlier readings ignored:

> the presence of the father as a constant point of reference, in a negative as well as a positive sense, is the expression of an explicitly secular and popular theologism, and indicates refusal of the pact that binds the Fathers, a pact that has been valid for centuries, a break with traditional patterns, and a struggle for a new awareness and autonomy.   (Decollanz 185)

Much thought has been given to the absence of all Christian, and even religious, references in *The Adventures of Pinocchio*. For Giorgio Bàrberi-Squarotti, Pinocchio is "the Voltairian Candide . . . who is in perfect syntony with the totally secular character of Collodi's world" (105). In that world, Collodi's imagination placed alternative forms of overpowering and capricious authority: the Green Fisherman and, most frighteningly, Fire-Eater, who is "an even too transparent metaphor of God, that Christian God who is so scandalously and clearly absent from Pinocchio's adventures" (94). Surely, once the issue of metaphysics was explicitly raised, the matter could not rest there; contradictory voices in fact proposed an entirely mythical reading of the marionnette's universe, most notably in the essays composing the volume *C'era una volta un pezzo di legno*, which addresses the symbolism of Pinocchio's story.

Given the diversity of readings the twentieth century has imposed on *The*

Adventures of Pinocchio, it is not surprising that the book's ending elicits op-posite responses. Collodi's Pinocchio does not return home, as Disney wanted us to believe. His existence began under the sign of rootlessness, once the wood he was made of ceased to be part of a tree; his life as a flesh-and-blood boy, sepa-rated from his earlier years, is again bound to be ambiguous and open to inter-pretation. Is his awakening from his dream a transformation or a metamor-phosis? A transformation implies learning and maturing, a metamorphosis the erasure of an earlier form. Critics with a salvific vision of human existence, whether in secular or religious terms, see in Pinocchio's changed essence a step forward, a redemption. Christian exegesis logically finds redemption. But Giu-seppe Decollanz also mentions the pain involved in that process, after speaking of the later Pinocchio's compassion, generosity, and acceptance of the human condition:

> It is this new reality, this greater existential awareness that are the bases of the last sentence in the book, a sentence that is neither banal nor rhetori-cal, but rather the simple, logical conclusion of a long and painful process of self-education. (187)

On the other hand, many readers of the last fifty years agree with Bàrberi-Squarotti's peremptory words: "Pinocchio cannot adapt . . . to this new, 'normal' condition; he must die. Normalcy and rules have killed him. . . . Normalcy is im-possible for the 'different' being that Pinocchio is" (107). Pinocchio has reached the depths of the process of erasure, the dark bottom of depersonalization (Gagliardi 11), which was foretold by what marked him, from the first, as the place of absence: absence of origin (he has no father), of traditional narrative (the nonexistent king), and of a mother. In a less somber vein, Glauco Cambon sighs, "What a delight . . . to follow Pinocchio's vagaries in his unreconstructed phase, and how poetically providential his transgressions were!" (54). Indeed, all read-ers, no matter how naive or experienced they may be, respond strongly to the controversial ending of one of world literature's most popular stories.

If critics express themselves in scholarly tones, two writers, Luigi Malerba and Giorgio Manganelli, use imaginative ways to bemoan the elimination of a crea-ture that, for them, embodied the saving graces of fantasy and rebellion.

For Malerba, chapter 35 of the original text documents Pinocchio's last obedi-ence. Searching for a new identity—or, more probably, as I believe, trying des-perately to hang on to his own—the puppet in Malerba's *Pinocchio con gli stivali* decides to run away for good when he reaches chapter 36: "I feel just fine as a puppet and I want to become neither a good nor a bad boy" (8). As the novella's title suggests ("Pinocchio in Boots"), the puppet attempts to enter the world of other fables, those that Charles Perrault wrote and Collodi translated into Ital-ian. Malerba's puppet meets Red Riding Hood and the Wolf, Cinderella, and Puss in Boots but fits in none of their stories and is always rejected. Ultimately, the carabinieri return him to the original concluding chapter, in what sounds like a final imprisonment: "Two mounted policemen took him back at a gallop into chapter 36, at the exact point from which he had run away" (25). Certainly, *The Adventures of Pinocchio*—as Malerba says—belong to the ancient world of fables that mirror the anxieties of the adults who invented them. And Malerba, as other late-twentieth-century readers do, believes that Pinocchio's adventures do not cause children harm, the harm of hypocrisy or inhuman perfection, but rather endow them with mental freedom. "Because ancient wise people knew, better than we do, that there is pleasure in life but also hard work" ("Pinocchio secondo Malerba").

The world's cruelty is a thematic constant in Collodi's novel, but more specifically, the drama of primary emotions revolves around the anxiety of belonging, which includes the fundamental issue of justice, most often experienced as suffered unfairness. The primal scene—pace Freud—takes place not at the door of a bedroom but when the child is confronted for the first time with injustice, as Collodi makes clear in the first pages of *Pinocchio*, when two carabinieri drag away an innocent Geppetto. Later, in the darkly humorous courtroom and prison scenes, skepticism about the authorities' morality is most evident. Those defining moments in Collodi's book were erased by Disney in his morality-conscious film but not by Italian readers. Italian writers, who have shown an abiding interest in social and political matters ever since Dante began his *Commedia*, have been inspired by Collodi's images, words, and scenes, which sleep in the depths of his readers' unconscious as a shared mythic presence. Antonio Tabucchi's work is an example of such inspiration.

Justice perverted haunts Tabucchi's pages. When, in one of his earliest novels, a poor and somewhat naive but rebellious man, Sesto, is taken to court, the guards metamorphose into mastiffs in his imagination. He understands "with no possibility of a mistake that [the court's presiding judge] was Pinocchio's gorilla, come back from his childhood" (*Piccolo naviglio* 175). The memory of the Collodian universe is pervasive in Tabucchi's fiction. In a later novel, Pinocchio's ghost appears with the incongruity of a dream when one of the protagonists, Firmino, a generous and inexperienced young newspaper reporter, attends a patently rigged political trial. As the mockery of justice drones on, the young man hovers between wakefulness and sleep:

> there was an interval of no more than a few seconds, to Firmino it seemed endless, a sort of limbo during which his memory carried him back to a white house on the shore at Cascais and his father's face, to a blue sea with white-crested waves, to a wooden Pinocchio doll with whom an infant Firmino had his bath in a zinc tub on a terrace.   (*Missing Head* 163)

Tabucchi said in *Requiem* that we are the ones who call into our dreams the people we wish to see again. It is not unexpected, then, that Collodi himself would appear in one of the most fascinating among Tabucchi's "dreams of dreams" ("Sogno"; trans. as "Dream").

Even more revealing is the fiction elaborated by Manganelli in his *Pinocchio: Un libro parallelo*. The "deliciously servile task of transcribing, deciphering, and solving enigmas" (v) is the route he chose to speak of Pinocchio. His parallel book takes shape inside the original, letting each episode and each image blossom thanks to the verve of his empathetic reading, which appeals to the sensibilities of today's readers. His reading of Collodi's Funland, for instance, is fully in tune with our experience. In Funland

> the terrible and lighthearted ecstasies of the young boys explode. The great nocturnal corruptor has built a city to receive them. In this metropolis of euphoria there is no joy . . . [Funland] is the capital of noise, of din as social rejoicing, a terrible prophecy.   (138)

That Funland is a males-only world is for Manganelli part of the adolescent boy's dream, and he senses in it a quality of loneliness that makes "Funland feel somewhat like a convent and at the same time a prison" (139). As for the ending, Manganelli also sees it in a melancholy and ambiguous way as the death of Pinocchio: "In the house of the new Pinocchio remains [a] dead and prodigious relic; the new and alive will have to cohabit with the old and dead" (171). The incorruptible wooden double of the conventionally handsome boy will never disappear. There is something menacing, Manganelli said once, in the puppet's unerasable presence, just as there is something "demonic, furious, disquieting . . . magical" in the entire book, at once elegant and ferocious. The most felicitous and fascinating thing Pinocchio does is to yield to temptations and use those temptations as instruments to learn about himself (19, 20).

The popularity of Collodi's book today is peculiarly disjointed from the popularity of its characters. In the heyday of its revival, from the 1950s to the 1980s, the immediate appeal of the puppet's image was exploited by the advertising industry to sell candy, toys, and even the most incongruous items. Now Pinocchio has almost disappeared from ads. Yet, "what has disappeared is not Pinocchio himself. . . . Social imaginary and cultural imaginary do not coincide" (Trequadrini 109). His presence has become more subtly pervasive, and his liveliness, his wit, and the skeptical eye he turns on the world have become the staples of contemporary reflection on world events. Pinocchio's subversive potential attracts readers of all colors and translators of all persuasions.

Emilio Garroni dramatically speaks of the book's modernity:

> Undoubtedly, a children's novel is modern if it fails its aim and turns against the very grown-ups who constructed it, in the same way an explosive device does when handled clumsily and in an unconsciously self-damaging way.   (150)

My own view is less apocalyptic: Pinocchio lives with us today in a new season of his life, because his adventures speak to us in ways similar to yet different from the ways he spoke to children and adults in the late 1880s. Is *The Adventures of Pinocchio* a timeless book, then? Only in the sense that any great work of literature is ever open to new readings. But let us remember that the book firmly belongs to its place and time. Pinocchio, I submit, has not found "paradoxically . . . an antiphrastic solution to his clash with the world's negativity by exiting the realm of history" (Bàrberi-Squarotti 108). On the contrary, *Pinocchio* emphatically belongs to history; but its central character has at last joined the company of Ulysses, Don Quijote, and Alice, having entered the world of literature without qualifiers.

NOTE

All English translations supplied in this essay are mine.

Recyling *Pinocchio* for Contemporary Audiences

Sandra L. Beckett

> Once upon a time there was Pinocchio. But not the one
> from the book about Pinocchio, another.
> —Gianni Rodari, "Pinocchio il furbo"

Although Pinocchio celebrated his one-hundredth birthday in 1981, he still thrives in contemporary children's literature everywhere. *Pinocchio* has an uncontested place in the canon of Western children's literature and is considered part of the literary heritage of all children. Generally, it is not Collodi's puppet that dominates the collective imagination but Disney's image from the 1940 animated film adaptation, which, like so many Disney remakes, has become the "original" version for most young people.[1] Few children today can name the author of *Pinocchio*, which has virtually become a text without an author, assuming the generic and autonomous status of many classic fairy tales.

Pinocchio continues to inspire countless retellings. The novel has been appropriated by authors, illustrators, cartoonists, and filmmakers; it has been recycled in every literary genre as well as in every other medium and in practically every aspect of contemporary culture.[2] Intertextual play with *Pinocchio* is a widespread phenomenon in children's literature, because authors can assume familiarity with some version of the story, albeit often an adulterated one. This essay examines the intertextual play with Collodi's *Pinocchio* in a wide selection of texts representing different genres and countries, to show how the diverse retellings present an exceptional opportunity to use a familiar story to introduce students to many important international authors and illustrators who all too often remain completely unknown in the English-speaking world. Such retellings can also initiate students to different genres and the various narrative strategies used to recast a classic story for a contemporary audience.

The countless illustrated editions of *Pinocchio* provide teachers with a rich source for examining the relation between text and image, between verbal and visual narrative. Many illustrators of Collodi's *Pinocchio* offer a highly original retelling of the story in their visual interpretation. Students can compare versions representing different cultures, historical periods, ideologies, and so forth. Pinocchio has inspired some of the finest illustrators in the world, working in every medium imaginable. Iassen Ghíuselev won the Illustrator of the Year Award at the Bologna Book Fair in 1994 for his remarkable rendition of *The Adventures of Pinocchio*. The Bulgarian illustrator admits that Collodi's story remains a favorite. Sakura Fujita illustrates the tale for young children in multimedia collage that makes use of fabrics, paper, and a variety of other materials. Yet at least one famous children's illustrator has confessed that he disliked Collodi's novel as a child and that his opinion did not change when he reread it as an adult. Although the twenty-year-old Maurice Sendak and his brother engineered an ingenious Pinocchio wooden mechanical toy that they took hopefully to FAO Schwarz in 1948, the author-illustrator of *Where the Wild Things Are* sees Collodi's "cruel and frightening tale," "full of ghastly, sadistic moments," of interest today chiefly "as evidence of the superiority of Disney's screenplay" (112, 114). Sendak's preference for the Disney movie contrasts with that of the many critics who lament the universal influence of the adulterated film version. It is a testimony to the story's timeless appeal that it survives even the most unmerciful dumbing down and continues to inspire some remarkable retellings.

The vast repertoire of works inspired by *Pinocchio* offers a wide range of examples for studying intertextuality in the classroom. Direct and indirect references to the story pervade Western literature. The young adult novel *Pinocchio's Sister* (Slepian), a chilling tale of jealousy and love between a girl and the pretty wooden doll in her ventriloquist father's famous vaudeville act, does not even mention Pinocchio other than through the direct paratextual reference in the title. Some allusions to the tale are strictly pictorial, as in Mitsumasa Anno's wordless picture book *Tabi no ehon II* (*Anno's Italy*). Unlike most of Anno's tiny figures, the puppet and the pursuing Geppetto are the sole occupants of one corner of an otherwise densely populated page, as if Anno wished to give a place of honor to Collodi's character in his vast iconic representation of Italian culture. Anno's allusion to *Pinocchio* will evoke the well-known tale for all readers, but the way in which that narrative is inserted into the frame story they invent in collaboration with the author-illustrator will be different for each.

Pictorial allusions to *Pinocchio* are common in picture books that use the technique of bricolage to meld several fairy tales in what Gianni Rodari calls an "insalata di favole" ("fairy-tale salad") in his *Grammatica della fantasia* (*Grammar* [38]), which presents various strategies for stimulating children's creativity and imagination with fairy-tale play. Many authors have used Rodari's successful recipe. An illustration in Tor Åge Bringsvaerd's *Alice lengter tilbake* ("Alice Longs to Go Back") prominently depicts a flesh-and-blood Pinocchio gazing up quizzically at a witch, probably the one of "Hansel and Gretel" fame looking for another gullible boy to fatten up. It is no accident that the self-willed puppet finds his way into Marion Zor's *La terrible bande à Charly P.* ("The Terrible Band of Charly P."), the story of a rebellious rock band composed of five of Charles Perrault's most famous fairy-tale characters and managed by his authoritarian great-great-great-grandson. Among the myriad of tiny, unrecognizable figures at their concert, the one large figure that stands out in the foreground is that of Pinocchio as a tall, thin, teen-aged figure reminiscent of the character imagined by Collodi's first illustrator, Enrico Mazzanti. In Alma Flor Ada and F. Isabel Campoy's *¡Feliz cumpleaños, Caperucita Roja!* (*Happy Birthday, Little Red Riding Hood!*), the Pinocchio allusion is textual as well as pictorial, because his name appears on the list of storybook characters Little Red Riding Hood is inviting to her birthday, while his image as a very young Pinocchio appears in a huge thought bubble beside the little girl who painstakingly composes the list. A series of transparent allusions to the Pinocchio story delights young readers: the house of Pinocchio and Geppetto is marked on the map of Little Red Riding Hood's neighborhood, Pinocchio's name appears on the open page of a phone book, and the grocery store features Pinocchio's Pizza and Geppetto's Spaghetti. A rather sophisticated allusion to Pinocchio occurs in the unique picture book *Magasin Zinzin ou Aux merveilles d'Alys* ("The Junk Shop; or, Alys's Wonders"), winner of the prestigious Bologna Prize in 1996, in which a peddler presents his rare collection of fairy-tale bric-à-brac (Clément). Among the items he classifies as "unique pieces" and "priceless relics," the very first is a fragment of Pinocchio's nose in a small, labeled container (16). The eccentric narrator turns Pinocchio's nose into the cultural artifact that it has indeed become and further elevates it to the status of a kind of religious relic.

Pinocchio is exploited for a ludic purpose in an endless array of children's books that fracture the fairy tale only to retain one or two elements and discard the rest. The character is often reduced by synecdoche, represented almost solely by his nose, but rarely with the aesthetic taste of *Magasin Zinzin*. In some picture-book retellings, Pinocchio becomes the protagonist of an entirely different story. One particularly original appropriation of the puppet is found in Ernst Jandl's *Fünfter sein* ("Fifth"), a touching depiction of the anxiety and fear of the unknown that pervades a doctor's waiting room. The wooden puppet has also been extremely popular with authors of poetry for children. Like most of Shel Silverstein's nonsense poetry, his humorous verse rendition "Pinocchio" relies heavily on repetition, rhythm, and rhyme. A simple aaba rhyming scheme is created in most of the eleven stanzas by the repetition of the eponymous hero's name and the addition of "-io" to other words, for example "bloke-io" is rhymed with "spoke-io" in the initial stanza, which introduces the lying little wooden puppet (*Falling* 46). Silverstein's humorous drawing of a Pinocchio whose nose is marked off, rather like a yardstick, from "lie 1" to "lie 14" is more than just decorative. The end of the long nose pointedly separates the first ten stanzas of the poem from the final verse, which describes the happy ending: now that the protagonist is a real boy, his nose has returned to normal and "everything's okey-dokey-o" (47).

Lane Smith's zany, postmodern *Pinocchio the Boy* can be used to broach the subject of postmodernism with students. The picture book begins with a comical summary of the main events of Collodi's novel on a double spread titled "Last Week in a Nutshell." Sixteen stamp-size pictures with short captions are joined by a broken line that leads readers up to the point where the Fairy arrives to grant Pinocchio's wish. However, Smith's story actually begins with the transformation of the puppet into a real boy, and the joke that underpins the hilarious adventures of this Pinocchio is that he is unaware of his transformation because a "nutty fairy" changed him while he was asleep. That explains the subtitle *Incognito in*

Collodi, which Smith puts on the back cover in a characteristic flouting of book-publishing conventions.

Luigi Malerba uses the "fairy-tale salad" or bricolage strategy to write a highly unique continuation, whose title, *Pinocchio con gli stivali* ("Pinocchio in Boots"), evokes "Puss in Boots." Malerba's humorous retelling demonstrates how effective intertextual and metafictive play can be in works for young children, who easily have the decoding skills necessary to appreciate this playful, self-reflexive narrative. For this reason, it provides an excellent text for studying both intertextuality and metafiction in the classroom. The metadiscourse is even more prominent in a second version adapted for the stage, since theater lends itself particularly well to the exposure of the fictional status of texts. It is underscored in the Spanish edition *(Pinocho con botas)* by illustrations that portray the characters as cutouts, either silhouettes or figures on a paper base or glued to a stick manipulated by a visible puppeteer's hand; the backdrop is a painting on folded paper. Quite conscious that he is playing a role based on a well-known script and discontent with the ending Collodi gave his story, Malerba's postmodern protagonist sets about to change it. *Pinocchio con gli stivali* begins at the end of chapter 35, when the protagonist decides he does not want to enter the final chapter, because the thought of being transformed into a good little boy is intolerable to him. As he explains in the prologue to the play, he gained his worldwide fame with his faults, not his virtues (which he is at a loss to name). In an attempt to find a role in a different story, Pinocchio intervenes in "Little Red Riding Hood," "Cinderella," and "Puss in Boots," whose characters are also aware of the roles they are playing and have no intention of relinquishing them to a wooden puppet, even one that seems to know their lines by heart.

In a manner accessible to young children, Malerba plays with the distinction between fiction and reality. Cinderella's prince asks what his subjects would think if he gave up his place to a wooden puppet, but Pinocchio points out that he is just a storybook prince with fictional subjects. In other words, whether they are in or out of their familiar stories, the characters are fictional. Yet sometimes Pinocchio distinguishes between the fictional world of the stories and a reality that, for readers, is no less fictional. The prince offers to hire Pinocchio as a buffoon, undoubtedly because insolence seems to come naturally to the puppet, but Pinocchio insists he wants a role "in the story" (45). Collodi himself intervenes in his fictive world when the Fairy desperately solicits his aid with the runaway puppet. The escape of the trouble-making protagonist threatens to ruin the book Collodi was just about to finish, and the author is concerned only with what he will tell his readers and his editor. A humorous twist at the end of Malerba's story turns the sequel into a kind of unedited in medias res episode. In the prologue to the theatrical version, Pinocchio informs readers-spectators that he is about to tell them "something that is not written in the book" (30). Malerba suggests, tongue in cheek, that Collodi has excised this embarrassing adventure from his version of *Pinocchio*. On the king's orders, Pinocchio is put into the sack to be hauled back to the exact spot in chapter 36 from which he escaped, and the theatrical version ends with the puppet's muffled protest that he does not want to become "a good little boy" (60). A kind of epilogue in the first version informs readers that the havoc Pinocchio wreaked in the age-old tale still disrupts the narrative from time to time.

The story of Pinocchio has not inspired as many feminist retellings as most popular fairy tales have. Anne Camp changes the gender of the protagonist in her novel *Das Mädchen Pinocchia* ("The Girl Pinocchia"). This is not the first time the German author feminized the protagonist of a classic, having devoted an earlier book to Doña Quixote (*Zwei Berühmtheiten*). The novel evokes Collodi's work only distantly, as in the chapter titles "Why Must One Go to School?" and "At the Theatre," but, as the original, it blends reality and fantasy. Set in modern times, *Das Mädchen Pinocchia* uses the story of Pinocchio to discuss the abuses of our time, in the hope of inciting a sense of responsibility in young readers. Students can examine the ideology that inspires this retelling of *Pinocchio*.

Retellings of *Pinocchio* can also be used to study various genres and generic codes. Pinocchio has been appropriated by the science fiction genre and cast in the role of a robot in a futuristic world. The most recent example is *P3K: Pinocchio 3000*, a film about a superrobot with a P3K processor, who is tricked into becoming involved in a devious scheme to turn all children into robots. Eventually the robot becomes a real boy thanks to the holographic fairy Cyberina.

The chapter book *Ram, le robot* ("Ram the Robot") has been categorized in the science fiction subgenre of "the technological fairy tale" (Le Brun 70). Although Daniel Mativat sets what he calls his "fantastical version" of Collodi's masterpiece (7) in a futuristic, scientifically advanced world on the star Sirius, he is quite faithful to the general plot of the original. The somewhat utopian world that relieves human beings of work (robots have taken over all the difficult jobs) and school (knowledge is hereditary) seems to contrast sharply with Collodi's worldview, but the moral of the two stories is essentially the same: the values with which Électro wants to program Ram are "kindness, the respect of others, the love of work" (17). Électro/Geppetto is the only person who must work, because he is the repairman who keeps the planet's robots functioning. Mativat seems to reject certain consequences of technology: the automation of work and the elimination of human beings.

Most retellings pay homage to Collodi's classic and invite us to read the pretext, but not Christine Nöstlinger's ambitious novel *Der neue Pinocchio*, which seeks to supplant the original work. Somewhat paradoxically, it is one of the most faithful: its thirty-five chapters, complete with descriptive titles, closely match Collodi's thirty-six. When the publisher asked Nöstlinger to revise Collodi's novel for contemporary readers, the Austrian author was not familiar with the classic. Although she tried hard to like *Pinocchio*, reading all the translations she could lay her hands on and even retranslating the original with the help of her daughter, she found the "reactionary" work obnoxious and admits that she would never have undertaken the project if she had known what it was like (Koppe). Afraid that today's children might still accept the moral of *Pinocchio*, she did not turn down the job but set about reworking the story according to her personal views on education and upbringing, views strongly influenced by Alice Miller's theories. *Pinocchio*'s didacticism appalled Nöstlinger, who insists that every single one of the puppet's adventures ends with his punishment, followed by repentance and total submission. Eventually the author realized that she could cast the moral of the story in an entirely different light without making major changes to Collodi's plot. She altered the story line only when forced to do so by her "respect for children, human beings, and their rights," as in the case of pointless cruelty. The illustrator, Nikolaus Heidelbach, does not seem to share the author's concern; whereas Nöstlinger passes over the episode of the blackbird in a single sentence, he portrays a nightmarish scene in which the frightening eyes of the "blind" cat stare at the reader as he cruelly devours a bird whose beak is open wide in protest. Ranging from tiny vignettes through full-page spreads to pictures that extend over several pages, Heidelbach's 110 colored illustrations provide a truly remarkable visual interpretation of a story that is at once familiar and new.

Nöstlinger takes care to announce clearly in the title of the last chapter that her story of Pinocchio has a "happy ending" (201). It is a poetic, open ending that diverges from Collodi's. The Blue Fairy manifests herself as a blue rose; Pinocchio holds it so tightly that a thorn pierces his thumb, making him aware that he has become a real, flesh-and-blood boy. Still in rose form, the Blue Fairy explains to Pinocchio that as a puppet he would never have grown up and she could never have married him. (The puppet confessed earlier that he wished to become a child so he could grow fast in order to become an adult and marry the Blue Fairy.) In Nöstlinger's version, the Blue Fairy shifts from a maternal role to the romantic one of potential partner for the protagonist. But Pinocchio remains a lovable child at the end. When he does a dance for joy and falls painfully on his backside, the narrator closes the story with the simple moral: "Flesh-and-blood children cannot do all the acrobatics that puppets can" (212).

Nöstlinger's book was quite controversial and sparked a great deal of argument as to whether or not a classic should be tinkered with—a great topic for classroom discussion. As the texts examined in this essay show, the Austrian writer is certainly not the only author who has reworked Collodi's classic. The famous tale has always been reinterpreted according to the sociocultural and literary preoccupations of the time. Its characters, motifs, and narrative structures are constantly being recontextualized, refashioned, and regenerated to convey new messages and to address new issues. Intertextual play with *Pinocchio* ranges from brief allusions to sophisticated, elaborate retellings in lengthy novel format. The story has been recycled in every literary genre, as well as in all areas of high and low culture, including all the mass media of our technological age. The puppet has inspired picture books, pop-up books, poems, plays, short stories, novels, and comics, as well as television shows, films, music, and computer games. The number and diversity of these works offer a wonderful opportunity to introduce students to a variety of theoretical issues, including intertextuality, parody, metafiction, genre, and narration. I have presented only a small sampling of the wide range of *Pinocchio* retellings that can be used to acquaint students with major international authors and illustrators, who often remain unknown in the English-speaking world. In addition, contemporary retellings of *Pinocchio* are a pretext to bring today's young readers back to the pre-text, which remains a classic of world literature.

NOTES

All English translations supplied in this essay are mine.

[1] For a detailed study of the fate of *Pinocchio* in the United States, see Wunderlich and Morrissey, *Pinocchio*.

[2] The wooden puppet with the trademark nose is a familiar icon in popular culture. Susan Tifft's article in the *Los Angeles Times*, 24 June 2003, went so far as to qualify contemporary culture as a "Pinocchio culture." The author laments what young people are learning from adult Pinocchios, like Bill Clinton, who have made lying the norm. During the Monica Lewinsky scandal, the image of a Pinocchio president adorned a host of products, including a series of watches by Worldwide Watch, on which Clinton's visibly lengthened nose served as a second hand. As of this writing, the most recent celebrity to be portrayed with the puppet's elongated nose is the style maven Martha Stewart.

Pinocchio on Screen: Teaching Filmic Versions of the Puppet's Tale

Rebecca West

From the early silent film version of *Pinocchio* directed by Giulio Cesare Anta-moro in 1911 and starring the French comedian Ferdinand Guillaume (known as Tontolini and then Polidor) to Luigi Comencini's 1971 made-for-television classic, from Disney's definitive 1940 animated *Pinocchio* to Roberto Benigni's less than successful 2002 live version starring himself as the puppet, Carlo Collodi's story has been adapted to the medium of cinema numerous times around the world. The tale has also been used in films that are not, strictly speaking, direct adaptations. For example, in Spielberg's *A.I.: Artificial Intelligence* a child robot who hears the puppet's story decides that he must find the Blue Fairy in order to ask her to make him a real boy. Pinocchio appears in many visual mass media venues as well—as an advertising device, a political icon of mendacity, or a globally recognizable symbol of Italy. Whether one is teaching Collodi's original tale or adaptations and versions of it as seen in contemporary literature, cinema, and popular culture, visual media are an essential component, from the very first illustrations to current images on screen.

A course on film versions of *Pinocchio* could follow a linear historical trajectory, not only in Italian but in several other national cinemas as well. In what follows I describe a different approach: I consider film versions in the context of other adaptations and uses of the original story and of the figure of Pinocchio in the twentieth century and beyond. Mine is not, strictly speaking, a film course but rather a course on what I call the puppet's afterlife in contemporary culture, cinema, and literature. But in this essay, which is concerned with cinematic versions of the tale, I concentrate on the part of my course that deals with films.

It is essential to begin a course on Pinocchio films with a close reading and discussion of Collodi's novel, either in Italian or in one of its many English translations. Context is also important: information on Collodi's life and career, on the social and political programs of the post-Unification period, and on Italian society and literary culture of the era. In analyzing the story itself, I seek to draw out its complexities and the ways in which it is much more than an anodyne pedagogical tale for children. Glauco Cambon, for example, emphasizes the novel's connections to Tuscan storytelling traditions. As other critics have done, Cambon connects it to the aulic literary tradition, in its allusions to the *Odyssey*, the *Aeneid*, and the *Divine Comedy*. Rodolfo Tommasi analyzes symbolic and allegorical elements, arguing that Collodi knew of Celtic and Nordic myths about talking trees, which had already been incorporated into the French and Italian fairy-tale traditions. With its many gothic, uncanny elements, *Pinocchio* is also allied to the genre of fantastic literature popular during the late nineteenth century. By learning about the many literary and popular texts and traditions on which Collodi drew, students come to understand the story as something other than a little moral tale for children. It has entered into the canon of Italian literature and is respected, even revered, by subsequent writers—Italo Calvino, Giorgio Manganelli, Luigi Malerba, and Gianni Celati, to name but a few—not because of their happy childhood memories of it but because it is a complex and engaging narrative work that both draws on and transcends its many sources and inspirations. That important cultural leaders such as Calvino, Benedetto Croce, and Alberto Asor Rosa deeply admired Collodi's tale and wrote seriously about it is a fact that students need to know as they begin their study of the novel.

Through these preliminary lectures and discussions of Collodi's tale and its illustrators I introduce some of the major themes and topics that will be relevant to specifically cinematic considerations. Because I am particularly interested in cinema's relation to the theme of the animate and inanimate, I ask students to consider how the novel treats this theme. Theories of the uncanny and of individual identity formation are useful here, including Freud's theories as well as studies by film scholars such as Tom Gunning. These discussions connect well with gender issues, for the feminine symbolic has always played an important role in psychiatric approaches to identity. The Fairy is a figure of great significance: she alone brings the feminine realm into the text's almost exclusively masculine world. Students need to pay close attention to her role in the story, asking what she might represent (a supernatural force, the maternal, the uncanny, the transcendental, the erotic, and so on). Finally, a discussion of the Dantesque aspects of Pinocchio's tale prepares the ground for an analysis of Benigni's film version. Benigni is a serious student of Dante's great poem, and in many interviews given before the release of his film, he often referred to Dante and Pinocchio in the same breath.

Having prepared the way for analyses of filmic versions of the tale, I introduce the general history of *Pinocchio* on screen, with particular emphasis on films made in Italy and the United States. I begin with Antamoro's 1911 film. According to Giacomo Manzoli and Roy Menarini, this was the first *lungometraggio* (full-length feature) done by the production company Cines, and it is all the more important for film history in that Antamoro was already a prestigious director and Ferdinand Guillaume, who played Pinocchio, was already a *divo* ("star") when the film was made. The film was ignored and undervalued until its restoration in 1994, which was done with the collaboration of the Centro Sperimentale di Cinematografia ("Experimental Center of Cinematography") and the Cineteca Nazionale ("National Film Archives"). Manzoli and Menarini call it "theatrical"; in fact, it draws on the already established theatrical tradition of on-stage representations of the Pinocchio tale. It begins with the opening of a curtain, which establishes a sort of "paratextual frame" for the introduction of the main characters, Pinocchio and Geppetto. The Web article's authors connect this mode of introduction to familiar techniques coming from *varietà*, Italian vaudeville. They also emphasize the importance of Attilio Mussino's illustrations of Collodi's tale, published by Bemporad in 1911, the year of Antamoro's film, but available in partial form before 1911. The look adopted by Polidor in the film is much closer to Mussino's Pinocchio than to earlier illustrations. Like Mussino's illustrations, Polidor's puppet is small, compact, and has a strange little cap that is nothing like the pointed paper hat that Ugo Fleres and Enrico Mazzanti drew in their earlier, more canonical versions. As Marco Arnaudo has so convincingly shown, Mussino drew heavily on the emergent comic strips of the period, and Manzoli and Menarini refer as well to posters of the era that seem to have conditioned not only the physical appearance of Polidor-Pinocchio but other characters as well, such as Mangiafoco (Fire-Eater) the puppet master, who looks like a stereotypical operatic baritone of the early twentieth century. Arnaudo also highlights the theatrical qualities of Collodi's original, which predispose the written text to translations into other visual semiotic systems such as comics and the cinema:

> So, if in *Pinocchio* everything that is thought and experienced is coupled with visible actions, recognizable postures and exchanges of dialogue, if, in short, the novel tends to be configured like a series of theatrical scenes, thus the novelistic version is predisposed also to an optimal translation into the new languages of the early twentieth century, precisely the cinema and the comic strip, which share with the theater the delegation of the narration in an author's voice to the interaction of characters who are directly offered to the public's sight. (73)

In presenting information about this early cinematic version, it is therefore possible to make connections with topics of theater (with references to Carmelo Bene's many theatrical presentations of the tale) and with early illustrations of the tale.

Because my aim is not in any sense historical completeness, I then jump many years to Comencini's 1971 made-for-television film version. The next and last Italian film I introduce is Benigni's 2002 *Pinocchio*. These films are only a small part of the complex history of *Pinocchio* on screen in Italy, including some films never made. Both Federico Fellini and Francis Ford Coppola wanted to film Collodi's tale; neither did so, although Fellini's last film, *La voce della luna*, starring Benigni, alludes to the puppet's story. Film versions have been made in France, Russia, Germany, Japan, and elsewhere. Japanese anime films featuring Astroboy owe a big debt to Collodi's story, for Astroboy was based on the Italian puppet. Because the remainder of the course is devoted to extensive analyses of films by Disney, Spielberg, Jan Švankmajer, and Benigni, I give only a general lecture on Disney's animated version as part of this historical overview, and I present clips from the 1996 film, *The Adventures of Pinocchio*, directed by Steve Barron and starring Martin Landau as Geppetto, Geneviève Bujold as the Fairy, and Jonathan Taylor-Thomas as the real-boy Pinocchio. A 1999 sequel, *The New Adventures of Pinocchio*, directed by Michael Anderson, also stars Landau as Geppetto, but Pinocchio is played by Gabriel Thomson, and Gemma Gregory is the Fairy.

Beginning the film analysis portion of the course with the minor films of Barron and Anderson may seem counterintuitive. But Barron's film follows Collodi's tale fairly closely and allows discussion of how film adaptations of books work and of whether fidelity to the original matters. It is also primarily a live-action film, and because animated films present a particular set of issues, I prefer to put off that discussion until later in the course when we analyze Disney's work. Barron's version, set in a vaguely eighteenth-century Italy, is much more sentimental and romantic than Collodi's tale. The film has it that years before the "birth" of Pinocchio, Geppetto carved a heart enclosing his and his beloved Leona's initials into a tree in the forest; from that very tree comes the piece of wood containing the magic puppet. Leona married Geppetto's brother, so Geppetto pined for her (pun intended!) for twenty-five years. Pinocchio is therefore the love child of Geppetto and the now-widowed Leona, and we know from the start that they will all end up as one happy family. In this love story, the mysterious Fairy is lost; we have instead the very human Leona (Bujold) as a potential mother for Pinocchio. Her sensible maternal presence differs from that of Collodi's haunting Fairy, who metamorphoses into many things and plays many roles. Beyond this fundamental plot change, the film condenses the important question of how the puppet might become a real boy into a school lesson: the ability to cry separates human beings from other creatures. When the puppet can cry, he becomes a real boy. Overall the film is a bit plodding, and the European and American elements in it sometimes clash oddly (as is also true in Disney's film). Despite these changes and the hybrid New World–Old World representation of the Italian tale, the film is a worthy and entertaining adaptation to the screen of Collodi's tale.

The remainder of the course focuses on Disney's and Benigni's films. If time permits, I also like to give some attention to Spielberg's *A.I.* and to Czech director Švankmajer's *Little Otik;* neither is a screen adaptation of Collodi's story, but both are thematically related and visually stunning. Like Disney's, they are films that address the line between the human and the nonhuman (or posthuman); the relationship between adults and children; and the power of children's needs and desires, which are often not as well understood by adults as we would like to believe.

American students today generally know about Disney's *Pinocchio*, and they often have had the experience either of seeing it or reading an illustrated book version derived from the Disney film. This is the only *Pinocchio* that many if not most of these students knew before reading Collodi's tale. Approaching the Disney version after having spent several weeks on other materials, they are ready to see it with new eyes and to understand that it is not by any means the authentic or only *Pinocchio* in existence. They are ready, in short, to receive it critically.

In the English-speaking world, no film of the puppet's tale approaches the sheer power of Disney's version, which for more than sixty years has conditioned the collective idea of and response to the puppet's story in the United States and even abroad. It has almost mythic stature, but still it should be seen for what it is: only one of many screen adaptations of Collodi's tale, and only one of the many animated films of its era—though it did transform and advance that particular art. I therefore seek to convey to students the great achievement that is this film, as well as the aspects of it that can and should be received with less than hagiographic awe.

From the time of its release in 1940, Disney's film was praised for its technical achievements. From the breaking of the frame to the use of a multiplane camera technique that created a sense of three-dimensionality and depth, Disney's team made one of the most innovative and visually captivating animated films ever put on screen. The Oscar-winning song "When You Wish upon a Star," the perfectly chosen voices for the animated characters, and the charmingly drawn figures add to the film's appeal. But the film has a dark side, both visually and thematically. Robin Allan notes, "The film is dark in content and in presentation, with 76 of its 88 minutes taking place at night or under water." He uses the word "bleakness" also, finding in this element the closest tie between Disney and Collodi (67).

In fairy tales, there is always a dangerous, frightening aspect to stories of magical kingdoms, princesses and princes, and "happily ever after" finales, and Collodi's tale of hunger, temptations, and loss is no exception. Yet, in Disney's version, the puppet is from the very beginning a darling, mischievous little innocent, much more a boy than a strange, talking wooden puppet. His cuteness, as well as that of kindly old Geppetto and the added characters of cuddly household pets— Cleo the fish and Figaro the kitten—creates a visual counterbalance to the film's darkness. In the odd blend of European and American characterizations, Jiminy Cricket is a Will Rogers type with a completely down-home American style of talking; Foulfellow, who shanghais Pinocchio to Pleasure Island, is Dickensian; the Fox and the Cat have elements of commedia dell'arte villains; and the setting itself, resembling a Bavarian Alpine village, distances the story from its Italian roots, although keeping it ensconced in an Old World environment. (The drawings of the settings were done by the Swedish artist Gustaf Tenggren, who had come to the Disney studios a few years before the film was made, and he based his conception of Pinocchio's village and home on his observations and photographs of an actual Bavarian town, Rothenburg ob der Tauber.) Although the film opens with a direct homage to Collodi's novel, it may well have owed more to a play by Yasha Frank that was performed in Los Angeles in 1937 and subsequently published in 1939. Frank's Pinocchio is a cuddly innocent, incapable of truly transgressive behavior, unlike Collodi's puppet, who seems to have a natural attraction to delinquency. The original Pinocchio's harshly selfish behavior vanishes in Disney's version, and we are given essentially a darling little boy whose curiosity, not delinquency, gets him into fixes.

The film also raises the important question of stereotyping and of racial, gendered, or ethnic representations in animated films. Cartoons have given us some of the most outrageously offensive portrayals of women, people of color, and diverse ethnicities, yet because they are "only" cartoons, a serious critique of them in this regard is seldom to be found in the critical literature on animated films. Particularly striking are the characterizations of Stromboli (Disney's version of Mangiafoco), the Fairy, and other feminine presences. The film critic Richard Schickel was the first to label the film anti-Semitic in his 1968 book on Walt Disney, asserting that Stromboli is represented as a Jew in terms of his gross, caricature-like Semitic facial features and his boundless greed. Given the era in which the film was made, when Hitler was promulgating his vicious attacks against Jews, it is especially important to give attention to this issue.

Similarly problematic, if less disturbing, is the characterization of the Fairy as a 1930s glamour girl, an animated equivalent of the dumb blonde of Hollywood manufacture, with none of the deeply mysterious and complex appeal of Collodi's Fairy. Like the few other females in the film, she is decorative and completely marginal. She flits in and out of some scenes to rescue Pinocchio and has no deeper resonance than an inanimate magic wand or potion would have. Her goal is to get Pinocchio to be a good, obedient boy, back in the warm protection of Geppetto's fatherly sphere, where mothers are not needed. Femaleness in any form in this film has merely superficial appeal to the (male) eye and plays a fundamentally conservative role. Students need to understand how animated films, like live-action ones, can both reflect and promulgate the values and stereotypes of their era.

Animated films call attention to the issue of animation more broadly speaking, and Disney's film is almost metafilmic in that it is an animated feature about an inanimate object that is animated, a piece of wood that becomes a moving, talking puppet and eventually a real human boy. This theme is highlighted in the lengthy sequences in Geppetto's cottage that feature the numerous clocks and toys that Geppetto has carved, all of which simulate human animation. His workshop is a prefilmic world of animation where little mechanical wooden figures are made to move, just as drawn figures will be made to move on the screen. Puppetry, the dominant mode of animation inscribed into the story, is of course embodied by Pinocchio himself, as well as by Stromboli's marionettes.

Gunning, among other scholars of early cinema, has studied contemporaneous responses to the earliest silent films, noting that there was much discussion of cinema's ability to capture life in motion, of the uncanny effect that animation had on audiences, as if cinema itself were creating life. A new realm was opened between the categories of reality and representation, living and inert, machine and soul, as modernity began to redefine Romantic opposition between machines and the imagination. The technology of cinema seemed able to make primitive, atavistic beliefs about the inanimate world come true, bringing childlike wishes to fulfillment (dolls coming alive, toys moving on their own). Sigmund

Freud deals with these and other issues in his essay *The Uncanny*, which serves as good preparation for a discussion of both the material and psychological aspects of animation. These issues are then brought back to the story of Pinocchio, in order for students to think once more about why the tale of a puppet should have such power and longevity for readers and audiences around the world.

Next on the syllabus is Benigni's *Pinocchio*. Benigni talked for years of doing his film version of the tale. By bringing the story to international filmgoers and playing the role of the puppet himself, he hoped not only to pay homage to a national icon but also to solidify his position as a contemporary embodiment of Italy, as a kind of living national icon. The film failed dismally at the box office, however, receiving cruelly negative reviews especially in the United States. One may ask why a film that tells a well-loved story, contains scenes of real beauty, and stars one of Italy's most acclaimed comic actors should fail so miserably. Does America still respond best to its own version of the puppet's tale, which is the one created by Disney decades ago, and does a re-Tuscanized, re-Italianized puppet ring false to audiences on this side of the ocean? Or are there other explanations for Benigni's ultimate failure to "embody Italy" for the world today? The film was poorly dubbed, and it was marketed as a Christmas movie for children, which may have been a mistake. Was there some sort of backlash against Benigni linked to the controversy that his award-winning *Life Is Beautiful* generated because of its comic treatment of the Holocaust? Finally, that the buildup for this movie in the press and other media was enormous may have contributed to the severity of the critical response.

If time permits, I end the course with brief discussions of Spielberg's *A.I.* and Švankmajer's *Little Otik*. Spielberg's film (an unfinished Kubrick project that Spielberg took on when Kubrick died) brings the issue of the line between the human and nonhuman into the realm of the posthuman, an issue pertinent to developments in current technologies of creation, both artistic and biological. Geoffrey O'Brien wrote, "*A.I.* is a meditation on its own components; the technical means that make possible the mechanical child are as one with the means used to make the film . . . now that we have the technology what are we going to use it for?" In Collodi's tale, in Disney's animated film, and in *A.I.*, the puppet (or robot) is created by a godlike father as a child figure intended to serve the material or emotional needs of the male parent. The idea of a motherless birth allows me to speak also about a gendered approach to texts and films. *A.I.* is explicitly tied to the tale of Pinocchio, in that David, the boy robot, longs to find the Fairy so that she will make him a real boy and thus as lovable as his human brother.

Little Otik finds its origin in Eastern European fables about tree children who have voracious appetites. Both Otik and Pinocchio are made of wood (Otik from a tree stump, Pinocchio from a simple *pezzo di legno*) and both are irrepressible children whose needs and desires rule supreme. No civilizing force can dampen the appetite of Otik, and he ends up eating the very parents who cared for him as their son. The film masterfully mixes live-action and stop-animation techniques, and it clearly shows Švankmajer's connections to the European modernist tradition of surrealistic art and filmmaking. Both *A.I.* and *Little Otik* engage topics, cinematic techniques, and visual styles that range far from Collodi's Tuscan world, yet as distant relations to *Pinocchio* they help place the puppet in a context that is much broader than that of any direct film adaptation.

Teaching *Pinocchio* on-screen enables scholars interested in both literary studies and film studies to unite these fields in numerous ways. Those interested in the history of film could use the many cinematic versions of *Pinocchio* to investigate developments in filmmaking art, as well as to consider how the popular and critical understanding and subsequent adaptation of the original book have been shaped and have changed over time and in different national contexts. Those who prefer to concentrate on particular auteurs have a rich panoply of films made by directors of renown (Disney, Comencini, Benigni), whose overall production could be the context in which their versions of *Pinocchio* are studied. Similarly, many writers have penned adaptations of the tale (Malerba, *Pinocchio*; Manganelli; Compagnone, *Vita nuova* and *Ballata*; Coover), and others have found inspiration in it for novels that are not strict rewritings or adaptations but that reveal fascinating connections with Collodi's story (Celati's *Le avventure di Guizzardi* is a prime example). However *Pinocchio* on screen is taught, it is an endlessly rich subject that holds surprises and delights for teachers and students alike. The persistent puppet has had an enduring afterlife, and his many heirs in film and literature go on animating the *pezzo di legno*, whose hold on the world's collective imaginary is stronger than his creator could ever have dreamed.

Pinocchio: From Italy to England at the Turn of the Twenty-First Century

Elena Paruolo

Carlo Collodi's *Pinocchio* was first translated into English by Mary Alice Murray (1892) in the Fisher Unwin series Children's Library, with original illustrations by Enrico Mazzanti. Other unabridged translations have followed since then, the most recent one in England being that by Ann Lawson Lucas (1996) for Oxford University Press (*Adventures*). To the translations one must add a great number of adaptations (literary, theatrical, cinematographic, etc.) and retellings. In this essay I discuss two recent theatrical adaptations in England, one of them by the Italian director Marcello Magni (see Hall). I also refer to three literary adaptations-retellings. This study explores some of the changes to which Collodi's *Pinocchio* is subject when it arrives north of the Alps and some of the reasons that might explain those changes.

Adaptations are active linguistic, social, and political choices that often conform to the censorship agenda of the country that controls the material, and nowhere is this conformity more relevant than in the education of children. To what extent censorship protects children instead of depriving them is still an open question. Anglo-Saxons and Italians have different attitudes toward censorship regarding *Pinocchio*. Normally, when editing books for a young audience, adults in Italy follow a moralistic, conservative publishing policy. Children's books are generally more censored than videos or other media (Denti). When reading or staging *Pinocchio*, however, adults present children with unabridged versions—both of the original text and of most of the innumerable adaptations produced domestically, some of which are very clever but also very disturbing. Collodi's polemical and satirical motivation and his ambivalence about issues of lying and education draw ever-increasing emphasis, and the text is presented to children in all its problematic complexity. This is true despite arguments over the suitability for children of Collodi's story or when they should read it. In England, on the other hand, Collodi's book is considered suitable for children on one condition: that cuts and omissions be made. Material considered boring for young readers-spectators or concepts that exceed their intellectual capabilities are cut, as well as passages that might disturb their innocence and happiness. In an age when children's literature is being enriched with new meanings, with texts in which real children confront real problems (Paruolo, "Grandes Tendances"), Collodi's work is seldom published in its entirety, whereas numerous adaptations and abridgments, in simplified language, have appeared for the very young. On those rare occasions that children have been exposed to uncut, uncensored versions of the story, critics have lambasted them, as happened with Magni's theatrical adaptation in London, 2000–01. The best known and the most loved version of *Pinocchio* in England is without a doubt Disney's 1940 film, which in the minds of both children and adults is the original.

In 1971, Franklyn S. Stych described cuts and omissions in *Pinocchio* translations, abridgments, and adaptations in Great Britain and Ireland (*Pinocchio*). The missing passages are often morbid, including death and cruelty toward the puppet and toward animals. Also cut are references to food—joyous moments of imagining vast feasts by one who, because of poverty, must settle for a pear core. In this way, the issue of poverty, a subject little discussed in well-off British society, is also avoided.

Things have not changed since 1971, as I observed in my analysis of three adaptations-retellings of *Pinocchio* available in London bookshops in the 1990s and early 2000s:

> *Pinocchio*, retold by Linda M. Jennings (for very young children), illustrated by Peter Stevenson, 24 pages, Favourite Tales, Ladybird, London, 1993.
> *Pinocchio*, translated and adapted by Jane Fior (for children under the age of eight), illustrated by Simon Bartram, 48 pages, Series Dorling Kindersley Classics, London, 1999.
> *The Adventures of Pinocchio*, retold by Helen Rossendale and Graham Philpot (for children under the age of eight), illustrated by Philpot, 96 pages, David Bennet Books, London, 2002.

Some of the cuts and omissions in these books echo those made in the past. The violent scenes still seem to be considered unsuitable for child readers. I cite two episodes as they appear in Collodi and in the three adaptations.

In chapter 4, Pinocchio kills the Talking Cricket: "taking a mallet from the workbench, he hurled it *at the Talking Cricket*. Maybe he didn't even mean to hit him, but unluckily he caught him squarely on the head. . . ." (111; italics mine). Rossendale and Philpot write, "Pinocchio . . . grabbing a mallet, hurled it *at the wall*. Now, Pinocchio had meant nothing more than to startle the Cricket, but the mallet stuck him squarely and the poor creature, who had been simply trying to offer some good advice, was flattened" (14; italics mine). Fior writes, "Pinocchio . . . picked up a wooden mallet and *hurled it*. Perhaps he didn't mean to hurt him, but the mallet flattened the poor cricket and struck him dead" (10; italics mine). Jennings writes, "But Pinocchio ignored the cricket."

In chapter 15, Pinocchio flees the assassins and sees the cottage shining in the distance:

> Realizing that knocking did no good, in desperation he began to kick the door and bang his head against it. Then there came to the window a beautiful Little Girl . . . who . . . said in a voice that seemed to come from the world beyond:

"There is nobody in this house. They are all dead."
"Well, then you at least open up for me!" cried Pinocchio, weeping and imploring.
"I am dead, too."
"Dead? But then what are you doing there at the window?"
"I am waiting for the bier to come and take me away."   (183, 185)

Rossendale and Philpot write, "At the window stood a beautiful young girl with blue hair. But she did not see Pinocchio and she closed the shutters" (34). Fior writes, "Pinocchio could see a cottage in the distance. If only he could reach it! But it was no good—the two robbers caught up with him" (16). Jennings cuts this scene completely.

In addition, in these adaptations the didactic passages of the original are cut, as are ironic passages that constitute an important aspect of Collodi's writing. The nature and length of Pinocchio's rebellion change. The world seems less harsh, cruel, and corrupt than the one portrayed by Collodi. This adapted Pinocchio emerges from his adventures without any great inner turmoil. Hardly anything remains of what Ann Lawson Lucas calls "the essential ambiguity . . . the pervasive ambivalence and interweaving of fantasy and reality" (xlv) of the original text.

The theatrical adaptations of *Pinocchio* in England, for a young audience, are numerous. The first presented, as Stych recalls in his study, seems to have been *Pinocchio for the Stage* directed and set by Remo Bufano and published in 1929. Among the more recent ones, that of Jatinder Verma (1997) is memorable. The work attempts to fuse the story of Pinocchio, Cyrano de Bergerac, and Ganesh—an Indian god—into a children's story called *Snira Ganesh*. This representation has multiple sources, from numerous legends, in which the nose is charged with different meanings. In some, the nose is a sign of punishment for sin; in others, especially in Indian and Japanese stories, the disproportionate nose appears in an ambivalent light, becoming the source of magical powers.

At the opening of the twenty-first century, *Pinocchio* provided the material for two theatrical adaptations in London: *The Adventures of Pinocchio* (for children 7 and over), by Magni (at the Lyric Hammersmith, Christmas 2000), dramatized by Lee Hall (a successful screenwriter, his name is also associated with the film *Billy Eliot*); *Pinocchio in the Park* (for children 6 to 11), by Emily Gray, staged by the children's theater company Unicorn in the open air of Regent's Park (Aug. 2001), dramatized by Michael Rosen (a well-known poet of children's poetry). In both adaptations, London critics discovered—and immediately condemned—the use of language unsuitable for children, including "pillock," "plonker," "balls," "bum," and "bastard." Apart from this similarity, the overall judgments were diametrically opposed: negative for Magni, positive for Gray. These two adaptations differ significantly in content (number of the scenes represented, criteria for selection, etc.); method of representation (commedia dell'arte for Magni, pantomime for Gray [Duchartre; Frow; Doglio; Fano]); and the image of childhood (achievement of a state of compassion for others or of one's own autonomy).

Magni's *The Adventures of Pinocchio* (Hall) remains faithful to Collodi's text. The director wants to give the English public the true *Pinocchio*, bitter and sad, far less saccharine than that portrayed in Disney's film. His production recalls the citrus of Tuscany, the Tuscan landscape. It is not Switzerland; it does not teem with little birdies.

Funny, moving, and full of pathos and great imagination, Magni's show does not censor violent scenes, most notably the scene in which Pinocchio is hanged. As Magni comments, "I did choose to put on a truly violent scene . . . but children see shoot-ups and incredible violence on TV. . . ." Also scary is the appearance of Fire Eater. If he is scary but not evil, the Cat and the Fox are truly evil, though they start off as good. "I wanted to show them as people with problems," the director comments. "They became bad because of money, because of a richness with which they were obsessed, in contrast with Pinocchio who, by opening his mind, saves himself." Magni believes that it is almost as if Collodi wrote a *Divine Comedy* for children, a journey of initiation that to a greater or lesser extent deals with facing difficulties, obstacles, and suffering. He stages many of the puppet's adventures—he would have liked to stage them all!—since "all the ups and downs, the positive and negative moments, the moments of success and often really bad luck that the hero has to go through constitute a good route with which the child can really identify." He believes Collodi used the repeated ups and downs purposefully, because only through repetition do children learn. It is only through "repetition of the same errors that they can escape from their own selfishness, sloth . . . and achieve an understanding of the world, and a state of compassion for others" (Personal interview).

Throughout the show Pinocchio wants to become a real boy, but at the end of the play, when he does become a child, he is not really happy. He sings an ironic song that expresses mixed emotions. Pinocchio has managed to find compassion and true generosity toward his father, but he has lost his former instinct of running around and being naughty, a typical childish trait. He has lost his joy of life:

> I'm a Boy, I'm a Boy,
> Oh, it's great to be a Boy;
> I'm a Boy, I'm a Boy,
> Oh, it's great to be a Boy.
>
> I will never get my feet burnt,
> I will never sit inside a whale,
> I will always do my homework; you
> Will see I'll never fail:

I will always help my father.
I will learn to tootle on the flute.
I will always eat bananas and
All kinds of healthy fruit.
                    (Hall 79–80)

Magni respects the Italianness of the puppet theater and of the commedia dell'arte, in which tradition Collodi seems to place himself. "I like the theater that derives from the commedia dell'arte," he says.

> You can find in it strong images and difficult situations, sometimes vulgar and grotesque, based on grand themes of hunger, money, sex. I used Arlecchino and Pantalone because the servant-master relationship is present in all theater, and also because we wanted a situation in which there was a narrative of repression and slaps.

Given Magni's fidelity to Collodi's text, it is not surprising that the critical reaction to the play was negative. As Magni observes, the English hero (Peter Pan, for example) is very different from Pinocchio. He is proud. Humiliated, he refuses to fall. Pinocchio, on the other hand, is constantly ridiculed—for example, when he becomes a donkey or is treated like a dog (this episode Magni was unable to include). Pinocchio is laughed at continually.

One critic has judged Pinocchio's story "an exceptionally tough way for the gullible woodentop to learn responsibility and earn his humanity"; another wrote, "There's a distinctly macabre feel to the Lyric Theatre's Christmas offering. The show based on Carlo Collodi's celebrated *Pinocchio* is not suitable for the under-7s."[1]

In Gray's *Pinocchio in the Park* (Rosen), on the other hand, the cuts and omissions in the adapted text resemble those traditionally undertaken when Collodi's tale moved north of the Alps. This adaptation tells the story of a son and a father instead of showing different adventures of the puppet. As the young director comments, "We didn't want it to be a totally *commedia* show . . . because particularly young people in this country don't know *commedia*. . . . I think the English like pantomime" (Personal interview). In the scene in which Pinocchio is drowning as a donkey, the Fairy appears and asks the audience to help him. The scene, in which words are repeated and chorused out loud by the audience, is in the tradition of English pantomimes in which there is usually a code of participation and intervention. This vocal intervention is organized but not chaotic.

Gray says further:

> [W]e wanted to give a sense of an adult world, a very controlling adult world, where the adults define what Pinocchio should be doing at any

point, but actually he wants to climb trees and chase butterflies and be human and be free of adults' control, rather than be taught what is right and what is wrong.

This is a play within a play. A group of English actors puts on a spectacle that has Italian origins, but when they are about to start, they find that the puppet has run away. George, the cleaner, ends up playing Pinocchio. The "real" person who plays the puppet is also an underdog, excluded from the inner core of the players. At the end he is allowed to become a player because he has played Pinocchio. Hence there is a double liberation, that of George and that of Pinocchio. As Rosen says, "I wanted to suggest something that is implied in Collodi's text as a whole but not stated: namely a liberationist idea. This is not to say that it preaches or commands liberation." This Pinocchio expresses the idea of a child as a self-identifying subject, who is not to be frightened by scenes of cruelty and violence. It is, in Rosen's words, "just about as un-warning, un-controlling, as it is possible to be without completely wrecking Collodi" (Personal interview).

Reaffirming the process of cuts and omissions (e.g., the episode of the Talking Cricket and that of the cottage and the beautiful Little Girl are cut) but also giving a personal interpretation of Collodi's text, this production did not arouse the anger of the London critics. One wrote, "With Dale Superville as good a Pinocchio as you can surely get . . . this is always entertaining . . . there is plenty to smile about." Another wrote, "A clumsy good Fairy, who sounds like an escapee from an East Enders set, provides more laughs aplenty." Another wrote:

> I must say, I developed a special sympathy for Jeff Diamond's carpenter-stepfather. Not only did he have to wear a wig that looked like ossified broccoli: he continued to dodder dotingly around when Pinocchio sold the reading primer [Geppetto had] pawned his own coat to buy and seemed remarkably unfazed when his quest for the runaway puppet forced him to do two hard years inside a shark. Parenthood can take less painful forms, at least in London right now.[2]

Some reasons for the cuts and omissions that characterize the English versions of Collodi's story lie in the peripheral status of children's literature that involves a lack of respect for the integrity of the original text (see Klingberg; Klingberg, Orvig, and Amor; Oitinnen); others lie in the differing images of childhood that emerge from the literary culture in England (Carpenter) and from that in Italy (Macchietti) when *Pinocchio* was first written. These images, which are tied to ancient mythologies, still condition and add to the childhood images transmitted today—and not only those images taken from the literary culture.

For example, Paul Hazard, in his book *Les livres, les enfants et les hommes* (1932), has shown that the ways of relating to childhood in Latin and Anglo-Saxon countries, and thus in the literature produced by those countries, differ. In Latin countries, children are seen as small candidates for the position of adult.

The first years of life are subordinate to those that will follow; they are a phase suspended in a time of waiting; they have no intrinsic value, being just a preparation. The Latin population begins to live and breathe only when maturity is reached. Anything before that is seen as a threat to development. Even children cannot wait for childhood to be over and done with (92).

In the Anglo-Saxon view, childhood has its own intrinsic value; it is an autonomous period of our lives, a blessed state in which happiness and innocence must be protected, one that often projects itself onto life as "nostalgia for a lost paradise" (92). Thus there is no hurry to leave the state of childhood behind: "for Latins, kids are just future adults; for the northerners, adults are just old kids" (94).

Hazard claims that climate explains this difference. The foggy northern climes provoke reveries, dreams, and introversion, while the south leans toward a clear and lucid vision of life, one that clips the wings of the imagination. This generalization is obviously based on clichés, tradition, and popular culture; it ignores the history, politics, and class stratification of the countries involved.

The problem with Hazard's north-south distinction remains open and is still debated. There are various souths in this world. In Europe, each country has its own south, well identifiable in less developed areas. How can north and south be defined in the field of children's literature? In an age of growing globalization, the Internet, and television, do the child and children's literature represent another realm altogether for Europeans and non-Europeans? Are there still different lifestyles, perceptions, and representations of childhood as opposed to adulthood? The definition of a child is complicated further, because, as Jacqueline Rose underscores, children can be differentiated on the basis of their social class, race, ethnicity, gender; they are not an objective, scientific entity. Karin Lesnik-Oberstein asks whether an objective, unique reader-child exists, and her answer is no (*Children's Literature* and "Defining").

Dieter Richter observes that different countries produce children's literature that reflects their own images of childhood. He distinguishes between a progressive and a regressive childhood novel. The former tells the story of the transformation from boy into man (and thus the story of the loss of childhood) and finds its greatest expression in *Pinocchio*. The latter—the product of the myth of childhood—tells the story of a rediscovered childhood. Its hero travels backward, toward a lost childhood, one of dreams, utopian. This second type of novel reaches its peak in England with Lewis Carroll's *Alice's Adventures in Wonderland* (1865) and James Matthew Barrie's *Peter Pan* (1904–11). The two types of novels, in Richter's opinion, can be read as parallel: themes, situations, and actions return but are lived differently. Both progressive and regressive deal with the refusal to become an adult but confront this refusal in a different way (*Pinocchio*).

The studies by Hazard and Richter provide food for thought. But Collodi's *Pinocchio*, although in some ways it can be considered progressive, does not fit in a single cage of interpretation. In an Italy in which children's literature was characterized by adulthood and a strong authoritarian aspect, his voice is inno-vative. He departs from the conventional and pedagogical viewpoints of his time. He sees the need for liberty and independence, the impatience with bonds and controls, the will for autonomy of judgment and action, as characteristics spe-cific to childhood. But these traits—also underlined in the adaptation of *Pinoc-chio* by Luigi Compagnone (*Ballata*)—encounter in his book the universe of norms represented through the voices of Geppetto, the Fairy, the talking ani-mals that succeed over the anarchic puppet, making him capitulate to the im-age of the good boy. Collodi perceives a new image of childhood that was emerg-ing in Europe, not the Romantic vision of innocence and purity that was gaining ground in nineteenth-century English literature and children's literature (Cambi). Collodi, Gianni Rodari writes, "does not stand in front of children as a teacher but as an adult . . . of the time . . . with all the contradictions that have filled his life" ("Pinocchio nella letteratura" 43). His novel and protagonist are full of contradictions.

The theatrical adaptations of *Pinocchio* produced in Italy today, while not avowedly produced for children, reach them as well. They tend to be faithful to the original version. If some display overall didactic purpose, others propose a highly complex reading. Childhood often becomes a metaphor for the human condition and thus a complex and difficult reality, rich in potential, creativity, anarchy, conflict, ambiguity, contradiction, and tragedy (Paruolo, "Les Pinoc-chio").

The English adaptations considered here reflect a process of domestication and purification, hewing to linguistic and cultural norms of the target reader. The authors-publishers tend to transmit through them images of childhood that aim to reflect less those in Collodi's text, more those prevalent in the great tradition of English children's literature, characterized by the elevation of childhood and by images of the beautiful child who must be protected from death and violence (Carpenter; Lurie). No doubt there is a reaction as well to the violence practiced on and by children today.

Collodi's *Pinocchio* contains many forms of violence. For Emilio Garroni the terrorist aspect of the book (the puppet's punishment is disproportionate to his guilt: he is hanged right away!) has been and continues to be the dominant mes-sage. But

> there is a complexity of meanings in the novel that is not immediately clear: children are not prepared to see beyond the most obvious content of the story. All the same they cannot avoid recognizing, *somehow*, *something* of the deeper messages carried along with the obvious contents.   (141)

Some contemporary Italian writers recall how often—as children from 4 to 11—they read Collodi with dismay, apprehension, and terror. Their first experi-ence of the text was negative and upsetting, at times because of the frighteningly ambiguous nature of the protagonist. Other writers thought it an important book, as it prompted them to reflect on certain shadowy corners of life (Bertacchini, "*Avventure*").

Is it suitable to present to children between 4 and 11 the original version of *Pinocchio*, or is it safer to turn to a purified version? The debate continues.

NOTES

[1] From a press clipping furnished by the theater staging Magni's *Pinocchio*. The first critic is Ian Johns (*Times*, 18 Dec. 2000). Other quotes read, "Beware, this is no Disney version. Strictly for the over-sevens" (*Guardian*, 24 Nov. 2000); "With the exception of some brilliant sequences—such as Pinocchio's flight on a bird's back over a green sheet field—the production suffers from the strongly episodic nature of the narrative . . ." (Lyn Gardner, *Guardian*, 6 Jan. 2001); "When [Pinocchio] winds up being lynched, some parents might have begun to feel a bit uneasy. . . . Pinocchio's final reconciliation with his long-lost 'Dad' in the bowels of the Whale is sure to bring a tear to the eye of the most hardened father. . . . I reckon 'adult' theatre should take note" (Oliver Jones, *What's On*, 13 Dec. 2000); "Fox and cat . . . attempt to kill Pinocchio before they hang his helpless puppet body from a tree. It's a shocking image some parents may take issue with" (Ronnie Haydon, *Time Out*, 12 Dec. 2000); "The threatre recommends the play for children over seven, but there may be some whimpering from the stalls" (*Independent*, 4 Feb. 2000).

[2] From a press clipping furnished by the theater staging Gray's *Pinocchio* (by Rosen). The first critic quoted is Colin Sheaman (*Stage*, 9 Aug. 2001); the second quotation is from *Romeike* (10 Aug. 2001); the third is by Benedict Nightingale (*Times*, 6 Aug. 2001). Another critic quoted was Maddy Costa: "The Pinocchio scampering about the Open Air Theatre . . . is a self-styled 'clever-clogs smarty-pants' who calls his father Geppetto 'wiggy-bum' and denounces his fairy guardian as a 'boring old bitch.' Even when a bout of particularly fruity fibbing causes his nose to sprout into an eighteen-inch baguette, he is more interested in nibbling the crust than expressing remorse" (*Guardian*, 13 Aug. 2001).

Between Collodi's *Ringmaster* and Manzoni's *Capocomico:* Antihumanism or the Circus of Life in Carmelo Bene's *Pinocchio*

Manuela Marchesini

Eccentric and gifted, Carmelo Bene was undoubtedly the greatest *guitto* ("barn-stormer") of the contemporary Italian stage—a term he relished. He was perceived as an iconoclast, a tyrant on stage, a genius, an impostor, a misanthrope and misogynist, and a controversial director for the 1966 Venice Biennale. I discuss one of his most celebrated versions of a classic text, Collodi's *Pinocchio.* Bene worked repeatedly on rewriting Collodi's novel and on its stage adaptation. A first edition of Bene's *Pinocchio* for the theater (in his words, an "adattamento scenico da Collodi" ["stage adaptation"]), staged by Teatro Laboratorio in Rome, 1961, is followed by a second (titled *Pinocchio '66* and staged by Teatro Centrale in Rome, 1966), then by a radio version (*Pinocchio*, in 1974) then by a third staged version (*Pinocchio*, with music by C. G. Luporini, at Teatro Verdi in Pisa, 5 Dec. 1981), and finally by a fourth in 1998 (*Pinocchio ovvero lo spettacolo della Provvidenza*, staged by Teatro dell'Angelo in Rome). Bene's long investment in Pinocchio takes the shape also of a printed text (*Pinocchio*, with *Proposte per il teatro*, published in Milan by Lerici, 1964). It is on this printed version of 1964, contained in Bene's *Opere*, that I focus my attention. It may or may not be in accord with the actual performances that Bene staged over a twenty-year period.[1] The distance separating the different instances of Bene's *Pinocchio* is striking enough to elicit an interest in a genetic study of that work according to the different media in which it morphed: print, stage, television and radio broadcasts.

The most striking feature of Bene's 1964 reappropriation and rewriting of *Pinocchio* for the stage is its fidelity to Collodi's text, whose words appear to be merely rearranged to suit the needs of scenic dialogue. There are two exceptions: one at the very beginning, the other at the very end of the play. In other words, Bene concentrates his personal interpretation of the puppet's story at the level of its structural framework. His rendition transforms the old tale of personal regeneration and coming of age, in accord with the values of the Italian Risorgimento, into something quite different. Through his use of the image of the artist as a clown, a topos of the nineteenth and early twentieth centuries whose importance is in no way limited either to a single artistic expression or to a single nation, Bene guides us to a performative grasp of what lies behind and ahead of Pinocchio—and thus to the *pinocchi* we all are. He reveals how behind Collodi's comforting tale looms Alessandro Manzoni's romantic irony and Samuel Beckett's postmodern, antihuman hero.

Bene's playscript *Pinocchio* opens with a prologue that is meant for us, the contemporary readers-spectators. It re-creates the ringmaster's ludicrous speech of chapter 33 of Collodi's novel, an episode recounted also in Bene's *Pinocchio*. In introducing himself and his play to us, Bene resorts to the same sort of clown-like *oratio soluta* that the circus manager uses to introduce the first public appearance of the famous donkey Pinocchio to his public of "worthy auditors" (397). The two extracts below give the speech in Bene's script (545) and Collodi's original:

From Bene's *Pinocchio*

Rispettabile pubblico ed inclita guarnigione dell'uno e dell'altro sesso essendo di passaggio per questa illustre Metropolitana mi sono voluto procreare il bene il piacere l'onore e il vantaggio di presentarvi davanti agli occhi un noto burattino sconosciuto finora in questi paesi e del quale forse avrete veduto il compagno ma non il simile.

Esso nasce da un padre di statura grande e da una madre parimenti piccolo. Non starò qui a far menzogna delle sue primizie giovanili né delle difficoltà da me soppressate per comprenderlo ma procediamo da ciò e per non intrattenerci più a lungo io passo alla vera e legittima presentazione. Avanti signori avanti si va subito ad incominciare per maggior comodo e distruzione di tutte le persone che sono dilettanti.

Esso è ghiottissimo del tobacco e lo prende nel naso e nella bocca che a chi lo crede è incredibile.

Parla la lingua dei cedri del Libano lingua che io bene intendo parlo ma non capisco e nella supposizione che nemmeno le signorie loro la intendano lo faremo ragionare nel forestiero idioma dei suoi paesi.

Balla magnificamente nel suo dialetto cosa che gli procurò dal Gran Turco la regalia di un orologio di argento vivo incrostato di pietre preziose pescate nel mar Caucaso.

Non vi starò qui a far menzogna di quanto sia ampia la sua capacità cerebrale io solo e null'altro lo sa. Io solo o signori che seguendo il sistema di galles ho anatomizzato la sua testa e vi ho trovato una piccolo cartilagine ossea sporgente in dentro che la stessa facoltà medicea di Parigi riconosce essere quello il Bulbo Occocchio della matematica solida e della geometria liquida.

Un solo esempio del mio burattino lungamente studiato ci rischiarerà meglio il proposito. Gli proporremo un problematico assioma e voi potrete conoscere quanta facoltà egli abbia nell'eliminarlo. Dato un bastimento della lunghezza di duecentottanta piedi della larghezza di centoventi della forza di quattrocento tonnellate della capacità di centottanta cavalli con l'albero maestro che sia alto quattrocento trentadue piedi si domanda quanti anni avrà il suo capitano.

Inoltre si domanderà qual differenza passa tra il timor panico e il peso specifico e come la dissoluzione di una dissenteria insorta fra i suoi concittadini esplose una sola botta e uccise ambo i quattro coorissanti.

Spero che vogliate favorirmi anche doman l'altro sera al diurno serale trattenimento. Ma nell'apoteosi che il tempo piovoso minacciasse acqua allora invece di doman l'altro sera il trattenimento sarà posticipato a doman mattina.

Intanto passino dentro o signori e vogliateci accordare un benevolo compatimento per i nostri involontari errori.

Honorable public and illustrious garrison of one and the other sex, while passing through this illustrious metropolitan I determined to procreate myself the good, the pleasure, the honor, and the advantage of presenting to you, before your eyes, a famous puppet unknown until now in these lands and whose companion perhaps you have seen, but nothing similar. He was born of a father of great stature and a mother equally small. I'm not about to make mendation about his youthful first fruits, nor about the difficulties suppressated in order to reprehend him, but let's go on from there, and in order not to linger any longer I pass to the true and legitimate introduction. Come forward, ladies and gentlemen, come forward, let's begin at once for greater comfort and destruction of all persons who are dilettantes.

He is a glutton for tobacco and he takes it up his nose and in his mouth, which, to he who believes it, is incredible.

He speaks the language of the cedars of Lebanon, a language that I apprehend, speak, but do not understand, and on the assumption that your lordships also do not understand it we will make him speak in the foreign idiom of his lands.

He dances magnificently in his dialect, something that won for him from the Great Turk the gift of a watch of bright silver encrusted with precious stones fished from the Caucasus Sea.

I'm not about to make mendation about how broad his cerebral capacity is, I alone and nobody else know it. I alone, O sirs and madams, who by following the system of Wales have anatomized his head, and have found there a small bony cartilage sticking inward that the same Medicean Faculty of Paris recognizes as being the Eye Bulb of solid mathematics and of liquid geometry.

A single example of my long-studied puppet will better reclarify the question. We shall put to him a problematic axiom and you can know how much faculty he has in eliminating it. Given a ship 280 feet long, 120 feet wide, with 400 tons of power and a capacity of 180 horses, and with a main mast that is 432 feet high, one asks how old its captain must be. Moreover, one asks what is the difference between panic fear and specific weight, and how the dissolution of a dysentery that arose among its citizens exploded a single blow and killed all four co-brawlers.

I hope that you will favor me also the day after tomorrow in the evening at the daytime evening entertainment. But in the apotheosis that the rainy weather threatens water, then instead of the evening of the day after tomorrow the entertainment will be postponed to tomorrow morning. In the meantime come inside, ladies and gentlemen, and accord benevolent pity upon our involuntary errors.

From Collodi's *Pinocchio*

"Rispettabile pubblico, cavalieri e dame!

"L'umile sottoscritto essendo di passaggio per questa illustre metropolitana, ho voluto procrearmi l'onore nonché il piacere di presentare a questo intelligente e cospicuo uditorio un celebre ciuchino, che ebbe già l'onore di ballare al cospetto di Sua Maestà l'imperatore di tutte le principali Corti d'Europa.

"E col ringraziandoli, aiutateci della vostra animatrice presenza e compatiteci!"...

"Miei rispettabili auditori! Non starò qui a farvi menzogna delle grandi difficoltà da me soppressate per comprendere e soggiogare questo mammifero, mentre pascolava liberamente di montagna in montagna nelle pianure della zona torrida. Osservate, vi prego, quanta selvaggina trasudi da' suoi occhi, conciossiaché essendo riusciti vanitosi tutti i mezzi per addomesticarlo al vivere dei quadrupedi civili, ho dovuto più volte ricorrere all'affabile dialetto della frusta. Ma ogni mia gentilezza, invece di farmi da lui benvolere, me ne ha maggiormente cattivato l'animo. Io però, seguendo il sistema di Galles, trovai nel suo cranio una piccolo cartagine ossea, che la stessa Facoltà medicea di Parigi riconobbe esser quello il bulbo rigeneratore dei capelli e della danza pirrica. E per questo io lo volli ammaestrare nel ballo, nonché nei relativi salti dei cerchi e delle botti foderate di foglio. Ammiratelo! e poi giudicatelo! Prima però di prendere cognato da voi, permettete, o signori, che io vi inviti al diurno spettacolo di domani sera: ma nell'apoteosi che il tempo piovoso minacciasse acqua, allora lo spettacolo, invece di domani sera, sarà posticipato a domattina, alle ore 11 antimeridiane del pomeriggio." (394, 396)

"Honorable public, cavalieres and noble ladies! Your humble undersigned passing through this illustrious metropolitan, I determined to procreate myself the honor not to mention the pleasure of presenting to this intelligent and conspicuous audience a celebrated donkey who formerly had the honor of dancing in the presence of His Majesty the Emperor of all the principal Courts of Europe.

"And by way to thank you, assist us with your animating presence and bear with us.". . .

"My worthy auditors! I will not here make mention of the mendacious difficulties suppressated by me in order to reprehend and subjugate this mammal while he was grazing freely from mountain to mountain in the plains of the torrid zone. Observe, I beg you, how much wild game transudes from his eyes, for inasmuch and insofar as all means of taming him to the life of civilized quadrupeds having proved vainglorious, I was obliged several times to resort to the amiable language of the whip. But every kindness of mine, instead of endearing me to him, has only won him over to me. I, however, following the system of Wales, found a small bony Carthage in his cranium, which the Medicean Faculty of Paris itself declared to be the bulb that regenerates hair and the pyrrhic dance. And for this reason I decided to train him in dancing, let alone the relative jumps through hoops and paper-sheathed barrels. Esteem him! And then judge him! However, before taking my lease from you, allow me, ladies and gentlemen, to invite you to tomorrow night's matinee. But in the apotheosis that the rain should threaten wet weather, then the show, instead of tomorrow night, will be postponed until tomorrow morning, at 11 A.M. in the afternoon."   (395, 397)

Bene's prologue creates an original and quite convincing piece of writing by repeating and transfiguring, literally point by point, his model. Bene resorts to the same rhetorical strategies of the model: paronomasia, and in general all sorts of substitutions, infractions, or disturbances of the normal order of language, at all levels—etymological, morphological, syntactic, semantic—as long as those devices serve the purpose of parody.

Bene takes the donkeyish dimension of Pinocchio as the interpretive key, the hallmark of his own, modern version of the nineteenth-century story. We are confronted with direct speech; no quotation marks, as in Collodi, put a reassuring distance between the tainted source of the words and the words themselves. Second, the gullibility of the circus audience in Collodi's book clearly extends, in Bene's application, to Bene's readers-spectators—in other words, to us. Lastly, the manipulative, clownlike quality of Collodi's ringmaster becomes the main trait of Bene's performative translation of Collodi's story—as Wolfgang Iser would call it (*Fictive*). Bene tranforms the donkeyish dimension of Pinocchio; the gullibility and simplemindness of his audience; and the manipulative, cynical buffoonery of his ringmaster from a sad but nonetheless transitory phase in Pinocchio's assured ascent toward moral soundness (i.e., the renewed Italian boy citizen of a newly forged Italy) to an overarching, ahistorical key of interpretation placed at the very beginning of the play.

Collodi's circus episode, clearly pointing to the tradition of popular arts (the puppet theater, the commedia dell'arte, the circus), also elicits another illustrious theme—the topos of the artist as clown. This topos has a remarkable history of its own, as Jean Starobinski argues. Coming from the faraway past of the medieval jugglers, the aesthetic interest in the world of buffoonery reaches, through Shakespeare, the core of Romantic poetics (Baudelaire and Rimbaud) and becomes one of the overarching images of modernity. Through the clown, the artist sheds light on the artist's own problematic identity.

Using the same image of the ringmaster as a tool of his Romantic irony, another Italian writer has hinted at the unsettling epistemological dimension in the artist's practice of literature: Alessandro Manzoni in *I promessi sposi*. Manzoni's novel explores the human capacity to signify our common words and our shared history.[2] It is a literary, performative scrutiny of the reliability (or unreliability) of all the words pronounced and the deeds performed in the sublunar world, in which we have lived and continue to live. The story is built on a paradox to which all three versions (*Fermo e Lucia* [1821–23], *I promessi sposi* [1825–27], and *I promessi sposi* [1840]) attest quite clearly. Bene, like the modern readers of Manzoni who stem from the seminal pages of Carlo Emilio Gadda's "Apologia manzoniana," notices and instinctively exploits this paradox for his own purposes.

Manzoni portrays the nineteenth-century narrator of the story, supposedly his double, as a manipulative *capocomico* ("leader of a troupe of actors") who addresses his audience as *rispettabile pubblico*. In this respect, he is a faithful follower of his eighteenth-century English models, mainly Henry Fielding and Laurence Sterne. In chapter 31, Manzoni describes how the seventeenth-century plague came into being with all its force once people of wisdom had yielded to the superstition of the many. Those few reasonable people, he writes, were persuaded by the superstition of the majority to believe in the existence of *untori*, people who viciously spread the disease by smearing the city doors. Reason, the alleged heir of the *siècle des lumières* and grandson of one of its champions (Cesare Beccaria), was vanquished by "l'opinione di quello che i poeti chiamavan volgo profano, e i capocomici, rispettabile pubblico" (1: 1208; "the opinion of that which the poets called the profane mob, and the leader of a troupe of actors called esteemed public"). We cannot fail to recognize ourselves in this *rispettabile pubblico*, simply because that is how we have been constantly referred to throughout the whole novel.

Of course Bene has no use, and no interest, in an ill-conceived textual or historical relation to Manzoni's novel—or Collodi's or anyone else's, for that matter. But his *variazione* of Collodi's *oratio soluta* quoted above, his making of the *capocomico* the signature of his rendition of *Pinocchio*, results from his intrinsic intelligence about the paradoxical core of Manzoni's work, and it shows that Bene opted for the unholy side of that work. As he explains in 1995, introducing the Bompiani reprint of his *Pinocchio*:

> *Pinocchio* è lo spettacolo dell'*infortunio sintattico* nel teatrino perverso
> della *Provvidenza* ("la bella bambina dai capelli turchini") e dell'indisciplina
> cieca d'un pezzo di legno crocifisso dai *pro-verbi* tricolori della *carne*: mor-
> talità natale e sciagurata *crescita umana*.   (537)

> Pinocchio is the spectacle of the syntactic accident in the perverse little
> theater of Providence ("the beautiful little girl with blue hair") and of the
> blind indiscipline of a piece of wood crucified by the tricolor *pro-verbs* of
> the *flesh*: native mortality and wretched human growth.

He sees in Collodi's *Pinocchio* and its underwriting of a lessened Manzonism a
"disastro linguistico" ("linguistic disaster") that heralds a broader semiotic and
interpretive disaster. Bene explodes both Manzoni's drive to linguistic-semiotic
unity as well as Collodi's edifying message of moral regeneration and growth.

A confirmation of Bene's distinctive, albeit unorthodox, take on Manzoni for
his own antirepresentative purposes can be found in *Adelchi o della volgarità del
politico* (1984, in Bene's *Opere*)—his rewriting of one of Manzoni's tragedies. According to Bene, the greatness of Manzoni's *Adelchi* lies precisely in what certain
academic criticism deems its limit: its supposed lack of completion, its "fami-
gerata incompiutezza" ("notorious incompleteness"). Quite the opposite, Bene
argues, thus offering another clear sign of his Gaddian grasp of Manzoni's work:

> Il Manzoni, così compiuto nei *Promessi* è vulnerabile, indifeso, imperfetto
> e soprattutto disperante(si) nel precendente *Adelchi*. E foss'anche? Ai
> sommelier s'ha da rispondere . . . Il valore "compiuto" dei *Promessi sposi*
> è il suo solo difetto, come la non definizione dell'*Adelchi* ne è il fascino e
> il suo pregio.   (1248)

> Manzoni, who was so complete in *The Betrothed*, is vulnerable, defense-
> less, imperfect and above all desperate in the earlier *Adelchi*. So what? To
> the sophisticated wine seller we would answer . . . the "complete" value of
> *The Betrothed* is its own defect, just as the nondefinition of *Adelchi* is its
> fascination and its value.

Bene clearly sympathizes with an anti-idyllic Manzoni, and he does so by focusing not only on the question of its semiotic tension (the *capocomico*) but also on
what is at the core of most modern readings of Manzoni's work: the issue of ending and of closure. The young protagonists of *I promessi sposi* may get married
in what traditional readings perceive as a conventional happy ending. But the
complex network of incommensurable points of view and languages, the in-
equities and power plays that make up human society will all continue beyond
such ending. Bene reminds us that it is not because Renzo and Lucia marry and
start a family that we will remember their story or read the novel.

Unsurprisingly, the theme of closure leads us to the second of Bene's innovations of Collodi's story—its ending: the protagonist of Bene's 1964 *Pinocchio* does not become a child; there is no final transformation. This scripted version of *Pinocchio* closes instead on the puppet's encounter with the Cat and the Fox, who are now down on their luck. Pinocchio utters a few words that are also the last words of Bene's playscript: "Addio mascherine! Ricordatevi del proverbio che dice: Chi ruba il mantello al suo prossimo, per il solito muore senza camicia" (444; "Farewell, pretty masqueraders! Remember the proverb that says: He who steals his neighbor's cloak is bound to die without a shirt" [445]). Bene's Pinocchio is, in other words, a marionette that remains forever such, eternally frozen in a fictive world that is managed by the *capocomico* and his like, a world where the very idea of the author's reliability coincides with the plain and simple fact of his prowess to manipulate anything and anyone.

Through his fidelity to Collodi's words, mediated by his awareness of Manzoni's subtext, Bene has given us a Pinocchio that could not be more removed from the edifying character of an edifying story. His *Pinocchio* is a coherent application of his long-standing reflections on theater and on communication and interpretation in general. As Gilles Deleuze argues, Bene's work is that of neither an avant-gardist nor a conservative, of neither a populist nor an elitist. Rather, his plays or adaptations break with constrictive mimesis, with the mere representation of conflicts—even in the Brechtian sense of "alienation" or, better, "dealienation" of the audience from conventional forms of identification and stereotypical modes of perception and understanding (see Brooker 191). Bene's *Pinocchio* is no longer an enclosed, claustrophobic, deadly text-container. Rather, it has become its staged, fertile, lively amputation (Deleuze 95).

Bene's betrayal of Collodi's text thus gives us the unsettling picture of a world reduced to a circus of lies (*menzogne*) with its crowd of *pinocchi*, its tragic clowns who never grow into adulthood, and its very respectable audiences of *hypocrite lecteurs*. Needless to say, it is a circus to which we all belong. Carmelo Bene, the last of the Romantics, has conjured up his *Pinocchio* in such a way as to undermine the very humanism that Collodi's edifying story was supposed to celebrate. Bene's Pinocchio will embrace not the supposed pleasures of a normal life but rather the inhumane challenges of Beckett's Molloy and Céline's desperate automatons.

NOTES

All English translations supplied in this essay, except those from Perella's bilingual edition of Collodi's *Avventure/Adventures*, are mine.

[1] One of Bene's *Pinocchios* I could screen—a RAI-TV version (*Pinocchio ovvero lo spettacolo della Provvidenza*) broadcast on 29 May 1999 by RAI 2—is remarkably different from the 1964 printed version, above all in the ending.

[2] For the difference between literature as an exploratory, as opposed to explanatory, enterprise, see Iser, "What Is Literary Anthropology?"

Digital *Pinocchio:* Teaching the Literary Text as Artificial Life-Form

Massimo Riva

> The most sublime labor of poetry is to give sense and pas-
> sion to inanimate things; and it is characteristic of chil-
> dren to take inanimate things in their hands and talk to
> them in play as if they were living persons. This philologico-
> philosophical axiom proves to us that in the world's child-
> hood men were by nature sublime poets.
>
> —Giambattista Vico, *The New Science*

> To be sure, contemporary molecular biologists still strenu-
> ously resist the most radical claims of artificial life in which
> digital or robotic constructions are assimilated with the or-
> ganisms they study (that is, with life-as-we-know-it). Never-
> theless, they live and work in a world in which what counts
> as an explanation has become more and more difficult to
> distinguish from what counts as a recipe for construction.
>
> —Evelyn Fox Keller, *Making Sense of Life*

The Adventures of Pinocchio, *beyond the Book*

In the one hundred and twenty years since his official birth as the protagonist of
a story, Pinocchio has become much more than a fictional character. The puppet
who turned into a boy has evolved even further, taking on a new life or many lives
of his own, perhaps the most successful cultural export ever made in (modern)
Italy.

The extraordinary dissemination of the Pinocchio character in modern and
contemporary popular culture makes it a perfect subject for a pedagogical experiment cutting across the traditional boundaries of comparative literary studies and cultural (Italian) studies. The course I teach at Brown University, entitled
Digital Pinocchio, is cross-listed between the departments of Italian Studies and
Modern Culture and Media and is divided into two sections: one taught in Italian and the other in English (covering slightly different materials but identically
structured). My approach differs from the more traditional comparative or cultural studies points of view, which have inspired such recent scholarly contribu-
tions to Pinocchiology (in English) as Harold B. Segel's *Pinocchio's Progeny* or
Richard Wunderlich and Thomas J. Morrissey's *Pinocchio Goes Postmodern.*
While these studies provide a useful background for my course, its real focus is
neither the position of Collodi's story in the framework of modernist and post-

modernist literature nor Pinocchio's dissemination into other cultures or media. Rather, it is the specific role played by technology in this dissemination. My students and I focus on Pinocchio as a cultural *and* technological construct, beyond its early embodiment as the character of a printed book.

Here is a short description of the course as it appears in the course announcement:

> Digital Pinocchio. The evolution of a universal icon from puppet to child to robotic computerized and virtual personage. Books, films, cartoons, hypertexts and interactive games directly or indirectly inspired by the nineteenth-century tale of Carlo Collodi.   ("IT0140")

As a cultural and technological construct, in its evolution from print to computer-based technology, *Pinocchio* perfectly embodies what, with a terminology widely adopted in recent years, we call a hyper- or cybertext: that is, a written text expanded, multiplied, evolved, mutated through the technological prism (see Landow; Aarseth; Murray; and Ryan, *Cyberspace Textuality* and *Narrative*). As a cultural-technological construct, *Pinocchio* also provides an ideal model for a series of experimentations with what, in contemporary jargon, we call intermedia theory: a cultural theory (and practice) encompassing the emerging discursive and artistic forms that, thanks to digital technology, cut across a variety of representational media (textual, visual, acoustic, dramatic) and their reciprocal combinations or remediations. The term *remediation*, introduced by Jay Bolter and Richard Grusin, is particularly useful in defining a task that my students and I have undertaken: creating a time line that represents *Pinocchio's* evolution from text to hyper- or cybertext. This time line is conceived as a fundamental resource for a Web site currently under construction. On it, crucial dates mark the emergence of new forms of Pinocchio life: 1911, for example, the year when *Pinocchio* came to the silver screen in Giulio Antamoro's silent film, or 1940, the year when Walt Disney's *Pinocchio* was released and another avatar of the puppet-boy, with whom we are all by now exceedingly familiar, made its debut.[1]

Constructing a time line of Pinocchio's evolution in a variety of media stimulates a critical understanding of how new media remediate old ones and of how new expressions take shape in older media, transformed by emerging visual techniques and technologies. The evolution of book illustrations, from Enrico Mazzanti to Gris Grimly, is an example. In particular, Pinocchio's cinematic or theatrical embodiments as a human actor and its animations as a synthetic character are the object of interesting discussions about the transformations of Pinocchio as both character and technological construct. Of course, Pinocchio's metamorphoses are not exclusively driven by technological change: linguistic, cultural, and historical factors play a fundamental role in the reception and adaptation of Collodi's story, throughout the twentieth century. However, the goal of the time line as a critical tool is to show how the advent of new technologies and media enables new interpretations, adaptations, and transformations of the puppet-boy and his adventures. They introduce new narrative or representational modes and codes that, by reelaborating, reframing, and remediating old ones, bring forth new virtual meanings embedded in the original text.

Let's take Steven Spielberg's film *A. I.*, for example, dubbed by some reviewers a sort of anti-*Pinocchio*. This film is particularly suggestive for our topic, because it projects a virtual avatar of the puppet-boy (the *mecha* David) into a distant technological future, whose characteristics, however, are still rooted in our contemporary discussions on artificial intelligence and life. My students view and discuss the film, along with related sci-fi narratives, such as Brian Aldiss's "Supertoys Last All Summer Long" (on which *A. I.* is based) and Philip K. Dick's classic *Do Androids Dream of Electric Sheep?* (which inspired Ridley Scott's cult film *Blade Runner*), and general-audience books on contemporary developments in artificial intelligence and artificial life, such as Rodney A. Brooks's *Flesh and Machines*. We also examine and discuss other, lesser-known adaptations and animations of the computer age: from Giuseppe Laganà and Guido Vanzetti's 1981 pioneering electronic *Pixnocchio* to Marc Perrier and Georges LaCroix's *Les nouvelles aventures de Geppetto* (in which Geppetto, a computer artist, creates a virtual Pinocchio). With Spielberg's visionary remake, these works help us reframe Collodi's story in the context of contemporary cyberculture, both in mainstream and avant-garde or experimental media.

Much of the original inspiration for my course was provided by Franz Fischnaller's software installation *Interactive Pinocchio (Pinocchio Interactive)*.[2] Fischnaller's installation is an experiment in interactivity: it combines elements of performance (theater, dance) and narrative. Pinocchio's story is folded into that of a real character, while the story of his virtual counterpart is projected on a screen behind him.

In Fischnaller's words:

> The literary Pinocchio becomes a robotic computerized puppet and a virtual personage. The robotic computerized puppet belongs to the real (physical) world. Digital Pinocchio belongs to the virtual (intangible) world. There is a dynamic and enigmatic relationship between Pinocchio Robot and virtual Pinocchio, the *avatar*.   ("Interview")

I was struck by the possibilities offered by this formulation for a rereading of the original story of the puppet-boy as well as for a new kind of pedagogical approach, an experiment in what I would call constructivist pedagogy.

For a final course project, I propose that my students design or perform their own Pinocchio, according to each student's intellectual interests, artistic tastes, and technical skills. Team projects are also accepted. We focus on how available tools (hardware and software) play a significant role in the formulation and execution of these ideas. The project is an experiment in visualization and may also be considered a contribution to an illustrated edition or representation of the text in digital form, should we decide to include Collodi's text on our Web site. Yet the construction of a cyber-Pinocchio is not the exclusive focus of my course. The most important pedagogical goal lies in the fundamental question that my students and I address throughout the semester: What is it about Pinocchio that inspires such a proliferation of offspring, such an extended virtual progeny?

Our cyber-Pinocchios are always based on a lively discussion of the potential meanings embedded in the story by Collodi, that is, on a close reading of the original. As Giorgio Manganelli wrote in his brilliant *Pinocchio: Un libro parallelo*:

> as a device of the imagination, Collodi's book is a "cubic" entity, a multidimensional map, in which the reader ventures, at every reading, choosing from a multiplicity of intersecting paths, always following in the footsteps of its runaway protagonist.

He adds, in a definition that unmistakably reminds us of another masterpiece of children's literature, *Alice in Wonderland*:

> *Pinocchio* is a text built on clues ["altamente indiziario"], an illusionist's book made of traces, footprints, pranks, riddles, jokes, a text in whose imaginative syntax silences are as essential as words while every word leads inevitably to a last stop.   (v–vi; trans. mine)

He concludes:

> One does not simply read *Pinocchio*, one plunges into it . . . . And when we finally get, not just to the center of the book but to one of its infinite centers, we realize that the book is not only boundless but also unique.
>   (101)

Adopting these words as a sort of pedagogical mantra, my students and I approach the labyrinth of the *Adventures* (not a novel, strictly speaking) with an exploratory and experimental attitude. If, as N. Katherine Hayles writes, "the present cultural moment is marked by a pervasive belief that information is more real than matter or energy," Pinocchio, a literary character evolved into multiple avatars, is a perfect specimen for a theoretical and pedagogical experiment with a new concept of "the literary text as artificial life form" (we might call it the Pinocchio code) capable of adapting to a variety of media environments and ecologies ("Artificial Life" 205, 209).[3] The first question we must ask, therefore, is, Who is Pinocchio, really? And what kind of information does it/he embody?

A (Cautionary) Tale concerning Technology

As a modern folktale, an ironic narrative designed for a preliterary audience (a story for children written by an adult, professional writer), the *Adventures* is built on a fundamental rhetorical ambivalence: its entertainment value (the pleasure its readers derive from it) and its pedagogical or moral message do not coincide. The pleasure of the text is linked to the open, playful nature of the puppet's story, while the edifying message depends almost entirely on the story's closure.[4] This ambivalence has interesting consequences for a reading of the *Adventures* as a (cautionary) tale concerning technology.

Reading the *Adventures* as a tale about technology and, more specifically, about the imaginative possibilities and ethical dilemmas that emerging forms of artificial intelligence or life offer us may sound at first like a contrived postmodern interpretation of Collodi's text. Of course, in discussing this approach with my students, I do not suggest that the "question concerning technology" (in Martin Heidegger's terms) was actually on the mind of Collodi when he conceived and wrote *Pinocchio*. But we cannot exclude the possibility that, at some unconscious level, it was indeed. As a literary character, Pinocchio emerges at the threshold between traditional and modern culture. Although his father (the author) belonged to a cultural context (post-Risorgimento Florence and Tuscany) not exactly at the forefront of modern European technological progress, he was not entirely ignorant of modernity, to which, as a writer, he characteristically reacted in a humoristic mode.

It is precisely this combination of traditional and modern that strikes us as original today. Collodi was a contemporary of Thomas Alva Edison and Auguste Villiers de l'Isle Adam. Villiers's novel *Tomorrow's Eve*, featuring an android ideal woman built by the Wizard of Menlo Park, was published in 1886, only three years after *The Adventures of Pinocchio* appeared as a book.[5] It seems therefore justified, in historical terms, to read Collodi's tale against the backdrop of a post-Romantic literary genealogy that harks back to E. T. A. Hoffmann's *Holzpüppchen* ("Wooden Puppet") Olympia in *The Sandman* (also an incunabulum of *Tomorrow's Eve*), focusing on the impact of technological imagination on the modernist literary mind.

But here we are immediately faced with the peculiarity of Collodi's creation. The connection between post-Romantic literature and technology, in contemporary critical studies, falls largely under the rubric of what Sigmund Freud (referring, among other things, to *The Sandman*) called the uncanny (*unheimlich*). In his essay on Collodi's book as a classic, Italo Calvino observes that Hoffmann would probably have liked the "little man more wide than tall, soft and oily like a lump of butter . . ." who drives Pinocchio and Lucignolo (Lampwick) to Funland. And Edgar Allan Poe would have definitely appreciated the disquieting apparition of the beautiful Little Girl with blue hair and a face as white as a wax image who, with eyes closed and hands crossed over her breast, without moving her lips at all, said in a voice that seemed to come from the world beyond: "There is nobody in this house. They are all dead." (*Romanzi* 1361)

Yet such instances of the uncanny, at the blurred boundary between the organic and the inorganic, the world of the living and the realm of the dead, are strange to encounter in a world, it is worth repeating, intentionally and ironically designed for children. Both Hoffmann's and Villiers's stories, written for adults, deal with the paradox of Romantic love between a man and a mechanical creature rather than with the Faustian and Promethean mythology of rebellion, which was embodied in another classic of the Romantic technological imagination, Mary Shelley's *Frankenstein*. In *The Sandman* and *Tomorrow's Eve* the source of the uncanny is the confusion provoked in the (male) protagonist by the ambiguous, natural-artificial, magical-mechanical nature of his beloved (a modern revival of the Pygmalion motif). Unlike Hoffmann's Olympia or Villiers's Hadaly, however, Collodi's Pinocchio is a male puppet.[6] Moreover, the confusion about Pinocchio's true nature does not evoke uncanny emotions. We know that the dual identity of the puppet-boy is precisely the reason for both the tale's entertaining power and its moral message. As a fictional character, until his final metamorphosis, Pinocchio is both puppet and boy—an artificial and a natural creature, a virtual and a real being.

But there is a crucial moment, early in the story, when Geppetto experiences something close to an uncanny sensation, a confusing and disturbing premonition of things to come. In chapter 3, happy at having found a perfect name for his puppet and having already carved its hair, forehead, and eyes, he suddenly realizes that the half-formed piece of wood is staring at him. Taken aback, the old craftsman says with a resentful tone, "Spiteful wooden eyes, why are you looking at me?" (97). Nobody answers.

This is one of those silences that Manganelli signaled as "most eloquent" in the elliptic syntax of the text (8).[7] We know that the piece of wood can see and talk, yet in the scene of its official birth, its manufacturing, it (the life-form hidden inside the piece of wood that will become Pinocchio) remains strangely silent, apparently waiting for its mouth to be carved out. But in the necessary order of its creation, proceeding from top to bottom, the nose comes first. As soon as it is carved, it begins to talk, figuratively speaking: growing disproportionately despite Geppetto's frantic attempts to cut it down (99). Then, for no reason (yet another symptomatic ellipsis in Collodi's text), Pinocchio's nose stops growing, perhaps—one is led to conjecture—because Geppetto simply gave up trying to stop it and turned to carving out the puppet's mouth. As soon as the mouth is carved, it bursts out in mocking laughter, thus confirming the rebellious but fundamentally comic nature of this mini-Frankensteinian golem.

The uncanny moment has quickly come and gone, framed between eloquent silence and mocking laughter. Now the adventures can begin, as soon as Pinocchio's body is completed. It seems reasonable to conclude that in *Pinocchio* the uncanny is only indirectly and ironically related to technology and its ambiguities. In the folktale mode of the story, the confusion between animate and inanimate, what is alive and what is dead, what is made by man and what grows naturally, and so on, is a playful premise (in rhetorical terms, the invention) of the story, a source of comedy rather than tragedy. But Geppetto's somber premonition is confirmed at every stage in the puppet's manufacturing (the eyes, the nose, the hands, the feet), and the scene turns into the ironic portrait of a melancholy artist ("At that insolent and mocking behavior, Geppetto became sadder and more dejected than he had ever been in his life" [101]—the Italian text reads, significantly, "tristo e melanconico" [100]). Of course, Geppetto is no Frankenstein and no Coppelius. He is no Wizard of Menlo Park either. Yet in that rapid exchange of oblique glances between father and son (maker and made), the fundamental contradiction in the puppet's nature—as a living and artificial creature, a life-form imprisoned in a manufactured body—has come unmistakably to light.

This discussion of the uncanny is crucial for our reading of Collodi's tale as a cautionary tale concerning technology. It is also crucial for our pedagogical experiment: students are invited to build their own Pinocchio, using technological tools unthinkable at the time of Collodi, tools that redefine Geppetto's original creation, reconceiving it as a cognitive exercise—puppet making for the digital age. The critical reader should never forget that Pinocchio is a special kind of technological construct, of artificial creature. Puppets have been around a long time in our culture, long before androids and automatons—therefore, on our Pinocchio time line, Collodi's character emerges only at midpoint, preceded by a long genealogy of ancestors and followed by its multifarious progeny. It has taken a long time to recognize puppets for what they really are: imperfect automatons, inanimate material beings that require (hidden) human energy (through strings, rods, etc.) to move and talk like living beings. The return of the puppet in Romantic, and post-Romantic culture is precisely a recognition of this dualistic nature, under the spell of the technological uncanny, at the interface between spiritualism and materialism. As a living puppet, Pinocchio, with his virtual progeny of robots and androids, is the modern embodiment of an ancient myth, caught in the peculiar moment of becoming modern, when other intangible forms of energy (electricity) and mechanical ways of capturing and reproducing the human voice (the phonograph) or image (photography and the cinema) begin to replace the hands and words of the puppeteer—as in Edison's talking doll. In Collodi's creation, two (unconsciously) gendered ideas about the nature of technology confront each other: a masculine desire, represented by the father, Geppetto, inspires the manufacturing of the puppet-boy, while a feminine secret power, represented by the sister-mother, the Blue Fairy, rules over its metamorphoses.

The Ambiguities of Closure:
Toward a Constructivist Pedagogy

Puppets are the secularized progeny of hieratic automatons, ancient technological constructs symbolically integrated into premodern culture. As a modern toy, the puppet is still linked to magical thinking, and yet it is also tied to the technological imagination of artificial beings, our own scientific and rational way of playing God. Here, in the puppet's simultaneous, conscious-unconscious ties with both premodern and contemporary (even futuristic) modes of thought and imagination, lie the deeper roots of Pinocchio's originality. As a coming-of-age story, the story of the puppet who turned into a boy may well be read as an original version of a post-Romantic tale: the return of the puppet, as the uncanny, in European modernist culture. The question is, What returns in or with the puppet, really? What is strangely familiar or disquietingly unfamiliar about Pinocchio for us today?

In the end, Pinocchio's story has a moral explanation. That the life-form temporarily embodied in the puppet must find its proper body, the body of "a proper boy," is a reassuringly humanistic and reasonable interpretation of Collodi's tale, one that definitely exorcises the uncanny nature of its protagonist's double identity. This moral and pedagogical happy ending, however, may be inadequate to condense the story's message, as our technological imagination has evolved to the point of making it literally possible to take inanimate things and turn them into artifacts that seem, indeed are, to all effects, alive.

If we take Roland Barthes's definition of myth as a type of speech—that is, as a message and a system of signification (109)—we can consider the Pinocchio myth as a signifying energy, a type of information (a magic formula or code) that can find its vehicle in a variety of media. As such, Pinocchio is an entirely virtual and metamorphic being. Yet, as Evelyn Fox Keller writes, we "live and work in a world in which what counts as an explanation has become more and more difficult to distinguish from what counts as a recipe for *construction*" (203). Our technological dream, the driving force of our evolution as a species, is still Geppetto's dream: the melancholy dream of a poor artisan turned into an (apprentice) wizard. As we increasingly treat the natural as artificial and the artificial as natural, in the process of becoming a technological construct ourselves (and our world along with us), new ideas about life begin to emerge. The message encoded in Pinocchio's character and story, the exemplary evolution of a cultural life-form that, imprisoned in the manufactured body of a protohuman puppet, undergoes a series of physical and moral metamorphoses (from vegetal to animal to fully human), thanks to an unconscious kind of magic, may thus be open to creative, playful, or serious reinterpretation. In the eternal return of the puppet, poetics, technology, and pedagogy implicate and challenge one another, as we (the explorers, the players, the apprentices) venture into the uncharted territory of an emerging cultural biology.[8]

NOTES

All English translations supplied in this essay, except those from Perella's bilingual edition of Collodi's *Avventure/Adventures*, are mine. The essay epigraph from Vico is translated by Thomas G. Bergin and Max H. Fisch (71).

[1] In this essay I take the word *avatar* in the same sense as O'Donnell: "in the sense of 'manifestation,' the form in which some abstract and powerful force takes palpable shape for human perception" (xi).

[2] See Fischnaller, *From Virtual Reality*. Fischnaller is art director and production coordinator for FABRICATORS, Architects of Culture, Fabricators of Ideas, an interdisciplinary group concerned with the integration of technology, communication, art, and design. He is also a professor at the University of Illinois, the Chicago School of Art and Design, and Università degli Studi di Firenze.

[3] More than anybody else, Hayles has explored the connection between "artificial life and literary culture," to quote the title of her essay. See also her *How We Became Posthuman*.

[4] From this point of view, the modernity of Collodi's tale (and the key to its success) lies in its original, peculiar mixture of traditional folk- and fairy tale and realistic elements. (This realism is either understood against the backdrop of late-nineteenth-century Italian society or translated and adapted to other cultural and social contexts.) Emphasizing one or the other aspect of the tale results in strikingly divergent interpretations, illustrations, or adaptations, which in turn reflect the social relevance of literary forms and institutions in their concrete historical context. Think, for example, of two Italian cinematic adaptations of *Pinocchio:* Luigi Comencini's neorealist film and Roberto Benigni's Felliniesque re-creation.

[5] Villiers's novel was probably conceived around the same time—the late 1870s or early 1880s—that Edison was at work on his talking doll. The doll was eventually released in 1889, but its first patent was issued in 1878, the same year that another of Edison's inventions, the phonograph, was shown at the Paris expo—where Villiers admired it. See Wood 145–63.

[6] One ancestor of Pinocchio could well be Pino Smalto, the "man made king" of a tale included by Basile in his *Pentamerone* or *Lo cunto de li cunti* (1634), the first collection of folktales in the Italian tradition, recently retranslated into Italian. "Once upon a time there was . . . 'A King!' my little readers will say right away" (83). In my course, I invite interested students to explore this particular lineage in the genealogy of Pinocchio.

[7] These silences (aphasic instances in the text) tend to occur at crucial junctures, where some uncanny epiphany is about to take place. In chapter 15, for example, right before the apparition of the melancholy wax doll, the first embodiment of the "beautiful Little Girl with blue hair," later to become the Fairy, we see the puppet, chased by the assassins, knocking at the door of the "little house as white as snow" that he saw "gleaming in the distance": "Nobody answered. He knocked again, harder, because he could hear his tormentors' footsteps nearing and their heavy labored breath. The same silence" (183).

[8] I take this expression from Dyens 3.

NOTES ON CONTRIBUTORS

Sandra L. Beckett, professor in the Department of Modern Languages, Literatures, and Cultures at Brock University, is a member of the Royal Society of Canada and was president of the International Research Society for Children's Literature from 1999 to 2003. She is the author of *Recycling Red Riding Hood* and *De grands romanciers écrivent pour les enfants* and has edited books on children's literature and francophone literature.

Holly Blackford, assistant professor of English at Rutgers University, Camden, teaches American literature, children's literature, feminist theory, and pedagogy and directs the writing program. She has published articles on children's literature and culture and on American women writers. She is the author of *Out of this World: Why Literature Matters to Girls.*

Amy Boylan teaches Italian language and literature at Colorado College. Her research is focused on issues of national and gender identity in late-nineteenth- and early-twentieth-century Italian literature and visual arts, particularly in monuments and war memorials. She has published articles on Giovanni Verga, Alessandro Manzoni, and Neera.

Nancy L. Canepa, associate professor of French and Italian at Dartmouth College, teaches and conducts research in the fields of early modern Italian literature and culture, fairy-tale studies, and dialect literature. She is the author of *From Court to Forest: Giambattista Basile's* Lo cunto de li cunti *and the Birth of the Literary Fairy Tale* and translator of Collodi's *The Adventures of Pinocchio* with the Steerforth Italia series. Her unabridged translation of Basile's *Lo cunto de li cunti* is forthcoming.

Lorinda B. Cohoon, assistant professor of English at the University of Memphis, does research in children's and young adult literature, American literature before 1900, and the construction of childhood citizenships. She has written articles on Eudora Welty's *The Shoe Bird,* Jacob Abbott's "Jonas Books," and Harriet Beecher Stowe.

Rossana Dedola, a researcher in contemporary Italian literature at the Scuola Normale Superiore in Pisa, has written on twentieth-century Italian narrative, focusing on such authors as Federigo Tozzi, Luigi Pirandello, Primo Levi, Leonardo Sciascia, and Italo Calvino. She is the author of *Pinocchio e Collodi*; *Storie sotto il cielo e sotto il mare,* a book of children's stories; and *La valigia delle Indie e altri bagagli,* which examines travel narratives by contemporary authors and filmmakers.

David Del Principe, assistant professor of Italian at Montclair State University, is the author of *Rebellion, Death, and Aesthetics in Italy: The Demons of Scapigliatura* as well as various articles. Focusing on the gothic in nineteenth- and twentieth-century Italian and European literature and culture, he is currently preparing a manuscript on gothic allegories of birth and nation in nineteenth-century Italian and European literature.

Jacqueline L. Gmuca, assistant professor of English at the University of Texas, El Paso, works principally in the field of British and North American children's literature and has published essays on the novels of Penelope Lively, Kenneth Grahame, and F. Anstey as well as the picture-book authors-illustrators Arnold Lobel, Anita Lobel, and Cynthia Rylant. With Lorinda B. Cohoon she is currently working on a textbook, "Invitations to Dialogue: Critical Theory and Children's Literature."

Angela M. Jeannet, Charles A. Dana Professor of Romance Languages Emerita at Franklin and Marshall Colleges, is the author of books and articles on modern Italian literature, especially the works of Italo Calvino and Natalia Ginzburg. She is currently translating Italian fiction into English and writing on Calvino, Ferdinando Camon, Maria Bellonci, and Giosuè Carducci.

Charles Klopp, professor of Italian and director of graduate studies in Italian at Ohio State University, teaches modern Italian literature and culture. He has written on Gabriele D'Annunzio, Antonio Tabucchi, Gianni Celati, the Tuscan writers Federigo Tozzi and Romano Bilenchi, and the writings of political prisoners in Italy. His most recent book is *Sentences: The Memoirs and Letters of Political Prisoners from Benvenuto Cellini to Aldo Moro.*

Dennis Looney, associate professor of Italian and assistant dean in the humanities at the University of Pittsburgh, is the author of *Compromising the Classics: Romance Epic Narrative in the Italian Renaissance.* With Deanna Shemek he is coeditor of *Phaethon's Children: The Este Court and Its Culture in Early Modern Ferrara.* He is editor and cotranslator of Sergio Zatti's *The Quest for Epic: From Ariosto to Tasso.*

Manuela Marchesini, assistant professor of Italian at Texas A&M University, studies the intersection of literature and criticism in modern and contemporary Italy. She is the author of *Scrittori in funzione d'altro: Contini, Longhi, Gadda;* has published articles on Boccaccio, Alessandro Manzoni, Antonio Pizzuto, and Carlo Emilio Gadda; and is working on a book titled "Merchants of Enchantment."

Cristina Mazzoni, professor of Romance languages at the University of Vermont, teaches Italian language, literature, and culture. She is the author of *Saint Hysteria* (1996), *Maternal Impressions* (2002), *The Voices of Gemma Galgani* (with Rudolph Bell; 2003), *Italian Made Simple* (2003), and *The Women in God's Kitchen* (2005). She is the editor and translator of Angela of Foligno's *Memorial* (1999).

Elena Paruolo, a researcher in English literature at the University of Salerno, works in the field of children's literature. She is studying the reception of *Pinocchio* in England and of *Alice in Wonderland* in Italy. She is the author of *Il mito di Oxbridge: L'università nel romanzo inglese.* She is a member of the board of the International Réseau Littératures d'Enfance of the Agence Universitarie de la Francophonie.

Massimo Riva, professor of Italian studies and modern culture and media and director of the Virtual Humanities Lab at Brown University, studies medieval and modern Italian literature and film and digital culture. He is the author of *Saturno e le Grazie* and *Malinconie del Moderno* and the editor of *Italian Tales: An Anthology of Contemporary Italian Fiction.*

Michael Sherberg, associate professor of Italian at Washington University, has written on Boccaccio, the Italian chivalric epic, Machiavelli, and the question of the language in sixteenth-century Italy. He also studies the Italian novel of the late nineteenth century and the literature of Sicily since the Unification.

Laura Stallings taught for several years as a lecturer in the Department of Romance Languages at Washington University and is particularly interested in second language acquisition. She is currently a lecturer in the Department of Foreign Languages and Literatures at Old Dominion University.

Carlo Testa, professor of Italian and French at the University of British Columbia, Vancouver, has written on the novel of education, the tradition of the superfluous man in the nineteenth and twentieth centuries, utopian themes in French and European Romanticism, nineteenth- and twentieth-century Italian narrative, twentieth-century Italian poetry, and Italian cinema. He is the author most recently of *Italian Cinema and Modern European Literatures, 1945–2000* and *Masters of Two Arts: Re-Creation of European Literatures in Italian Cinema.*

Maria Truglio, assistant professor of Italian at Pennsylvania State University, works in the fields of nineteenth-century Italian literature, especially symbolist and gothic literature; women writers; children's literature; psychoanalytic critical methodologies; and Italian American culture. Her first book, *Beyond the Family Romance: The Legend of Pascoli,* is forthcoming.

Rebecca West, William R. Kenan Jr. Professor in the Department of Romance Languages and Literatures and on the Committee on Cinema and Media Studies at the University of Chicago, has written articles on modern Italian poetry and narrative as well as on cinema. Her books include *Eugenio Montale: Poet on the Edge* (awarded the MLA's Howard Marrero Prize in 1982) and *Gianni Celati: The Craft of Everyday Storytelling* (awarded the MLA's Scaglione Prize in 1999).

SURVEY RESPONDENTS

Gillian Adams, *University of Texas, Austin*
Holly Blackford, *Rutgers University, Camden*
Lucinda Cassamassino, *Lucechiara Translations Ltd.*
Luisetta Elia Chomel, *University of Houston*
David Del Principe, *Montclair State University*
Angela M. Jeannet, *Franklin and Marshall College*
Charles Klopp, *Ohio State University*
Joseph Luzzi, *Bard College*
Manuela Marchesini, *Texas A&M University*
Umberto C. Marian, *Rutgers University, New Brunswick*
Ida Marinzoli, *Old Bridge High School West*
E. Ann Matter, *University of Pennsylvania*
Rita M. Mignacca, *State University of New York, Albany*
Nicolas J. Perella, *University of California, Berkeley*
Massimo Riva, *Brown University*
Maria Truglio, *Pennsylvania State University*
Rebecca West, *University of Chicago*

WORKS CITED

Aarseth, Erspen. *Cybertext: Perspectives on Ergodic Literature.* Baltimore: Johns Hopkins UP, 1997.

Abiuso, Giuseppe L., and M. Giglio, eds. Le avventure di Pinocchio: *Adapted as a Beginning Reader.* Skokie: Natl. Textbook, 1977.

Ada, Alma Flor, and F. Isabel Campoy. *¡Feliz cumpleaños, Caperucita Roja!* Miami: Alfaguara, 2002. N. pag. Trans. as *Happy Birthday, Little Red Riding Hood.* Trans. A la Carte Langs.

The Adventures of Pinocchio. Dir. Steve Barron. 1996. VHS. New Line Studios, 1997.

Aesop. *The Complete Fables.* Trans. Olivia Temple and Robert Temple. New York: Penguin, 1998.

Agnew, John. "The Myth of Backward Italy in Modern Europe." *Revisioning Italy: National Identity and Global Culture.* Ed. Beverly Allen and Mary Russo. Minneapolis: U of Minnesota P, 1997. 23–42.

A. I.: Artificial Intelligence. Dir. Steven Spielberg. Warner Brothers, 2001.

Aldiss, Brian. *"Supertoys Last All Summer Long" and Other Stories of Future Time.* London: Orbit, 2001.

Allan, Robin. *Walt Disney and Europe: European Influences on the Animated Feature Films of Walt Disney.* Bloomington: Indiana UP, 1999.

L'altra metà di Pinocchio: Un burattino e le sue illustratrici. Ed. Walter Fochesato and Donatella Curletto. Genoa: Provincia di Genova, 2002.

Annibaletto, Stefano, and Francesco Luchi. "Pinocchio da Collodi a Disney a Comencini." *Pinocchio sullo schermo* 19–27.

Anno, Mitsumasa. *Tabi no ehon II.* Tokyo: Fukuinkan, 1978. Trans. as *Anno's Italy.* New York: Collins, 1980.

Apostolidès, Jean-Marie. "Pinocchio; or, A Masculine Upbringing." *Merveilles et contes* 2.2 (1988): 75–86.

Applebee, Arthur N. "Problems in Process Approaches toward a Reconceptualization of Process Instruction." *The Teaching of Writing: Eighty-Fifth Yearbook of the National Society for the Study of Education.* Ed. Anthony R. Petrosky and David Bartholomae. Chicago: Natl. Soc. of the Study of Educ., 1986. 95–113.

Ariosto, Ludovico. *Cinque canti.* Trans. David Quint and Alexander Sheers. Introd. Quint. Berkeley: U of California P, 1995.

———. *Orlando Furioso.* Trans. Allan H. Gilbert. New York: Vanni, 1954.

Arnaudo, Marco. "Attilio Mussino, autore di *Pinocchio*: Un esempio di ibridazione tra letteratura, fumetto e cinema nel primo Novecento italiano." *Contemporanea* 2 (2004): 67–93.

Ascoli, Albert Russell, and Krystyna Clara von Henneberg. *Making and Remaking Italy: The Cultivation of National Identity around the Risorgimento.* Oxford: Berg, 2001.

Asor Rosa, Alberto. "*Le avventure di Pinocchio: Storia di un burattino* di Carlo Collodi." *Genus italicum: Saggi sulla identità letteraria italiana nel corso del tempo.* Turin: Einaudi, 1997. 551–618.

Astroboy: The Complete Series. DVD. Columbia-Tristar, 2005.

Le avventure di Pinocchio. Dir. Luigi Comencini. 1971. Twentieth Century Fox, 2002.

Bacigalupi, Marcella, and Piero Fossati. *Da plebe a popolo: L'educazione popolare nei libri di scuola dall'Unità d'Italia alla Repubblica.* Milan: U Cattolica, 2000.

Bacon, Martha. "Puppet's Progress: *Pinocchio.*" *Children and Literature: Views and Reviews.* Ed. Virginia Havilland. Glenview: Scott, 1973. 71–77.

Bakhtin, Mikhail Mikhailovich. *The Dialogic Imagination: Four Essays.* Ed. Michael Holquist. Trans. Caryl Emerson and Holquist. Austin: U of Texas P, 1981.

Baldini, Antonio. "La ragion politica di *Pinocchio.*" 1876. *Fine Ottocento: Carducci Pascoli D'Annunzio e minori.* Florence: Le Monnier, 1947. 118–24.

Balzac, Honoré de. *Lost Illusions.* Trans. Herbert J. Hunt. London: Penguin, 1986.

———. *Old Goriot.* Trans. David Bellos. Cambridge: Cambridge UP, 1987.

Banti, Alberto. *La nazione del Risorgimento.* Turin: Einaudi, 2000.

Barański, Zygmunt G., and Rebecca J. West, eds. *The Cambridge Companion to Modern Italian Culture.* Cambridge: Cambridge UP, 2001.

Bàrberi-Squarotti, Giorgio. "Gli schemi narrativi di Collodi." *Studi collodiani* 87–108.

Barthes, Roland. *Mythologies.* Trans. Annette Lavers. New York: Hill, 1984.

Basile, Giambattista. *Il racconto dei racconti, ovvero, Il trattenimento dei piccoli.* Trans. Ruggero Guarini. Milan: Adelphi, 1994.

Beckett, Sandra L. *Recycling Red Riding Hood.* New York: Routledge, 2002.

Bellini, Renato. "Pinocchio." *Fifty-One Piano Pieces from the Modern Repertoire: Representing Composers of Thirteen Nationalities.* New York: Schirmer, 1940. 138–42.

Bell, Sandra, Marina Morrow, and Evangelia Tastsoglou. "Teaching in Environments of Resistance: Toward a Critical, Feminist, and Antiracist Pedagogy." *Meeting the Challenge: Innovative Feminist Pedagogies in Action.* Ed. Maralee Mayberry and Ellen Cronan Rose. New York: Routledge, 1999. 23–46.

Bene, Carmelo. *Pinocchio.* 1964. *Opere con l'autografia d'un ritratto.* Milan: Bompiani, 1995. 539–80.

Bertacchini, Renato, ed. *Le "avventure" ritrovate: Pinocchio e gli scrittori del Novecento.* Pescia: Fondazione Nazionale Carlo Collodi, 1983.

———. "Carlo Collodi." *Letteratura italiana: I minori.* Vol. 8. Milan: Marzorati, 1962. 2821–35.

———. *Collodi narratore.* Pisa: Nistri-Lischi, 1961.

———. *Il padre di Pinocchio: Vita e opera del Collodi.* Milan: Camunia, 1993.

———. "'Pinocchio' centenario e vent'anni di critica collodiana." *Cultura e scuola* 23 (1984): 22–39.

———. "Pinocchio tra due secoli: Breve storia della critica collodiana." *Carlo Lorenzini-Collodi nel centenario* 121–64.

Bettelheim, Bruno. *The Uses of Enchantment: The Meaning and Importance of Fairy Tales.* New York: Knopf, 1976.

Biaggioni, Rodolfo, ed. *Pinocchio: Cent'anni di* Avventure *illustrate: Bibliografia delle edizioni illustrate italiane di C. Collodi,* Le avventure di Pinocchio: *1881/83–1983.* Florence: Giunti-Marzocco, 1984.

Biffi, Giacomo. *Contro maestro Ciliegia: Commento teologico a* Le avventure di Pinocchio. Milan: Jaca, 1977.

———. *Il "mistero" di Pinocchio.* Turin: Elledici, 2003.

Bjornson, Richard. *The Picaresque Hero in European Fiction.* Madison: U of Wisconsin P, 1977.

Blackford, Holly. *Out of This World: Why Literature Matters to Girls.* New York: Teachers Coll., 2004.

Blake, William. "The fields from Islington to Marybone." *Blake's Selected Poems.* Ed. David Erdman and Virginia Erdman. Mineola: Dover, 1995. 68.

Boero, Pino, and Carmine De Luca. "Carlo Collodi e *Le avventure di Pinocchio.*" *La letteratura per l'infanzia.* Rome-Bari: Laterza, 1995. 49–57.

Bolter, Jay David, and Richard Grusin. *Remediation: Understanding New Media.* Cambridge: MIT P, 1999.

Braine, George. "Beyond Word Processing: Networked Computers in ESL Writing Classes." *Computers and Composition* 14 (1997): 45–58.

Bringsvaerd, Tor Åge. *Alice lengter tilbake.* Illus. Judith Allan. Oslo: Gyldendal, 1983.

Brooker, Peter. "Key Words in Brecht's Theory and Practice." *The Cambridge Companion to Brecht.* Ed. Peter Thomson and Glendyr Sachs. Cambridge: Cambridge UP, 1994. 187–95.

Brooks, Rodney A. *Flesh and Machines: How Robots Will Change Us.* New York: Pantheon, 2002.

Bufano, Remo, dir. *Pinocchio for the Stage, in Four Short Plays from Collodi's Original, Dramatized and Illustrated.* New York: Knopf, 1929.

Bull, Anna Cento. "Social and Political Cultures in Italy from 1860 to the Present Day." Barański and West 35–61.

Burnett, Frances Hodgson. *The Secret Garden.* New York: Harper, 1998.

Calvino, Italo. *Romanzi e racconti.* Ed. Mario Barenghi and Bruno Falcetto. Vol. 2. Milan: Mondadori, 1992.

Cambi, Franco. *Collodi, De Amicis, Rodari: Tre immagini d'infanzia.* Bari: Dedalo, 1985.

Cambon, Glauco. "*Pinocchio* and the Problem of Children's Literature." *Children's Literature: The Great Excluded.* Birmingham: Intl. Federation of Lib. Assns., 1973. 50–60.

Camp, Anne. *Das Mädchen Pinocchia.* Frankfurt: Fisher, 1992.

———. *Zwei Berühmtheiten auf den Kopf gestellt: Doña Quijote und der Herr von Stein: Erzählungen.* Munich: Weiss, 1986.

Campa, Riccardo. *La metafora dell'irrealtà.* Lucca: Maria Pacina Fazzi, 1999.

Campbell, Joseph. *The Hero with a Thousand Faces.* Princeton: Princeton UP, 1949.

Capuana, Luigi. *Tutte le fiabe.* Ed. Maurizio Vitta. 2 vols. Milan: Mondadori, 1983.

Card, Claudia. "Pinocchio." *From Mouse to Mermaid: The Politics of Film, Gender, and Culture.* Bloomington: Indiana UP, 1995. 62–71.

Carlo Lorenzini-Collodi nel centenario. Rome: Istituto della Enciclopedia Italiana, 1992.

Carne-Ross, Donald S. "The One and the Many: A Reading of *Orlando Furioso*: Cantos 1 and 8." *Arion* 5 (1966): 195–234; ns 3 (1976): 146–219.

Carpenter, Kevin. *Desert Isles and Pirate Islands: The Island Theme in Nineteenth-Century English Juvenile Fiction: A Survey and Bibliography.* Frankfurt am Main: Lang, 1984.

Castellani Pollidori, Ornella. Introduction. Collodi, *Avventure* [Castellani Pollidori] xi–lxxxiv.

Catani, Tommaso. *Pinocchio nella luna.* Florence: Bemporad, 1924.

Cech, John. "The Triumphant Transformations of *Pinocchio.*" *Triumphs of the Spirit in Children's Literature.* Ed. Francelia Butler and Richard Rotert. Hamden: Lib. Professional, 1986. 171–77.

Celati, Gianni. *Le avventure di Guizzardi.* Turin: Einaudi, 1973.

C'era una volta un pezzo di legno: La simbologia di Pinocchio. Milan: Emme, 1981.

Cherubini, Eugenio. *Pinocchio in Africa.* Florence: Bemporad, 1903.

Chiappelli, Fredi. "Sullo stile del Lorenzini." *Letteratura* 1 (1953): 110–18.

Citati, Pietro. *Il velo nero.* Milan: Rizzoli, 1979.

Clément, Frédéric. *Magasin Zinzin ou Aux merveilles d'Alys.* Paris : Ipomée–Albin Michel, 1995.

Clemente, Pietro, and Mariano Fresta, eds. *Interni e dintorni del Pinocchio: Atti del Convegno "Folkloristi italiani del tempo di Collodi."* Montepulciano: Grifo, 1986.

Collodi, Carlo. *The Adventures of Pinocchio.* Trans. Ann Lawson Lucas. New York: Oxford UP, 1996.

———. *The Adventures of Pinocchio: Story of a Puppet.* Trans. Nancy Canepa. Illus. Carmelo Lettere. South Royalton: Steerforth, 2002.

———. *Le avventure di Pinocchio.* Milan: Mondadori, 1995.

———. *Le avventure di Pinocchio.* Introd. Luigi M. Reale. Perugia: Guerra, 1995.

———. *Le avventure di Pinocchio.* Ed. Cesare Zavattini. Turin: Einaudi, 1961.

———. *Le avventure di Pinocchio / The Adventures of Pinocchio.* Trans. Nicolas J. Perella. Berkeley: U of California P, 1986.

———. *Le avventure di Pinocchio: Storia di un burattino.* Ed. Amerindo Camilli. Florence: Sansoni, 1946.

———. *Le avventure di Pinocchio. Storia di un burattino.* Ed. Ornella Castellani Pollidori. Pescia: Fondazione Nazionale Carlo Collodi, 1983.

———. *Divagazioni critico-umoristiche.* Florence: Bemporad, 1893

———. *Note Gaie.* Florence: Bemporad, 1893.

———. *Opere.* Ed. Daniela Marcheschi. Milan: Mondadori, 1995.

———. *Pinocchio.* 1972. Ed. Fernando Tempesti. Milan: Feltrinelli, 2004.

———. Pinocchio: *Ristampa anastatica dell'edizione originale dal* Giornale per i Bambini, *1881–1883.* Florence: Pagliai Polistampa, 2002.

———. *Pinocchio: The Tale of a Puppet*. Trans. Mary Alice Murray and Giovanna Tassinari. London: Penguin, 2001.

Colombo, Fausto. "Pinocchio intarsiato: Varianti narrative nelle versioni audiovisive de *Le avventure di Pinocchio*." *Pinocchio sullo schermo* 95–120.

Compagnone, Luigi. *La ballata di Pinocchio*. 1980. Milan: Mondadori, 2002.

———. *La vita nuova di Pinocchio*. Florence: Vallecchi, 1971.

Coover, Robert. *Pinocchio in Venice*. New York: Linden, 1991.

Coveney, Peter. *The Image of Childhood: The Individual and Society: A Study of the Theme in English Literature*. Harmondsworth: Penguin, 1967.

Cro, Stelio. "Collodi: When Children's Literature Becomes Adult." *Merveilles et contes* 7 (1993): 87–112.

Cummins, June. "Comparisons between *Goblin Market* and *The Tale of Peter Rabbit*." Roanoke: Children's Lit. Assn. Conf., 2000.

D'Angeli, Concetta. "L'ideologia 'moderata' di Carlo Lorenzini, detto Collodi." *Rassegna della letteratura italiana* 86 (1982): 152–77.

D'Angelo, Marco. "Lettore avvisato, burattino salvato." Pezzini and Fabbri 75–94.

Dante Alighieri. *Paradiso*. Trans. Allen Mandelbaum. New York: Bantam, 1986.

Davis, John A., ed. *Italy in the Nineteenth Century, 1796–1900*. Oxford: Oxford UP, 2000.

De Amicis, Edmondo. *Cuore*. Ed. Luciano Tamburini. Turin: Einaudi, 1972.

Decollanz, Giuseppe. "Educazione e politica nel *Pinocchio*." *Studi collodiani* 169–87.

Dedola, Rossana. *Pinocchio e Collodi*. Milan: Mondadori, 2002.

Del Beccaro, Felice. "Premesse ad una lettura di *Pinocchio*." *Studi Collodiani* 191–204.

Deleuze, Gilles. "Un manifesto di meno." Trans. J.-P. Manganaro, Carmelo Bene, and Deleuze. *Sovrapposizioni*. Macerata: Quodlibet, 2002. 85–113.

Denti, Roberto. *Lasciamoli leggere. Il piacere e l'interesse per la lettura nei bambini e nei ragazzi*. Turin: Einaudi, 1999.

De Sanctis, Francesco. *Storia della letteratura italiana*. Ed. Gianfranco Contini. Turin: UTET, 1968.

Desideri, Saverio. "Collodi giornalista." *Studi Collodiani* 247–62.

Di Biasio, Rodolfo. "Il notturno in *Pinocchio*." *Studi collodiani* 263–72.

Dick, Philip K. *Do Androids Dream of Electric Sheep?* New York: Ballantine, 1996.

Disney, Walt. *Pinocchio*. Burbank: Walt Disney Productions, 1940.

Doglio, Federico. *Storia del teatro: Il '500 e il '600*. Milan: Garzanti, 1999.

Ducharte, Pierre Louis. *La commedia dell'arte*. Paris: d'Art et Industrie, 1955.

Dusi, Nicola. "Pinocchio nella balena." Pezzini and Fabbri 175–202.

Dyens, Ollivier. *Metal and Flesh: The Evolution of Man: Technology Takes Over*. Trans. Evan J. Bibbee and Dyens. Cambridge: MIT P, 2001.

Dyer, Brenda. "L1 and L2 Composition Theories: Hillcocks' 'Environmental Mode' and Task-Based Language Learning." *ELT Journal* 50 (1996): 314–17.

The Erotic Adventures of Pinocchio. Dir. Corey Allen. Warner Brothers, 1971.

Eusebietti, Dora. *Piccola storia dei burattini e delle maschere*. Rome: ERI, 1966.

Faeti, Antonio. *Guardare le figure: Gli illustratori italiani dei libri per l'infanzia.* Turin: Einaudi, 1972.

Fano, Nicola. *Le maschere italiane.* Bologna: Il Mulino, 2001.

Ferrari, Vittorio. *Letteratura italiana moderna e contemporanea (1748–1903).* Milan: Hoepli, 1904.

Ferretti, Roberto. "Gli animali nella narrativa orale e in *Pinocchio*." Clemente and Fresta 215–40.

Ferroni, Giulio. *Storia della letteratura italiana: Dall'Ottocento alla Novecento.* Turin: Einaudi, 1991.

Ferrucci, Franco. "Il teatro dei burattini." *Paragone* Aug. 1970: 129–46.

Fiedler, Leslie. "An Eye to Innocence: Some Notes on the Role of the Child in Literature." *Collected Essays of Leslie Fiedler.* New York: Stein, 1971. 471–511.

Fischnaller, Franz. *From Virtual Reality to Mixed Reality? The Twilight within the Real and the Virtual.* 2 Jan. 2006 <http://www.noemalab.org/sections/gallery/fischnaller/pdf/vr_to_mr.pdf>.

———. "Interview with a 3D Artist." *Webspace.* 2 Jan. 2006 <http://web.tiscali.it/3dfantasia/1issue/franz.htm>.

Frank, Yasha. *Pinocchio: A Musical Legend.* New York: Marks Music, 1939.

Frattini, Alberto. "Appunti sulla tecnica del racconto e sulle strutture espressive nelle *Avventure di Pinocchio*." *Studi collodiani* 287–94.

Freud, Sigmund. *The Uncanny.* Trans. David McClintock. New York: Penguin, 2003.

Frittelli, Ugo. *Lorenzo Pignotti favolista.* Florence: Barbera, 1901.

Frosini, Vittorio. *Filosofia politica di Pinocchio.* Rome: Lavoro, 1990.

Frow, Gerald. *"Oh, Yes it is!": A History of Pantomime.* London: BBC, 1985.

Frye, Northrop. *Anatomy of Criticism: Four Essays.* Princeton: Princeton UP, 1973.

Fujita, Sakura, illus. *Pinocchio.* Text by Ann Herring. Tokyo: Gakken, 1971.

Gadda, Carlo Emilio. "Apologia manzoniana." *Saggi giornali favole e altri scritti.* Ed. Liliana Orlando, Clelia Martignoni, and Dante Isella. Milan: Garzanti, 1991. 679–86.

Gagliardi, Antonio. *Il burattino e il labirinto.* Turin: Einaudi, 1980.

Gaillard, Jone. "Pinocchio sovversivo: Un'altra lettura del capolavoro di Carlo Collodi." *Romance Languages Annual* 8 (1997): 179–85.

Gannon, Susan. "A Note on Collodi and Lucian." *Children's Literature* 8 (1980): 98–102.

Garroni, Emilio. *Pinocchio uno e bino.* Bari: Laterza, 1975.

Gasparini, Giovanni. *La corsa di Pinocchio.* Milan: Vita e pensiero, 1997.

Gaylin, Willard. *Adam and Eve and Pinocchio: On Being and Becoming Human.* New York: Viking, 1990.

Genot, Gérard. "Le corps de Pinocchio." *Studi Collodiani* 299–314.

Geppetto. Dir. Tom Moore II. 2000. VHS. Walt Disney Home Video, 2000.

Ghíuselev, Iassen, illus. *The Adventures of Pinocchio: The Story of a Puppet.* By Carlo Collodi. Turin: Ideogramma, 1994.

Gilbert, Allan H. "The Sea-Monster in Ariosto's *Cinque Canti* and in *Pinocchio.*" *Italica* 33 (1956): 260–63.

Giornale per i bambini. Ristampa anastatica della prima edizione originale. 3 vols. L'Aquila: L'Acacia, 1990.

Goethe, Johann Wolfgang von. *Wilhelm Meister's Apprenticeship.* Trans. Eric A. Blackall with Victor Lange. Princeton: Princeton UP, 1989.

Goncharov, Ivan Aleksandrovich. *Oblomov.* Trans. Ann Dunnigan. New York: New Amer. Lib., 1963.

Grant-Schaefer, George Alfred. *Adventures of Pinocchio: An Operetta in Three Acts.* Chicago: Hoffman, 1935.

Grassi, Antonio. "Pinocchio nell'ottica mitologico-archetipica della psicologia analitica di C. G. Jung." *C'era una volta* 71–92.

Gray, Emily. Personal interview. 15 Aug. 2001.

Guglielmoni, Luigi, and Fausto Negri. *Le notti di Pinocchio: Riflessioni per giovani, provocazioni per adulti.* Leumann (Turin): Elledici, 2002.

Gunning, Tom. "The Ghost in the Machine: Animated Pictures at the Haunted Hotel of Early Cinema." *Living Pictures: The Journal of the Popular and Projected Images before 1914* 1 (2001): 4–17.

Hall, Lee. The Adventures of Pinocchio, *by Carlo Collodi: A New Adaptation.* London: Methuen, 2000.

Hamilton, Virginia. *The People Could Fly.* Illus. Leo Dillon and Diane Dillon. New York: Knopf, 1985.

Hayles, Nancy Katherine. "Artificial Life and Literary Culture." Ryan, *Cyberspace Textuality* 205–23.

———. *How We Became Posthuman: Virtual Bodies in Cybernetics, Literature, and Informatics.* Chicago: U of Chicago P, 1999.

Hazard, Paul. *Les livres, les enfants et les hommes.* Paris: Flammarion, 1932.

Hearder, Harry. *Italy: A Short History.* Ed. Jonathan Morris. Cambridge: Cambridge UP, 2001.

Heidegger, Martin. *Philosophical and Political Writings.* Ed. Manfred Stassen. New York: Continuum, 2003.

———. *"The Question concerning Technology" and Other Essays.* Trans. William Lovitt. New York: Harper, 1977.

Heins, Paul. "A Second Look: *The Adventures of Pinocchio.*" *Horn Book* 7 (1982): 200–04.

Heisig, James W. "Pinocchio, Archetype of the Motherless Child." *Children's Literature* 3 (1974): 23–35.

Hoffmann, E. T. A. *The Sandman.* Trans. John Oxenford. Virginia Commonwealth U Dept. of Foreign Langs. 9 Sept. 1999. 2 Jan. 2006 <http://www.fln.vcu.edu/hoffmann/sand_e.html>.

Hunt, Peter, ed. *International Companion Encyclopedia of Children's Literature.* London: Routledge, 1996.

L'immagine nel libro per ragazzi: Gli illustratori di Collodi in Italia e nel mondo. Ed. Piero Zanzotto. Trent: Assessorato Attività Culturali, 1977.

Iser, Wolfgang. *The Fictive and the Imaginary: Charting Literary Anthropology.* Baltimore: Johns Hopkins UP, 1993.

———. "What Is Literary Anthropology? The Difference between Explanatory and Exploratory Fictions." *Revenge of the Aesthetic: The Place of Literature in Theory Today.* Ed. M. Clark. Berkeley: U of California P, 2000. 157–69.

"IT0140: Literature and Adolescence: Digital Pinocchio." *Brown Online Course Announcement.* Spring 2006. 6 Mar. 2006 <http://boca.brown.edu/topicsdet.asp>.

Jakobson, Roman. "On Linguistic Aspects of Translation." *On Translation.* Ed. Reuben A. Brower. Cambridge: Harvard UP, 1959. 232–39.

Jandl, Ernst. *Fünfter sein.* Illus. Norman Junge. Weinheim, Ger.: Beltz, 1997.

Jones, Dudley, and Tony Watkins, eds. *A Necessary Fantasy? The Heroic Figure in Children's Popular Culture.* New York: Garland, 2000.

Jurkowski, Henryk, and Francis Penny. *A History of European Puppetry.* Vol. 2. Lewiston: Mellen, 1998.

Kashi no Ki Mokku [Le nuove avventure di Pinocchio]. Dir. Shotaro Hara. Tatsunoko, 1972.

Keller, Evelyn Fox. *Making Sense of Life.* Cambridge: Harvard UP, 2002.

Kertzer, David I., and Mario Barbagli, eds. *Family Life in the Long Nineteenth Century, 1789–1913.* New Haven: Yale UP, 2002. Vol. 2 of *The History of the European Family.*

Kincaid, Jamaica. *Annie John.* New York: Farrar, 2001.

Klingberg, Göte. *Children's Fiction in the Hands of the Translator.* Lund, Swed.: Bloms Boktryckeri, 1986.

Klingberg, Göte, Mary Orvig, and Stuart Amor, eds. *Children's Books in Translation: The Situation and the Problems: Proceedings of the Third Symposium of the International Research Society for Children's Literature, August 26–29 1976.* Stockholm: Almqvist, 1978.

Knoepflmacher, U. C. Introduction. Sadler 1–11.

Koffolt, Kimberly, and Sheryl L. Holt. "Using the 'Writing Process' with Non-native Users of English." *New Directions for Teaching and Learning* 70 (1997): 53–60.

Kohl, Herbert R. "Wicked Boys and Girls: Three Takes on Pinocchio." *Should We Burn Babar? Essays on Children's Literature and the Power of Stories.* New York: New, 1995. 94–124.

Koppe, Susanne. "Darf man Pinocchio verändern? Antworten von Nöstlinger und Heidelbach." *Eselsohr* 7 (1988): 16.

Krashen, Stephen. *Principles and Practice in Second Language Acquisition.* Hertfordshire, Eng.: Prentice, 1995.

Kuznets, Lois Rostow. *When Toys Come Alive: Narratives of Animation, Metamorphosis, and Development.* New Haven: Yale UP, 1994.

La Fontaine, Jean de. *The Complete Fables.* Ed. and trans. Norman B. Spector. Evanston: Northwestern UP, 1988.

Landow, George P. *Hypertext 2. The Convergence of Contemporary Critical Theory and Technology.* Baltimore: Johns Hopkins UP, 1997.

Lavinio, Cristina. "Modalità narrative tipiche del racconto popolare in *Pinocchio.*" Clemente and Fresta 257–81.

Le Brun, Claire. "Il était/sera une fois: Le conte de fées technologique des années 80." *Canadian Children's Literature* 74 (1994): 63–74.

Lesnik-Obserstein, Karin. *Children's Literature: Criticism and the Fictional Child.* New York: Oxford UP, 1994.

———. "Defining Children's Literature and Childhood." Hunt 17–31.

Levine, George, and U. C. Knoepflmacher, eds. *The Endurance of* Frankenstein: *Essays on Mary Shelley's Novel.* Berkeley: U of California P, 1979.

Little Otik. Dir. Jan Švankmajer. 2001. DVD. Zeitgeist Films, 2003.

Lucas, Ann Lawson. "Enquiring Mind, Rebellious Spirit: Alice and Pinocchio as Nonmodel Children." *Children's Literature in Education* 30 (1999): 157–69.

———. Introduction. Collodi, *Adventures* [Lucas] vii–lvi.

Lucian. True History *and* Lucian; or, The Ass. Trans. Paul Turner. Bloomington: Indiana UP, 1958.

Lurie, Alison. *Boys and Girls Forever: Reflections on Children's Classics.* London: Chatto, 2003.

Macchietti, Sira Serenella, ed. *Il sentimento dell'infanzia in Toscana nell'ultimo Ottocento.* Rome: Bulzoni, 1993.

Magni, Marcello, dir. *The Aventures of Pinocchio.* By Carlo Collodi. Dramatized by Lee Hall. Lyric Theatre Hammersmith. Nov. 2000.

———. Personal interview. 15 Aug. 2001.

Malerba, Luigi. *Pinocchio con gli stivali.* Rome: Cooperativa Scrittori, 1977.

———. "Pinocchio secondo Malerba." Pinocchio's Centennial. Florence, 1981.

———. *Pinocho con botas.* Trans. Fabio Morádito. Illus. Damián Ortega. Mexico City: Fondo de Cultura Económica, 1992.

Manganelli, Giorgio. *Pinocchio: Un libro parallelo.* Turin: Einaudi, 1977.

Manzoli, Giacomo, and Roy Menarini. *Pinocchio, comico muto.* Rev. of Pinocchio, dir. Gant. Dipartimento di Musica e Spettacolo, U di Bologna. 20 Nov. 2005 <http://www.muspe.unibo.it/period/fotogen/num045/14MANZOLIPinocchioI.htm>.

Manzoni, Alessandro. *I promessi sposi.* Ed. Mario Martelli. 2 vols. Florence: Sansoni, 1973.

Marcheschi, Daniela. "Collodi e la linea sterniana nella nostra letteratura." Collodi, *Opere* xi–lxii.

Martini, Carlo, ed. *Pinocchio nella letteratura per l'infanzia.* Urbino: QuattroVenti, 1999.

Martini, Ferdinando. "Come andò." *Giornale per i bambini* 7 July 1881: 1–2.

Mativat, Daniel. *Ram, le robot.* Montreal: Héritage, 1984.

McGillis, Roderick. *The Nimble Reader: Literary Theory and Children's Literature.* New York: Twayne, 1996.

Meirieu, Philippe. *Frankenstein pédagogue.* Paris: ESF, 1996.

Merivale, Patricia. "The Telling of Lies and 'The Sea of Stories': 'Haroun,' 'Pinocchio,' and the Postcolonial Artist Parable." *Ariel* 28 (1977): 193–208.

Muñoz Ryan, Pam. *Esperanza Rising.* New York: Scholastic, 2000.

Murray, Janet H. *Hamlet on the Holodeck: The Future of Narrative in Cyberspace.* New York: Free, 1997.

Negri, Renzo. "Pinocchio ariostesco." *Studi collodiani* 439–43.

The New Adventures of Pinocchio. Dir. Michael Anderson. Pinocchio II Productions, 1999.

The New Jerusalem Bible. Ed. Henry Wansbrough. New York: Doubleday, 1990.

Nietzsche, Friedrich. *The Joyful Wisdom.* Trans. Thomas Common. Ed. Oscar Levy. New York: Russell, 1964. Vol. 10 of *Complete Works.*

Nikolejeva, Maria. *From Mythic to Linear: Time in Children's Literature.* Lanham: Rowman, 2000.

Nodelman, Perry. "Pleasure and Genre: Speculations on the Characteristics of Children's Fiction." *Children's Literature* 28 (2000): 1–14.

Nöstlinger, Christine. *Der neue Pinocchio.* Illus. Nikolaus Heidelbach. Weinheim, Ger.: Beltz, 1988.

O'Brien, Geoffrey. "Very Special Effects." *New York Review of Books* 9 Aug. 2001: 13.

O'Donnell, James J. *Avatars of the Word: From Papyrus to Cyberspace.* Cambridge: Harvard UP, 1998.

Oittinen, Riitta. *Translating for Children.* New York: Garland, 2000.

Omaggio a Pinocchio. Pescia: Quaderni della Fondazione Nazionale Carlo Collodi, 1967.

Ottevaere–van Praag, Ganna. *Le roman pour la jeunesse: Approaches, définitions, techniques narratives.* New York: Lang, 1996.

P3K: Pinocchio 3000. CinéGroupe, 2004.

Pancrazi, Pietro. "Elogio di Pinocchio." *Scrittori d'oggi: Serie prima.* Bari: Laterza, 1946. 229–35.

———. "Vita di Collodi." *Tutto Collodi.* Ed. Pancrazi. Florence: Le Monnier, 1948. vii–xxxviii.

Parenti, Marino. "Il papà di Pinocchio." *Rarità bibliografiche dell'Ottocento.* Vol. 1. Florence: Sansoni, 1953. 129–55.

Paruolo, Elena. "Les grandes tendances de l'édition jeunesse en Italie à travers la réaction de la presse italienne à la 41e édition de la Foire Internationale du Livre pour Enfants (Bologne 14–17 avril 2004)." *Littératures d'Enfance: Un réseau pluridisciplinaire sur les littératures d'enfance.* Agence Universitaire de la Francophonie. 20 Nov. 2005 <http://www.lde.auf.org/Texte-de-Elena-Paruolo>.

———. "Les Pinocchio de Luigi Compagnone." Perrot 227–40.

———. Pascoli, Giovanni. *Opere.* Vol. 1. Ed. Federico Goffis. Milan: Rizzoli, 1970.

Perella, Nicolas J. "An Essay on *Pinocchio.*" *Italica* 63.1 (1986): 1–47.

———. "An Essay on *Pinocchio.*" Collodi, *Avventure/Adventures* 1–69.

———. "When Children's Literature Becomes Adult." *Merveilles et contes* 7 (1993): 87–112.

Perrot, Jean, ed. Pinocchio: *Entre text et image*. Brussells: Lang, 2001.

Petronio, Giuseppe. *L'attività letteraria in Italia: Storia della letteratura italiana*. 1963. Palermo: Palumbo, 1989.

Pezzini, Isabella, and Paolo Fabbri. Le avventure di Pinocchio: *Tra un linguaggio e l'altro*. Rome: Meltemi, 2002.

Phaedrus. *The Fables of Phaedrus*. Trans. P. F. Widdows. Austin: U of Texas P, 1992.

Pico della Mirandola, Giovanni. *On the Dignity of Man*. Trans. Charles Glenn Wallis. Indianapolis: Bobbs, 1965.

Pinocchio. Dir. Roberto Benigni. Miramax, 2002.

Pinocchio. Dir. Ron Field and Sid Smith. VCI Home Video, 2000.

Pinocchio. Dir. Hamilton Luske and Ben Sharpsteen. Disney Productions, 1940, 1984.

Pinocchio. Dir. Gianluigi Toccafondo. Arte, 1999.

Pinocchio fra i burattini: Atti del Convegno del 27–28 marzo 1987, Firenze-Pescia. Ed. Fernando Tempesti. Florence: Nuova Italia, 1993.

Pinocchio Interactive. FABRICATORS. 2005. 2 Jan. 2006 <http://www.fabricat.com/ VRI_PINOCCHHome.htm>.

Pinocchio nella pubblicità. Ed. Pier Francesco Bernacchi. Florence: Nuova Italia, 1997.

Pinocchio oggi: Atti del Convegno Pedagogico Pesci-Collodi, 30 settembre–1 ottobre 1978. Pescia: Fondazione Nazionale Carlo Collodi, 1980.

Pinocchio's Revenge. Dir. Kevin Tenney. Trimark Home Video, 1996.

Pinocchio sullo schermo e sulla scena: Atti del Convegno internazionale di studio dell' 8–9–10 novembre 1990. Ed. Giuseppe Flores d'Arcais. Florence: Nuova Italia, 1994.

Pinocchio Yori Piccolino no Bokken [The Adventures of Piccolino]. Dir. Hiroshi Saitô and Shigeo Koshi. Tatsunoko, 1976–77.

Pixnocchio. Dir. Giuseppe Laganà and Guido Vanzetti. 1981.

Prezzolini, Giuseppe. *La cultura italiana*. 1923. Milan: Corbaccio, 1938.

Propp, V. *Morphology of the Folktale*. Trans. Laurence Scott. Austin: U of Texas P, 1968.

Quiet Fire: A Historical Anthology of Asian American Poetry, 1892–1970. Ed. Juliana Chang. New York: Asian Amer. Writers' Workshop, 1996.

Quint, David. *Epic and Empire: Politics and Generic Form from Virgil to Milton*. Princeton: Princeton UP, 1993.

Rabkin, Eric S. *Fantastic Worlds: Myths, Tales, and Stories*. Oxford: Oxford UP, 1979.

Raimes, Ann. "Out of the Woods: Emerging Traditions in the Teaching of Writing." *TESOL Quarterly* 25 (1991): 407–30.

Reid, Joy. "English as a Second Language Composition in Higher Education: The Expectations of the Academic Audience." *Richness in Writing: Empowering ESL Students*. Ed. Donna M. Johnson and Duane H. Roden. New York: Longman, 1989. 220–34.

Rhu, Lawrence F. *The Genesis of Tasso's Narrative Theory: English Translations of the Early Poetics and a Comparative Study of Their Significance*. Detroit: Wayne State UP, 1993.

Richardson, Alan. "Childhood and Romanticism." Sadler 121–30.

Richardson, Brian. "Questions of Language." Barański and West 63–79.

Richter, Dieter. *Pinocchio o il romanzo d'infanzia.* Rome: Storia e Letteratura, 2002.

Rigutini, Giuseppe, and Pietro Fanfani. *Vocabolario italiano della lingua parlata.* Florence: Tipografia Cenniniana, 1875.

Rodari, Gianni. *The Grammar of Fantasy.* Trans. Jack Zipes. New York: Teachers and Writers Collaborative, 1996.

———. *Grammatica della fantasia.* Turin: Einaudi, 1973.

———. "Pinocchio il furbo." *Tante storie per giocare.* Illus. Tomi di Paola. Rome: Riuniti, 1971. 11–16.

———. "Pinocchio nella letteratura per l'infanzia." *Studi collodiani* 37–57.

Rodari, Gianni, and Raul Verdini. *La filastrocca di Pinocchio.* Rome: Riuniti, 1974.

Rose, Jacqueline. *The Case of Peter Pan; or, The Impossibility of Children's Fiction.* London: Macmillan, 1984.

Rosen, Michael. Personal interview. 15 Aug. 2001.

———. *Pinocchio in the Park.* Dir. Emily Gray. Open Air Theatre, Regent's Park, London, 2001.

Rosenthal, M. L. "Alice, Huck, Pinocchio, and the Blue Fairy: Bodies Real and Imagined." *Southern Review* 29 (1993): 486–90.

———. "The Hidden *Pinocchio*: Tale of a Subversive Puppet." *Literature and Revolution.* Ed. David Bevan. Atlanta: Rodopi, 1989. 49–61.

Rossetti, Christina. *"The Goblin Market" and Other Poems.* New York: Dover, 1994.

Russell, David L. "Pinocchio and the Child-Hero's Quest." *Children's Literature in Education* 20 (1989): 203–13.

Ryan, Marie-Laure, ed. *Cyberspace Textuality, Computer Technology, and Literary Theory.* Bloomington: Indiana UP, 1999.

———. *Narrative as Virtual Reality: Immersion and Interactivity in Literature and Electronic Media.* Baltimore: Johns Hopkins UP, 2001.

Sachse, Nancy. *Pinocchio in USA.* Pescia: Fondazione Nazionale Carlo Collodi, 1981.

Sadler, Glenn Edward, ed. *Teaching Children's Literature: Issues, Pedagogy, Resources.* New York: MLA, 1992.

Sale, Roger. *Fairy Tales and After: From Snow White to E. B. White.* Cambridge: Harvard UP, 1978.

Sapegno, Natalino. *Disegno storico della letteratura italiana.* Florence: Nuova Italia, 1977.

Sax, Boria. *The Mythical Zoo: An Encyclopedia of Animals in World Myth, Legend, and Literature.* Oxford: ABC CLIO, 2001.

Schickel, Richard. *The Disney Version: The Life, Times, Art, and Commerce of Walt Disney.* New York: Simon, 1968.

Scrittura dell'uso al tempo del Collodi: Atti del Convegno del 3–4 maggio 1990. Ed. Fernando Tempesti. Florence: Nuova Italia, 1994.

Scrivano, Riccardo. "Gioco del caso e fantasia nelle *Avventure di Pinocchio.*" *Studi Collodiani* 563–72.

Segel, Harold B. *Pinocchio's Progeny: Puppets, Marionettes, Automatons, and Robots in Modernist and Avant-Garde Drama.* Baltimore: Johns Hopkins UP, 1995.

Sendak, Maurice. *Caldecott and Co.: Notes on Books and Pictures.* New York: Noonday, 1988.

Shelley, Mary Wollstonecraft. *Frankenstein.* Norton Critical Ed. Ed. J. Paul Hunter. New York: Norton, 1996.

———. *Mary Wollstonecraft Shelley's* Frankenstein; or, The Modern Prometheus. Ed. Susan J. Wolfson. New York: Longman, 2003.

She's All That. Dir. Robert Iscove. 1999. DVD. Miramax Home Entertainment, 2003.

Silverstein, Shel. *Falling Up.* New York: Harper, 1996.

———. *The Giving Tree.* New York: Harper, 1964.

Slepian, Jan. *Pinocchio's Sister.* New York: Philomel, 1995.

Smith, Lane. *Pinocchio the Boy; or, Incognito in Collodi.* New York: Penguin, 2002. N. pag.

Solan, Miriam. *A Woman Combing.* West Stockbridge: Hard, 1997.

Starobinski, Jean. *Portrait de l'artiste en saltimbanque.* Geneva: Skira, 1970.

Stone, Jennifer A. "Pinocchio and Pinocchiology." *American Imago* 51(1994): 329–42.

Studi collodiani: Atti del I Convegno Internazionale. Pescia: Cassa di Risparmio di Pistoia e Pescia, 1976.

Stych, Franklyn S. *Pinocchio in Gran Bretagna e Irlanda.* Pescia: Fondazione Nazionale Carlo Collodi, 1971.

Sullivan, Nancy, and Ellen Pratt. "A Comparative Study of Two ESL Writing Environments: A Computer-Assisted Classroom and a Traditional Oral Classroom." *System* 24 (1996): 491–501.

Tabucchi, Antonio. "Dream of Carlo Collodi, Writer and Theatre Censor." *Dream of Dreams.* Trans. Nancy J. Peters. San Francisco: City Lights, 1999. 43–45.

———. *The Missing Head of Damasceno Monteiro.* Trans. J. C. Patrick. New York: New Directions, 1999.

———. *Il piccolo naviglio.* Milan: Mondadori, 1978.

———. *Requiem–uma alucinaçã.* Lisbon: Quetzal, 1991. Trans. as *Requiem: A Hallucination.* Trans. Margaret Jull Costa. New York: New Directions, 1994.

———. "Sogno di Carlo Collodi, scrittore e censore teatrale." *Sogni di sogni.* Palermo: Sellerio, 1992. 47–49. Trans. as "Dream of Carlo Collodi, Writer and Theatre Censor."

Tang, Gloria, and Joan Tithecott. "Peer Response in ESL Writing." *TESL Canada Journal* 16 (1999): 20–38.

Tarchetti, Iginio Ugo. *Tutte le opere.* 2 vols. Ed. Enrico Ghidetti. Bologna: Cappelli, 1967.

Tempesti, Ferdinando. "Chi era il Collodi" and "Come è fatto Pinocchio." Collodi, *Pinocchio* [Tempesti] 7–135.

———. Letter to the author. 13 Aug. 1994.

Tifft, Susan E. "Kids Learn from Our Pinocchio Culture." *Los Angeles Times* 24 June 2003: B17.

Tommasi, Rodolfo. *Pinocchio: Analisi di un burattino.* Florence: Sansoni, 1992.

Toy Story [and] Toy Story 2. Dir. John Lasseter. DVD. Disney-Pixar, 2000.

Trequadrini, Franco. "L'eclisse di Pinocchio: Ipotesi sulla scomparsa dal mercato e dall'immaginario sociale." *Pinocchio nella pubblicita* 103–09.

Tropp, Martin. *Mary Shelley's Monster.* Boston: Houghton, 1977.

Turner, Victor. *The Ritual Process: Structure and Anti-structure.* Chicago: Aldine, 1966.

Ulivi, Ferruccio. "Manzoni e Collodi." *Studi Collodiani* 615–20.

Vico, Giambattista. *The New Science.* Trans. and ed. Thomas G. Bergin and Max H. Fisch. Ithaca: Cornell UP, 1991.

Villiers de l'Isle Adam, Auguste. *Tomorrow's Eve.* Trans. Robert Martin Adams. Champaign: U of Illinois P, 2001. Trans. of *L'Ève future.*

Volpicelli, Luigi. *Bibliografia collodiana, 1883–1980.* Pescia: Fondazione Nazionale Carlo Collodi, 1980.

Vygotsky, L. S. *Mind in Society: The Development of Higher Psychological Processes.* Cambridge: Harvard UP, 1978.

Warner, Marina. *Six Myths of Our Time: Little Angels, Little Monsters, Beautiful Beasts, and More.* New York: Vintage, 1995. Rpt. of *Managing Monsters.* London: Vintage, 1994.

Webb, Charles Harper. *Reading the Water.* Boston: Northeastern UP, 1997.

Weird Science. Dir. John Hughes. 1997. VHS. Universal Studios, 1997.

Wilder, Laura Ingalls. *Little House in the Big Woods.* New York: Harper, 1953.

Winnicott, D. W. *Playing and Reality.* New York: Basic, 1971.

Wolfram von Eschenbach. *Parzival.* Trans. Helen M. Mustard and Charles E. Passage. New York: Knopf, 1961. Trans. of *Parzival.* Bibliotheca Augustana. 13 Dec. 2005. 21 Dec. 2005 <http://www.fh-augsburg.de/~harsch/germanica/Chronologie/13Jh/Wolfram/wol_pa09.html>.

Wood, Gaby. *Edison's Eve. A Magical History of the Quest for Mechanical Life.* New York: Knopf, 2002.

Wunderlich, Richard. "De-radicalizing *Pinocchio.*" *Functions of the Fantastic: Selected Essays from the Thirteenth International Conference on the Fantastic in the Arts.* Ed. Joe Sanders. Westport: Greenwood, 1995. 19–28.

Wunderlich, Richard, and Thomas J. Morrissey. "Death and Rebirth in *Pinocchio.*" *Children's Literature* 11 (1983): 64–75.

———. *Pinocchio Goes Postmodern: Perils of a Puppet in the United States.* New York: Routledge, 2002.

Zangheri, Marta, and Roberto Maini, eds. *Pinocchio e pinocchiate: Nelle edizioni fiorentine della Marucelliana.* Florence: Aida, 2000.

Zatti, Sergio. *The Quest for Epic: From Ariosto to Tasso.* Ed. Dennis Looney. Trans. Sally Hill with Looney. Toronto: U of Toronto P, 2006.

Zellermayer, Michal, Gavriel Salomon, Tamar Globerson, and Hanna Givon. "Enhancing Writing-Related Metacognitions through a Computerized Writing Partner." *American Educational Research Journal* 28 (1991): 373–91.

Zipes, Jack., ed. and trans. *Beauties, Beasts, and Enchantment: Classic French Fairy Tales*. New York: New Amer. Lib., 1989.

———. "Carlo Collodi's *Pinocchio* as Tragic-Comic Fairy Tale." Zipes, *When Dreams* 141–50.

———. *Fairy Tales and the Art of Subversion: The Classical Genre for Children and the Process of Civilization*. New York: Wildman, 1983.

———. "Toward a Theory of the Fairy-Tale Film: The Case of *Pinocchio*." *The Lion and the Unicorn* 20 (1996): 1–24

———. *When Dreams Came True: Classical Fairy Tales and Their Tradition*. New York: Routledge, 1999.

Zolla, Elémire. "L'esoterismo di Pinocchio." *C'era una volta* 165–67.

Zor, Marion. *La terrible bande à Charly P.* Illus. Yan Thomas. Paris: Rue du monde, 1997.

INDEX

Hoffmann, E. T. A., 27n1, 148, 149
Holt, Sheryl, 96, 101
Horace, 45

Iser, Wolfgang, 140, 143n2
Ives, Burl, 8

Jakobson, Roman, 104
Jandl, Ernst, 114
Jeannet, Angela, 11, 13, 14
Jennings, Linda M., 128, 129
Jervis, Giovanni, 3
Jesus Christ, 25, 26, 38
Johns, Ian, 135n1
Jonah, Book of, 38, 77, 83, 89
Jones, Dudley, 63
Jones, Oliver, 135n1
Jurkowski, Henryk, 5

Kaplan, Robert, 100
Karloff, Boris, 28
Keller, Evelyn Fox, 144, 151
Kertzer, David I., 79n1
Kincaid, Jamaica, 69
Klingberg, Göte, 132
Klopp, Charles, 11, 13, 14
Knoepflmacher, U. C., 28, 75
Koffolt, Kimberly, 96, 101
Kohl, Herbert, 73, 84
Koppe, Susanne, 117
Krashen, Stephen, 95, 96, 98
Kubrick, Stanley, 125
Kuznets, Lois, 5, 66, 69, 73

LaCroix, Georges, 146
La Fontaine, Jean de, 92
Laganà, Giuseppe, 146
Landau, Martin, 7–8, 121, 122
Landow, George P., 145
Lavinio, Cristina, 36
Le Brun, Claire, 116
Leopardi, Giacomo, 30, 43
Leopold II, 17
Lesnik-Oberstein, Karin, 133
Levine, George, 28
Lewinsky, Monica, 118n2
Long, Michael H., 100
Looney, Dennis, 14
Loredo, Armando, 8
Lorenzini, Domenico, 16
Lucas, Ann Lawson, 3, 6, 37, 39, 63, 127, 129
Luchi, Francesco, 105
Lucian, 38, 89
Luporini, C. G., 136
Lurie, Alison, 5, 134
Luzzi, Joseph, 11

Macchietti, Sira Serenella, 132
Magni, Marcello, 127, 129–31, 135n1
Maini, Roberto, 7
Malerba, Luigi, 108–09, 115, 120, 126
Malthus, Thomas, 21
Manganelli, Giorgio, 80, 84, 108, 110, 120, 126, 147, 149
Manzoli, Giacomo, 120
Manzoni, Alessandro, 41, 43, 62n3, 136, 141, 142–43
Marcheschi, Daniela, 3, 4, 5, 103
Marchesini, Manuela, 11, 13, 14
Martini, Carlo, 7
Martini, Ferdinando, 41, 45–47
Mary, mother of Jesus, 25
Mativat, Daniel, 116
Matter, E. Ann, 12
Mazzanti, Enrico, 113, 121, 127, 145
Mazzini, Giuseppe, 17, 19
Mazzoni, Cristina, 14
Mazzoni, Guido, 45
McGillis, Roderick, 65
McGroarty, Mary, 100
Meirieu, Philippe, 33n1
Menarini, Roy, 120
Merivale, Patricia, 6
Mignacca, Rita, 12, 13
Miller, Alice, 117
Milton, John, 32
Montessori, Maria, 11
Monti, Vincenzo, 43
Morrissey, Thomas, 4, 6, 68, 70, 104, 118n1, 144
Morrow, Marina, 84
Murray, Janet H., 145
Murray, Mary Alice, 3, 104, 127
Mussino, Attilio, 121

Namjoshi, Suniti, 8
Negri, Fausto, 7, 40n3
Nightingale, Benedict, 135n2
Nikolejeva, Maria, 69
Nietzsche, Friedrich, 56
Nodelman, Perry, 79
Noone, Peter, 8
Nöstlinger, Christine, 116–17

O'Brien, Geoffrey, 125
O'Donnell, James J., 152n1
Oitinnen, Riitta, 132
Orvig, Mary, 132
Ottevaere–van Praag, Ganna, 5, 105
Orzali, Angela, 16

Pancrazi, Pietro, 5, 43
Parenti, Marino, 6
Paruolo, Elena, 14, 127, 134

Approaches to Teaching World Literature

Joseph Gibaldi, series editor

Achebe's Things Fall Apart. Ed. Bernth Lindfors. 1991.

Arthurian Tradition. Ed. Maureen Fries and Jeanie Watson. 1992.

Atwood's The Handmaid's Tale *and Other Works*. Ed. Sharon R. Wilson, Thomas B. Friedman, and Shannon Hengen. 1996.

Austen's Emma. Ed. Marcia McClintock Folsom. 2004.

Austen's Pride and Prejudice. Ed. Marcia McClintock Folsom. 1993.

Balzac's Old Goriot. Ed. Michal Peled Ginsburg. 2000.

Baudelaire's Flowers of Evil. Ed. Laurence M. Porter. 2000.

Beckett's Waiting for Godot. Ed. June Schlueter and Enoch Brater. 1991.

Beowulf. Ed. Jess B. Bessinger, Jr., and Robert F. Yeager. 1984.

Blake's Songs of Innocence and of Experience. Ed. Robert F. Gleckner and Mark L. Greenberg. 1989.

Boccaccio's Decameron. Ed. James H. McGregor. 2000.

British Women Poets of the Romantic Period. Ed. Stephen C. Behrendt and Harriet Kramer Linkin. 1997.

Brontë's Jane Eyre. Ed. Diane Long Hoeveler and Beth Lau. 1993.

Emily Brontë's Wuthering Heights. Ed. Sue Lonoff and Terri A. Hasseler. 2006.

Byron's Poetry. Ed. Frederick W. Shilstone. 1991.

Camus's The Plague. Ed. Steven G. Kellman. 1985.

Cather's My Ántonia. Ed. Susan J. Rosowski. 1989.

Cervantes' Don Quixote. Ed. Richard Bjornson. 1984.

Chaucer's Canterbury Tales. Ed. Joseph Gibaldi. 1980.

Chaucer's Troilus and Criseyde *and the Shorter Poems*. Ed. Tison Pugh and Angela Jane Weisl. 2006.

Chopin's The Awakening. Ed. Bernard Koloski. 1988.

Coleridge's Poetry and Prose. Ed. Richard E. Matlak. 1991.

Collodi's Pinocchio *and Its Adaptations*. Ed. Michael Sherberg. 2006.

Conrad's "Heart of Darkness" *and* "The Secret Sharer." Ed. Hunt Hawkins and Brian W. Shaffer. 2002.

Dante's Divine Comedy. Ed. Carole Slade. 1982.

Defoe's Robinson Crusoe. Ed. Maximillian E. Novak and Carl Fisher. 2005.

DeLillo's White Noise. Ed. Tim Engles and John N. Duvall. 2006.

Dickens' David Copperfield. Ed. Richard J. Dunn. 1984.

Dickinson's Poetry. Ed. Robin Riley Fast and Christine Mack Gordon. 1989.

Narrative of the Life of Frederick Douglass. Ed. James C. Hall. 1999.

Early Modern Spanish Drama. Ed. Laura R. Bass and Margaret R. Greer. 2006

Eliot's Middlemarch. Ed. Kathleen Blake. 1990.

Eliot's Poetry and Plays. Ed. Jewel Spears Brooker. 1988.

Shorter Elizabethan Poetry. Ed. Patrick Cheney and Anne Lake Prescott. 2000.
Ellison's Invisible Man. Ed. Susan Resneck Parr and Pancho Savery. 1989.
English Renaissance Drama. Ed. Karen Bamford and Alexander Leggatt. 2002.
Works of Louise Erdrich. Ed. Gregg Sarris, Connie A. Jacobs, and
    James R. Giles. 2004.
Dramas of Euripides. Ed. Robin Mitchell-Boyask. 2002.
Faulkner's The Sound and the Fury. Ed. Stephen Hahn and Arthur F. Kinney. 1996.
Flaubert's Madame Bovary. Ed. Laurence M. Porter and Eugene F. Gray. 1995.
García Márquez's One Hundred Years of Solitude. Ed. María Elena de Valdés and
    Mario J. Valdés. 1990.
Gilman's "The Yellow Wall-Paper" and Herland. Ed. Denise D. Knight and
    Cynthia J. Davis. 2003.
Goethe's Faust. Ed. Douglas J. McMillan. 1987.
Gothic Fiction: The British and American Traditions. Ed. Diane Long Hoeveler
    and Tamar Heller. 2003.
Hebrew Bible as Literature in Translation. Ed. Barry N. Olshen and
    Yael S. Feldman. 1989.
Homer's Iliad *and* Odyssey. Ed. Kostas Myrsiades. 1987.
Ibsen's A Doll House. Ed. Yvonne Shafer. 1985.
Henry James's Daisy Miller *and* The Turn of the Screw. Ed. Kimberly C. Reed and
    Peter G. Beidler. 2005.
Works of Samuel Johnson. Ed. David R. Anderson and Gwin J. Kolb. 1993.
Joyce's Ulysses. Ed. Kathleen McCormick and Erwin R. Steinberg. 1993.
Kafka's Short Fiction. Ed. Richard T. Gray. 1995.
Keats's Poetry. Ed. Walter H. Evert and Jack W. Rhodes. 1991.
Kingston's The Woman Warrior. Ed. Shirley Geok-lin Lim. 1991.
Lafayette's The Princess of Clèves. Ed. Faith E. Beasley and
    Katharine Ann Jensen. 1998.
Works of D. H. Lawrence. Ed. M. Elizabeth Sargent and Garry Watson. 2001.
Lessing's The Golden Notebook. Ed. Carey Kaplan and Ellen Cronan Rose. 1989.
Mann's Death in Venice *and Other Short Fiction*. Ed. Jeffrey B. Berlin. 1992.
Medieval English Drama. Ed. Richard K. Emmerson. 1990.
Melville's Moby-Dick. Ed. Martin Bickman. 1985.
Metaphysical Poets. Ed. Sidney Gottlieb. 1990.
Miller's Death of a Salesman. Ed. Matthew C. Roudané. 1995.
Milton's Paradise Lost. Ed. Galbraith M. Crump. 1986.
Molière's Tartuffe *and Other Plays*. Ed. James F. Gaines and
    Michael S. Koppisch. 1995.
Momaday's The Way to Rainy Mountain. Ed. Kenneth M. Roemer. 1988.
Montaigne's Essays. Ed. Patrick Henry. 1994.
Novels of Toni Morrison. Ed. Nellie Y. McKay and Kathryn Earle. 1997.
Murasaki Shikibu's The Tale of Genji. Ed. Edward Kamens. 1993.
Pope's Poetry. Ed. Wallace Jackson and R. Paul Yoder. 1993.

Proust's Fiction and Criticism. Ed. Elyane Dezon-Jones and
     Inge Crosman Wimmers. 2003.
Novels of Samuel Richardson. Ed. Lisa Zunshine and Jocelyn Harris. 2006.
Rousseau's Confessions *and* Reveries of the Solitary Walker. Ed. John C. O'Neal
     and Ourida Mostefai. 2003.
Shakespeare's Hamlet. Ed. Bernice W. Kliman. 2001.
Shakespeare's King Lear. Ed. Robert H. Ray. 1986.
Shakespeare's Othello. Ed. Peter Erickson and Maurice Hunt. 2005.
Shakespeare's Romeo and Juliet. Ed. Maurice Hunt. 2000.
Shakespeare's The Tempest *and Other Late Romances*. Ed. Maurice Hunt. 1992.
Shelley's Frankenstein. Ed. Stephen C. Behrendt. 1990.
Shelley's Poetry. Ed. Spencer Hall. 1990.
Sir Gawain and the Green Knight. Ed. Miriam Youngerman Miller and
     Jane Chance. 1986.
Song of Roland. Ed. William W. Kibler and Leslie Zarker Morgan. 2006.
Spenser's Faerie Queene. Ed. David Lee Miller and Alexander Dunlop. 1994.
Stendhal's The Red and the Black. Ed. Dean de la Motte and Stirling Haig. 1999.
Sterne's Tristram Shandy. Ed. Melvyn New. 1989.
Stowe's Uncle Tom's Cabin. Ed. Elizabeth Ammons and Susan Belasco. 2000.
Swift's Gulliver's Travels. Ed. Edward J. Rielly. 1988.
Thoreau's Walden *and Other Works*. Ed. Richard J. Schneider. 1996.
Tolstoy's Anna Karenina. Ed. Liza Knapp and Amy Mandelker. 2003.
Vergil's Aeneid. Ed. William S. Anderson and Lorina N. Quartarone. 2002.
Voltaire's Candide. Ed. Renée Waldinger. 1987.
Whitman's Leaves of Grass. Ed. Donald D. Kummings. 1990.
Woolf's To the Lighthouse. Ed. Beth Rigel Daugherty and Mary Beth Pringle. 2001.
Wordsworth's Poetry. Ed. Spencer Hall, with Jonathan Ramsey. 1986.
Wright's Native Son. Ed. James A. Miller. 1997.